CRITICAL PERSPECTIVES ON WORK AND ORGANISATIONS

Series editors:

David Knights, Department of Management, University of Keele
Chris Smith, School of Management, Royal Holloway, University of London
Paul Thompson, Department of Human Resource Management, University
  of Strathclyde
Hugh Willmott, Manchester School of Management, UMIST

Published:

Alan Felstead and Nick Jewson *Global Trends in Flexible Labour*

Craig Prichard, Richard Hull, Mike Chumer and Hugh Willmott
  Managing Knowledge

Paul Thompson and Chris Warhurst *Workplaces of the Future*

Critical Perspectives on Work and Organisations Series
Series Standing Order ISBN 0-333-73535-8
(outside North America only)

You can receive future titles in this series as they are published by placing a standing order.
Please contact your bookseller or, in case of difficulty, write to us at the address below with
your name and address, the title of the series and the ISBN quoted above.

Customer Services Department, Macmillan Distribution Ltd
Houndmills, Basingstoke, Hampshire RG21 6XS, England

Customer Service

Empowerment and Entrapment

Edited by Andrew Sturdy, Irena Grugulis and Hugh Willmott

palgrave

First published 2001 by
PALGRAVE
Houndmills, Basingstoke, Hampshire RG21 6XS and
175 Fifth Avenue, New York, N. Y. 10010
Companies and representatives throughout the world

PALGRAVE is the new global academic imprint of
St. Martin's Press LLC Scholarly and Reference Division and
Palgrave Publishers Ltd (formerly Macmillan Press Ltd).

ISBN 0-333-94607-3

This book is printed on paper suitable for recycling and
made from fully managed and sustained forest sources.

A catalogue record for this book is available
from the British Library.

10   9   8   7   6   5   4   3   2   1
10   09   08   07   06   05   04   03   02   01

Copy-edited and typeset by Povey–Edmondson
Tavistock and Rochdale, England

Printed and bound in Great Britain by
Antony Rowe Ltd, Chippenham, Wiltshire

Contents

1

Servicing Societies? – Colonisation, Control, Contradiction and Contestation

Andrew Sturdy

> The enlarged market has become at once more impersonal and more intimate. What is there that does not pass through the market? Science and love, virtue and conscience, friendliness, carefully nurtured skills and animosities? This is a time of venality (instrumentality).
>
> (Mills, 1951:161)

Introduction

This quote is as relevant today as it was when first published, 50 years ago. Only now, its applicability stretches well beyond the US middle classes of the 1950s. Also, for Wright Mills, the focus was on sales; now this would be replaced or subsumed by the ostensibly less instrumental ethos of *customer service*. This is presented by many in business, the public sector and politics as of universal benefit or, at least, benign in its endeavours to tailor products to the needs ascribed to customers. The very idea of a critical approach to customer service, the aim of this volume, may then seem perverse to some – 'we all want good service don't we?'.[1] Indeed, we may well do, and increasingly so. However, this certainly does not preclude the need for critique.

The key questions addressed in this volume include the following. Who defines the nature and scope of 'service', 'customer needs' and 'relationships'? Under whose terms is service/consumption organised? What are the consequences for individuals and societies? What alternative ways of understanding and organising service are there? As service language, values and practices spread to more and more activities and places, the importance of these questions increases. Their relevance extends way beyond how long one waits in a queue, or whether or not one receives 'appropriate' behaviour from service providers. How service is defined, organised, enacted and contested affects our lives, not only as employees, but as consumers and citizens.

1

interaction, albeit without the local community and employment/career structures of earlier times (e.g. local shops, branches). In retail banking for example, a shift from 'teller to seller/server to relater' is evident, whereby customer contact is ascribed higher status than previously. Moreover, new, albeit limited, career paths are emerging for some employees (Morgan and Sturdy, 2000). Elsewhere, in cases cited by service protagonists (e.g. FedEx and Scandinavian Airlines), organisational structures are flattened and notionally inverted with the customer at the top (cf. Ritzer and Stillman, in this volume). More recently, customer service has been repackaged as Customer Relationship Management with a new acronym, CRM, to accompany it:

> Customer Relationship Management is all the rage at the moment but behind the hype lies a fundamental truth: the customer relationship is important to any company . . . . It is really about owning a customer base and managing and satisfying that base; looking after people better than anyone else . . . . [It] involves changing people, technology and processes. (Huntington, 2000:44; see Fitchett and McDonagh, this volume)

Of course, there are clear market-based rationales for such changes, beyond fuelling the management consultancy/ideas market. Notably, there is the attraction of cutting the costs of customer turnover; the concomitant selecting out of unprofitable market segments (i.e. excluding people) and services; and using 'relationships' to sell-on connected services to existing customers (Sturdy and Knights, 1996; Hodgson and Fitchett and McDonagh, this volume).

But, the significance of customer service is now seen to extend far beyond its economic or employment-based rationales and consequences. It feeds the symbolic world of consumption, the changing meanings and experiences of it. As the distinction between manufacturing and service breaks down, so too do those of production–consumption, economy–culture, worker–consumer and authentic-enacted self (Allen and du Gay, 1994). Here, post-structuralism has shifted critical attention away from essentialist concepts such as consumer alienation, needs and false consciousness, to the joys and aesthetics of consumption and service work (as well as to associated processes of subjectification). McDonald's, for example, is said to create pleasure and innovations in habits and culture (Finkelstein, 1999). Similarly, accounts that point to the loss of authenticity we may experience in consuming and providing standardised service are critiqued as reflecting middle class humanism (Munch, 1999; cf. Ritzer, 1999). Others also eschew negative judgements on new forms of service such as 'Disneyisation' (which coexists with the more modernist phenomenon of 'McDonaldisation') (Bryman, 1999; cf. Ritzer and Liska, 1997). Here, service is centred on explicit symbolism, 'themeing', merchandising and deep (cf. surface) emotional labour from service workers and consumers – 'a new experience economy' (see Fitzsimmons and Fitzsimmons, 2000; also Nickson *et al.*, this volume). The way in which such labour is prescribed, performed and experienced remains however, a question of power and/or control. But, even here, traditional divisions and relationships are becoming less clear, namely that of employer–employee, to which we now turn.

Control

The distinctions between service and manufacturing labour processes are sometimes overdrawn. For example, it is not only in service work that personal characteristics of employees, such as attitudes and, to a lesser extent, appearance have been important (Thompson, 1967; Macdonald and Sirianni, 1996b). This is especially true in current times where a customer service ethos has entered manufacturing, in terms of 'quality' and culture management. Nevertheless, there are important differences, which condition the nature, experience and problems of control. In particular, the role of the customer/supplier introduces a 'new' third party to the traditional employer–employee relationship that problematises both the practice and theorising of control in the labour process (Leidner, 1993; Weatherley and Tansik, 1993). Macdonald and Sirianni (1996a) note how, in theory, management influence customers through employees, but in practice management may join with employees to manipulate consumers (Leidner, 1996) or with customers to supervise employees (Fuller and Smith, 1991); workers too, may use their understanding of customers or service (i.e. 'customer first') discourse to influence management; and, customers may oversee or even override/replace management (Lopez, 1996). Of course, and as already intimated, management may also use others, through the development and use of technologies, to control customers remotely through phone data entry or service tills for example. Nevertheless, it is clear that the active role and increased profile of the customer/'outsider' opens up the possibility or even, necessity for studies of work and organisation to connect more directly with broader issues of culture and politics or, in more critical terms, the superstructure or governmentality (Sturdy, 1998; Hodgson, in this volume).[4] This requirement is reinforced by the other key characteristic of service work, the perceived importance of the personal–cultural characteristics of employees.

It is often considered that managerial attention to employees' appearance, moods and attitudes was focused mostly on those with careers, rather than jobs, with 'white collar work'. As service work and ideas have expanded in scope, so too have these invasive forms of control since the producer, in many cases, *is* the product in services (Macdonald and Sirianni, 1996a:15). This has led to continued and expanding standardisation and/or commodification of personal characteristics. This has a long history. For example, Wright Mills wrote of it in terms of the increased bureaucratic attention

2

Academic Discourses of the Customer: 'Sovereign Beings', 'Management Accomplices' or 'People Like Us'?

Patrice Rosenthal, Ricardo Peccei and Stephen Hill

Introduction

'Customer sovereignty' has been cast as the dominant discourse of the current socio-economic-political sphere (du Gay, 1996; Gabriel and Lang, 1995; Keat and Abercrombie, 1991; Sturdy, 1998). The primacy now accorded customers has been traced to related core phenomena, including increased competition, the rise of the service sector, changing consumer expectations and a dominant political ideology of 'enterprise'. One manifestation of these shifts is that the customer, historically absent from academic analyses of organisation (Danet, 1981; Dean and Bowen, 1994), has now begun to pervade them. Strands of literature which used to take scant notice are now busy 'working the customer in' to existing perspectives. At one level, then, the sovereign customer has arrived. The representation of the customer as an inescapable, powerful (and legitimate?) force now permeates diverse perspectives on organisation (see for example, Hill and Wilkinson, 1995 and Lengnick-Hall, 1996 on TQM; Heery, 1993 on industrial relations; Rosenthal *et al.*, 1997 on HRM; Fuller and Smith, 1991 on management control; Hall, 1993 on gender and work; and Ashforth and Humphrey, 1993 on emotional labour).

At a deeper level, there are important tensions within and across academic texts in how customers, and their implications for organisations and for service work, are being constituted. This can be seen from exploring the multiplicity of metaphors and images that now populate the literature. In this chapter we begin to map some of these representations. Six selected images (or groups of images) are briefly sketched. These are then used to illustrate a set of broader points about metaphorical thinking and multiple tropes to understand organisational phenomena.

Some cautionary notes are in order. We are aware that 'mapping is not an innocent act' (Dunford and Palmer, 1996:701). We are imposing our own

18

parameters on literatures that are complex, internally differentiated and overlapping. Further, in some cases, we are (consciously) constructing metaphors that remain implicit in the texts we are considering. Other researchers may conjure alternate images and classifications. Our presentation of images is not meant to be exhaustive, but rather to highlight some important and contrasting positions in the literature.

We proceed for a number of reasons. First, to do so seems to us an interesting exercise. Images of the customer have begun to proliferate and to fragment in the literature: the presentation of *one* map of this territory for debate seems an intriguing and worthwhile task. Gabriel and Lang (1995) have addressed the fragmentary and undecided nature of consumption in contemporary society and in so doing explored differing faces worn by the consumer, including that of hedonist, citizen, victim and rebel. This insightful analysis is located within macro level debates of politics, sociology and cultural theory, in contrast to our concern with the literature on organisation and management. We are unaware of other attempts to map varying representations of the *customer* (an entity acting in relation to workers and management) within that domain.

Second, we believe that consideration of these varying representations can contribute to the debate on metaphorical thinking and the use of multiple metaphors to understand organisational phenomena. We offer four observations on this issue. The first concerns consideration of the contexts within which one dominant trope (here, the 'sovereign customer') can offer different meanings. The second addresses explicitness and implicitness of representations in the literature. The third explores tensions and indeterminacy within, as well as across, texts, in how phenomena are constituted. The fourth considers the production and consumption of metaphors in the process of identity construction among academics. In the final part of the chapter we consider some implications of our analysis for research on organisations and management.

In the next section, we introduce some representations of the customer that appear in various strands of the literature on organisation. We then turn to a consideration of metaphorical thinking and its usefulness in understanding customers and their implications for organisations and for service work.

Representations of the Customer in Academic Analyses

Traditionally, management and workers have been the important actors in academic accounts of organising and its fundamental problems. These constituencies and their (conflicting and/or overlapping) interests, resources, behaviours and so forth have largely defined the research territory. More recently the academic gaze has shifted to include customers, but the object reflected back is not uniform. In other words, while the

> [Individuals who identify with their work roles are] most truly them-
> selves when they are fulfilling the role say, of the extroverted salesperson
> or the sympathetic guidance councillor. (Ashforth and Humphrey,
> 1993:94)

The gendered nature of service work is privileged in analyses of patriarchy
and organisation. Here the customer is painted, inherently, as a *consumer of
sexuality*, and where engaged in more conscious participation in sexualised
exchanges, as a *punter* or a *buyer of sexuality*.

> You ask the [young men] why they come in here . . . and they'll say it's
> because of the girls. What Ricky wants up here is the figures (quick at the
> tills and good at the sums), the personality, and the bums. (from Filby,
> 1992:28)

> The vast majority of the agents we select are women. If we are honest
> about it [we] select women sometimes because they are women rather
> than anything they've particularly shown in the interview. (from Taylor
> and Tyler, 2000:83–4.)

> Women more often react to subordination by making defensive use of
> sexual beauty, charm and relational skills. For them, it is these capacities
> that become most vulnerable to commercial exploitation, and so it is these
> capacities they are more likely to become estranged from. (Hochschild,
> 1983:164)

Finally, the customer takes a set of shifting and diverse images in the
services management literature, including that of *resource . . . worker . . .
buyer . . . beneficiary . . . product* (Lengnick-Hall, 1996:796), *motivator of
employees* (Bowen and Schneider, 1988:53), *enemy, source of uncertainty*
(Bowen and Schneider, 1988:55), *free actor* (Bowen and Schneider,
1988:73); *audience for a performance* (Deighton, 1994).

   The gallery of images sketched above juxtaposes important and contrasting representations of the customer. The nature of these tropes depart from
Gabriel and Lang's (1995) exploration of consumers as citizens, explorers,
identity seekers and so on. As stated above, Gabriel and Lang's (1995)
analysis is located within macro level debates concerning consumerism in
wider society. In contrast our customer(s) – be they sovereigns, spies or
emotional drains – emerge as entities acting in relation to workers and
managers within organisations.

   Underlying these contrasting representations is an often complex ontol-
ogy/epistemology. A full consideration of these is beyond the scope of the
chapter. Our purpose here, rather, is to use this play of tropes to illustrate
some broader observations about metaphorical thinking in the analysis of
organisation. We turn to this in the following section.

Observations on the Use of Multiple Metaphors in Organisation Studies

Customer sovereignty: internal differentiation in dominant tropes

Our first observation concerns the emergence of dominant tropes in the analysis of organisational phenomena, and how these tropes may be internally differentiated depending upon the perspective of the enunciator. Often in the early stages of analyses, there emerges a dominant metaphor which aids in conceptualisation of phenomena (for example, the machine metaphor in analyses of organisation; see Morgan, 1986). The 'sovereign customer' is one illustration of this. Indeed, du Gay (1996:80) locates it as the 'primary image informing representations of economic life'. Yet dominant metaphors are not monolithic. In the section below we explore the image of customer sovereignty and its presentation within two discourses: Total Quality Management and sociological accounts of post-modernity and enterprise. We show how the image becomes internally differentiated depending upon the enunciators' perspective; in other words, depending upon the context within which the trope is being used.

The discovery of the sovereignty of the consumer in contemporary managerial and academic discourse reflects two developments. First there are changes in product markets, namely the increased competition between producers which has extended consumer choice. Then there is the rise to discursive dominance of the ideology or discourse of enterprise,[1] which is said to have become established as the dominant interpretative framework among American and British elites (Keat *et al.*, 1994; du Gay, 1996). Customers may be sovereign in different ways: they may rule producers, who therefore stand as the subservient party in a relationship of authority (Abercrombie, 1994); or they may now simply be more able to satisfy their own wishes in the exchange with producers, because the contractual relationship is no longer biased towards the producer as it was in the past. Customer sovereignty is first, self-evidently a metaphor that conceptualises customers. Sovereignty is secondly a metaphor for governance (including issues of rule, authority, power, governmentality). However, in contemporary usage the metaphor covers such a variety of ways of conceptualising customers and consumer–producer relations, that it may obscure as much as it reveals.

The managerial literature is long on the rhetoric of the customer, but remarkably short on the analysis of this agent (or, if one were to take an extreme post-structuralist turn, this artefact). Of all the current managerial discourses, Total Quality Management is the one that most explicitly enthrones the customer. Yet external customers are curiously under-represented in the TQM literature. Customers would seem to have causal powers – in this they resemble deities and some pre-modern sovereigns –

logical sturdiness of the various images, seeking the 'truest' or most 'useful' metaphor. Or, we could attempt a synthesis of the varying (but often divergent or contradictory) images of the customer. Or, we could adopt a contingency approach, seeking to clarify the circumstances under which the various portraits would have more or less resonance. Citing the difficulties of 'stepping outside fundamental differences in epistemology and ontology', Dunford and Palmer (1996:701) suggest a fourth strategy, one of reflexivity, wherein researchers develop a critical awareness of the underlying intellectual assumptions that are driving their construction of metaphors.

This brings us on to our fourth observation on the use of multiple metaphors in organisation studies. We note that all four of the strategies considered by Dunford and Palmer (1996) (and by implication, our endeavour here), privilege the notion of intellectual assumptions driving metaphor construction. That is, the 'point' of proliferating metaphors is taken to be, if not the pursuit of 'truth', then of meaningful or useful insights on organisation. There is the assumption that intellectual assumptions (with essentialist overtones) are driving the process. Drawing (playfully) from post-modern analyses, we suggest an alternative perspective on metaphor proliferation among academics, wherein the privileging of deeper intellectual assumptions may be somewhat off the mark.

If post-modernists are correct about the current nature of consumption (i.e. that we construct our identities through consumption, as ever, but that in post-modernity we seek through consumption to *differentiate* ourselves from others) this may have implications for our analysis.

> The construction of identity is an active process, but what is distinctive about the current period is the number and significance of consumables in that process. In modern Western society it is through consumption that individuals are continuously transformed into subjects who secure a meaning, personal significance and a sense of identity through a socially mediated relation with the object or symbol consumed. (Knights and Morgan, 1993:225)

> [In the post-modern era] product differentiation, alongside market segmentation, are the ways in which organisations seek to create a niche for themselves, offering commodities which make individuals or groups of people feel special, exclusive and individual. It may be *designer label clothes, the latest model of a particular car.* . . . (Knights and Morgan, 1993:226, our emphasis)

Or the latest metaphor?

That is, it may be useful to see metaphor production and consumption as a process of identity construction among academics. The salient point of a metaphor may be to differentiate *me* from *you*. If so, perhaps we were wrong to concern ourselves with surfacing deeper assumptions. Perhaps a key point is that of identity construction through differentiation, as opposed to (in addition to?) the development of 'deep insights' about organisations and service work.

But according to this post-modern line of analysis, metaphors, like luxury goods, *must* then proliferate:

> As previously privileged and prestigious cultural items become available to a mass-market, elite leaders and cultural, avant-garde groups were forced to create new forms of taste, different and distinct to preserve their cultural superiority over the aspiring masses. However, given contemporary means of mass cultural production, changes within the cultural fields are so rapid that it becomes increasingly difficult to identify the leading-edge of either the art-world or the market place of consumer goods. (Turner, 1988:74)

If this analysis is fruitful, it may be useful to think of academics as 'diverse groups of consumers ceaselessly searching for distinctive meanings and identities' (Knights and Morgan, 1993:228). The production and consumption of proliferating metaphors among academics may, therefore, have as much to do with the construction of a distinctive (and therefore valued) identity as arising from 'deeper intellectual assumptions'? In other words, it raises the question of the *nature* and *timing* of relations between a niche in the metaphor 'market' – within which individual distinctiveness may be asserted – and the development of deeply held intellectual positions.

Such a conclusion may well arise from a post-modern 'take' on the academy, or a materialised one which views knowledge as a commodity. Yet those researchers who, like us, cleave both to the possibility of, and responsibility for, the development of meaningful insights on organisations, see these differing images as representing something a little more substantive than an academic game. The issue that we need to address therefore is the implications that these multiple and shifting tropes have for organisation research. It is this issue we turn to in the final part of the chapter.

Conclusions

The sovereign customer is cast as 'the primary image informing representations of economic life' (du Gay, 1996:80). The representation of the customer as a powerful and inescapable force now appears common to diverse academic perspectives on organisation. At one level, then, there is congruence. At a deeper level, there are interesting differences in how customers are being constituted in academic texts. Our purpose in this paper has been twofold. First we have begun to map some of these images and the assumptions that have generated them. And second, we have used these representations to illustrate some broader observations about the use of multiple tropes to understand organisational phenomena. These relate first, to the importance of the enunciator's perspective, within which one dominant metaphor can have different meanings. Second, the extent to which explicitness of tropes differ across texts. And third, the existence of tensions within, as well as across, texts.

What significance do these observations carry for management and organisation studies? Below we outline a set of implications for research on the changing role and significance of the customer. These pertain to (1) analyses of the wider literature on organisation, (2) researchers' critical awareness of their own position on the meaning of 'the customer' in contemporary society and (3) attention to the views of service workers within organisations.

With respect to analyses of the wider literature, we have sought to undermine the position of a dominant, monolithic discourse of the customer. While the sovereign customer may be 'the primary image informing representations of economic life' (du Gay, 1996), this chapter has demonstrated that the phenomenon is variously constituted in different strands of literature. This chapter has taken a first step towards mapping and critically examining some of these images and in so doing has suggested ways of 'reading' texts. Researchers might usefully extend this analysis, through development of alternative maps and/or more focused and detailed critical analyses of customer representations. This can aid in understanding of particular texts and positions, for example by surfacing unacknowledged assumptions and tensions. It can also contribute to a broader understanding of the much remarked fragmentation of organisation studies (Burrell and Morgan, 1979; Pfeffer, 1993), using the lens of a particular phenomenon and the different ways it is constituted. This in turn may become a basis for constructive dialogue across perspectives (Fabian, 2000).

A second set of implications concerns researchers' understanding of their own positions. This takes us back to arguments for a reflexive approach, whereby researchers can arrive at a critical awareness of the assumptions underlying their own use of metaphors to conceptualise phenomena such as customers. This in turn is linked to debates concerning the constraining vs. liberating nature of metaphors in pursuit of knowledge of management and organisations (see for example, Tsoukas, 1993). It is in this vein that Morgan (1986:232) speaks of metaphors creating 'partial truth', and that Dunford and Palmer (1996:707) urge researchers to be aware of the extent to which their own perceptions 'are "saturated" by the metaphors they use to discuss and analyse [phenomena]'. These cautionary points, we would argue, are all the more important to bear in mind given the implicitness of much metaphorical thinking in organisational analysis, as well as the unavoidable tensions and indeterminacy inherent in most metaphorical representations.

A final set of research implications concerns attention to the perceptions of actors within organisations. Proceeding from arguments positing a dominant discourse of customer sovereignty, this chapter has examined various ways in which the customer is represented in academic texts and examined tensions within and across them. This raises empirical questions about how the customer is conceptualised by those engaged in service work. In other words, do workers constitute customers in similar or different ways to academic commentators? Further, what are the implications of *employee* discourses of the customer?

Such questions may be a useful for researchers operating within various perspectives. For example, Sturdy (1998) writing within a critical sociological vein, calls for empirical research on employees' experience of and reaction to consumerist ideas within organisations and in the wider socio-political context. He argues that the lack of such research on employees' subjectivity may have the effect of exaggerating 'the dominance and coherence of (consumerist) discourse' (Sturdy, 1998:46). For mainstream researchers, an understanding of how employees conceptualise customers would be useful, for example, in evaluations of the success of customer care interventions. It would also be useful in advancing understanding of how front-line employees experience service work, for example, the conditions under which it is experienced as stressful, fulfilling and so on. Critical analyses of the changing role and significance of the customer should not proceed in the absence of the views of those who actually engage in service work. We suspect empirical analyses of service workers' conceptualisations may render the concept of a 'dominant discourse' of customer sovereignty increasingly fragile.

Notes

1   Definitions of both ideology and discourse are contested and subject to ongoing debates. We use both terms, in the first instance, to refer to a system of beliefs organised around a set of core values (in this case those associated with enterprise). The notion of ideology differs here from discourse in that the former assumes the existence of an objective reality which may be known by people (i.e. they may 'see through' attempts to manipulate them through use of propaganda). The term discourse is contrasted here in a post-structuralist sense, in which 'reality' is held not to exist in objective terms, but rather is inseparable from and constituted through language (see Deetz, 1992; du Gay, 1996; Keat *et al.*, 1994; Rosenthal *et al.*, 1997).

References

Abercrombie, N. (1994) 'Authority and Consumer Society', in Keat, R., Whiteley, N. and Abercrombie, N. (eds), *The Authority of the Consumer*, 43–57, London: Routledge.

Alvesson, M. (1993) 'The Play of Metaphors', in Hassard, J. and Parker, M. (eds), *Post–modernism and Organisations*, 114–31, London: Sage.

Ashforth, B. and Humphrey, R. (1993) 'Emotional Labour in Service Roles: The Influence of Identity', *Academy of Management Review*, 18:1, 88–115.

Bowen, D. and Schneider, B. (1988) 'Services Marketing and Management: Implications for Organisational Behaviour', *Research in Organisational Behaviour*, 10, 43–80.

Burrell, G. and Morgan, G. (1979) *Sociological Paradigms and Organisational Analysis*, London: Heinemann.

Danet, B. (1981) 'Client Organisation Relationships', in Nystron, P. and Starbuck, W. (eds), *Handbook of Organisation Design*, New York: Oxford University Press.

Dean, J. and Bowen, D. (1994) 'Management Theory And Total Quality Management: Improving Research And Practice Through Theory Development', *Academy of Management Review*, 19, 392–418.

Deetz, S. (1992) 'Disciplinary Power and the Modern Corporation', in Alvesson, M. and Willmott, H. (eds), *Critical Management Studies*, London: Sage.

Deighton, J. (1994) 'Managing Services When Services is a Performance', in Rust, R. and Oliver, R. (eds), *Service Quality: New Directions in Theory and Practice*, 123–38, Thousand Oaks, Ca.: Sage.

Deming, W. (1986) *Out of the Crisis*, Cambridge: Cambridge University Press.

du Gay, P. (1996) *Consumption and Identity at Work*, London: Sage.

Dunford, R. and Palmer, I. (1996) 'Conflicting Uses of Metaphors: Reconceptualising Their Use in The Field of Organisational Change', *Academy of Management Review*, 21:3, 691–717.

Fabian, F. (2000) 'Keeping the Tension: Pressures to Keep Controversy in the Management Discipline', *Academy of Management Review*, 25:2, 350–71.

Filby, M. (1992) ' "The Figures, the Personality And the Bums": Service Work and Sexuality', *Work, Employment and Society*, 6:19, 23–42.

Fiol, C. (1990) 'Narrative Semiotics: Theory, Procedures and Illustration', in Huff, A. (ed.), *Mapping Strategic Thought*, Chichester: John Wiley and Sons.

Fuller, L. and Smith, V. (1991) 'Consumers' Reports: Management by Customers in a Changing Economy', *Work, Employment and Society*, 5:1, 1–16.

Gabriel, Y. and Lang, T. (1995) *The Unmanageable Consumer – Contemporary Consumption and its Fragmentations*, London: Sage.

Gersuny, C. and Rosengren, W. (1973) *The Service Society*, Cambridge, MA: Schenkman Publishing Company.

Hall, E. (1993) 'Smiling, Deferring and Flirting: Doing Gender by Giving "Good Service" ', *Work and Occupations*, 20:4, 452–71.

Heery, E. (1993) 'Industrial Relations and the Customer', *Industrial Relations Journal*, 24:4, 284–95.

Hill, S. and Wilkinson, A. (1995) 'In Search of TQM', *Employee Relations*, 17:3, 8–25.

Hochschild, A. (1983) *The Managed Heart – Commercialisation of Human Feeling*, Berkeley, Ca.: University of California Press.

Juran, J., Gryna, F. and Bingham, R. (1974) *Quality Control Handbook*, 3rd edn, New York: McGraw Hill.

Keat, R. and Abercrombie, N. (1991) *Enterprise Culture*, London: Routledge.

Keat, R., Whiteley, N. and Abercrombie, N. (1994) 'Introduction', in Keat, R., Whiteley, N. and Abercrombie, N. (eds), *The Authority of the Consumer*, 1–22, London: Routledge.

Knights, D. and Morgan, G. (1993) 'Organisation Theory and Consumption In A Post–Modern Era', *Organisation Studies*, 14:2, 211–34.

Lakoff, G. (1986) 'A Figure of Thought', *Metaphor and Symbolic Activity*, 1(3), 215–225.

Lengnick–Hall, C. (1996) 'Customer Contributions to Quality: A Different View of the Customer–Oriented Firm', *Academy of Management Review*, 21:3, 791–824.

Linstead, S. (1995) 'Averting the Gaze: Gender and Power on the Perfumed Picket Line', *Gender, Work and Organisations*, 2:4, 190–206.

Morgan, G. (1986) *Images of Organisation*, Beverly Hills: Sage.

Oakland, J. (1995) *Total Quality Management*, Oxford: Butterworth Heinemann.

Parker, M. (1992) 'Post-Modern Organisation or Post-modern Organisation Theory?', *Organisation Studies*, 13:1, 1–17.

Peters, T. and Waterman, R. (1982) *In Search of Excellence*, London: Fontana/Collins.

Pfeffer, J. (1993) 'Barriers to the Advance of Organisational Science: Paradigm Development as a Dependent Variable', *Academy of Management Review*, 18, 599–620.

Pratt, J. and Zeckhauser, R. (1985) *Principals and Agents: The Structure of Business*, Boston: Harvard Business School Press.

Rosenthal, P., Hill, S. and Peccei, R. (1997) 'Checking Out Service: Evaluating Excellence, HRM and TQM in Services', *Work, Employment and Society*, 11:3, 481–503.

Sturdy, A. (1998) 'Customer Care in a Consumer Society: Smiling and Sometimes Meaning It?', *Organisation*, 5:1, 27–53.

Taylor, S. and Tyler, M. (2000) 'Emotional Labour and Sexual Difference in the Airline Industry', *Work, Employment and Society*, 14:1, 83–4.

Tsoukas, H. (1993) 'Analogical Reasoning and Knowledge Generation In Organisation Theory', *Organisation Studies*, 14:3, 323–46.

Turner, B. (1988) *Status*, Milton Keynes: Open University

Wilkinson, A., Redman, T., Snape, E. and Marchington, M. (1998) *Managing with Total Quality – Theory and Practice*, Basingstoke: Macmillan.

3
Representing Customer Service: Telephones and Texts

Edward Wray-Bliss

Introduction: Serving the Customers of our Texts

In writing this chapter,[1] I experience there to be an expectation that I write about 'customer service' as something that exists independently of what I or the other contributors and the editors are doing in producing this text. The interesting social phenomena are happening 'out there', in factories, nurseries, schools, hospitals, telephone banks and shopping arcades, and the book is merely a frame through which these outside events and occasions may be viewed and understood. And (to be honest) to an extent that is what I will be doing by reflecting upon the meaning(s) of 'customer service' for a group of call centre workers. However, I am also concerned to challenge this felt expectation that positions the contributors, like myself, as privileged observers and commentators upon others' celebrations of, colonisation by, or battles with discourses of 'customer service'. To this end I aim to exploit a 'customer service' discourse to encourage us to think of the effects of our texts and our research for those we study. Specifically, I hope to make central to your/our readings and production of these texts consideration of the 'service' or otherwise we are giving to those we research. Such consideration is not always as common as those we research might have legitimate right to expect. Normalised practices of textual construction in organisational studies act in intersecting ways to separate off the representations produced from the social, ethical, organisational context of their production. The author's role becomes seen as a responsibility to produce an authoritative and interesting account, rather than to feel particularly responsible for how this then reflects upon the lives of those from whom it was constructed. Conventions of academic textual construction such as corroboration with existing literatures, processes of selection, silencing, and appropriation, and implicit and explicit claims to interpretive authority, encourage us to understand a narrative as non-narrated: as authoritative, as truthful, as expertly researched, as a story of the real that must be told (Edwards and Potter, 1992; hooks, 1989; Opie, 1992; Said 1978; Seidman, 1992; Smith, 1990a; Spivak, 1990; Van Maanen, 1988). I wish to encourage us to view chapters in this book, and by implication other texts, somewhat differently. Like Smith (1990a:162), I understand texts to 'enter into and order courses of action and relations among individuals'. Texts:

> are social relations. They are more than simply an expansion of communication beyond the local. They reorganize relationships among local everyday worlds within them and by relating them to others through common participation in the textually mediated discourse. People scattered and unknown to one another are coordinated in an orientation to the same texts. Public textual discourse creates new forms of social relations. (Smith, 1990a:168)

Following Smith, questions then of just what social relations (what 'relations with otherness' (Jodelet, 1991:18)) we encourage becomes a central, if not the central, criterion for our evaluation and production of texts. What are the likely or intended 'truth effects' of the representations we choose to produce or read? In this context, the production, dissemination and reception of a text then becomes a matter of our ethical–political agency – our intervention into existing and future social relations. As Opie (1992) asks, 'Who are we writing for? What kinds of authority should we claim for our text? What kind of texts should we be producing?' Or to rephrase this, what future or existing social relations do we want to legitimise, enable or pathologise? What 'service' do we want to give to our 'customers': the researched, whose existence and resistance we cite as tacit authority for our critiques?

I suggest here that at present many of our texts do a disservice to those we research. Our representations can, and often do, encourage and embody subordinating and pathologising relations: relations of distance from and denouncement of others. I make this argument through exploring the effects of different representations of call centre clerks' use of a discourse of 'customer service'. These representations are made through drawing upon existing organisational studies literatures. These include du Gay and Salaman's (1992) critique of enterprise; Knights and Collinson's (1987) representation of gendered subjectivity; and Bauman's (1989, 1993) examination of organisational amorality. Before exploring these representations and their effects I provide an introduction to the call centre, the clerks, and their understanding of 'customer service' below.

Background to a Call Centre or 'Dark Satanic Mill'

Much of the physical, social and technical background of the call centre that I explore in this chapter is, regrettably, probably familiar to many readers of this book. Regrettably familiar because the levels of surveillance, monitoring and intensification of labour in call centres, and the associated redundancies and rationalisations of other non-call centre staff, have already carved out a unenviable space in organisational folk-lore. As one author has evocatively phrased it, call centres are the 'dark satanic mills' of the modern era (Wylie, 1997). I am happy (?) to let this imagery stand as a general-emotional representation for the call centre I focus upon here. But to draw out issues of 'customer service' as experienced and negotiated within the day-to-day life of the call centre I add to this now some more detail about the micro-practice of labouring as a call centre clerk.[2]

Call centre clerks' performance is measured on the number of calls answered. The target at the time of this study (it has since been raised) is set by management as 95 to 115 calls a day for full-time staff, proportionally less for part-time staff. Clerks are paid and evaluated in relation to their meeting, exceeding, or failing to meet this target. To meet the target clerks depend upon being sent enough calls by the central, call-managing, computer. Calls are sent to the clerk who has been logged by the computer as 'available' the longest. To be 'available' a clerk must not be on the telephone to another customer and must not be on 'wrap-up' – that is temporarily removed from the queue by the clerks' own initiation to perform a task which could not be completed within the time that the customer was on the phone. A clerk can thus ensure that they receive a high number of calls by maximising 'available' time and minimising time on calls or wrap-up. To do this clerks have to apply at least three techniques of micro-task/self-management, namely the management of customers, the management of the computer, and the management of time. A typical call demonstrates these techniques in process. In the following example, to indicate the multi-layered aspect of clerks' work I have used **bold** to represent the conversation between clerk and customer, and *italics* to explain the encounter and indicate the tasks a clerk performs.

Background: transfer of money requests made by previous customers have been written down by the clerk to be performed in between calls. A transfer of money involves the clerk performing several processes. Rather than press 'wrap-up' after each call and thus taking her/himself from the call queue, clerks typically save transfers and other time consuming tasks until there is not another customer immediately waiting. This they know by checking the two LED displays around the department and by the light on their telephone turrets. They then conduct the transfer while still logged as available. As frequently happens a call arrives while the clerk is still making the transfer.

Headset.	**'Beep'** *automatic call feeding has given the clerk a call*
Clerk.	*control tone/emotion, clerk must be efficient and pleasant, tone of voice moderated to disguise the fact that clerk is working on another customer's account, carries on with transfer while answering phone* **'Good afternoon Telephone Bank, how may I help you?'** *listens to answer, while it is being given enters:*

number of transfer account to be debited, tab across, amount, tab across, and number of account to be credited.

Customer. **'I'd like a balance please'**

Clerk. **'A balance, certainly'** *repeating the demand buys a little time; checks information entered . . . ok . . . hits function key to complete transaction, enters 5 digit code for next screen* **'Could you tell me at which branch your account is held please'** *controls conversation, minimises unnecessary chat – if the transfer is not going well, if clerk is hitting wrong keys etc, s/he might ask about the weather or how the business is doing, this buys more time. Use of this technique depends on clues about the emotional state of the customer, some customers clearly don't want to chat – while listening to answer begins to input note about transfer onto computer notepad screen on other customer's account XFER 200.00 FROM A/C 9107554-00 TO 9107554-02 AS CUST. REQ.*

Customer. **'Leeds, New Street'**

Clerk. **'Leeds'** *repeating this buys another split second, presses function key to confirm transfer of money, returns to start screen, only now starts to work on screen on current customer's account; types in sort code for Leeds New Street if s/he doesn't recall it clerk finds number in folder to her right, while looking s/he buys more time by asking* **'And your account number please?'**

Customer. **'8107595'**

Clerk. *while listening, finds sort code, enters it, tabs across, and enters account number, tabs down, enter pass number screen code* **'Ok, could you tell me your pass number please?'**

Customer. **'1970'**

Clerk. *enters pass number, waits for confirmation . . . ok . . . enters balance information screen code, buys time while waiting for the screen to catch up by asking . . .* **'Ok, and it was a balance you wanted?'**

Customer. **'That's right'**

Clerk. **'Your closing balance at the end of business last night was . . .'** *speaking this introduction fills in time it takes for information to appear on screen, by this stage clerk may be curious to see how much they have, s/he is careful to control the emotional tone of her voice here, pleasant and professional, no hint of judgement or surprise whatever the amount in/or how overdrawn the account* **'Six thousand, four hundred and thirty five pounds and sixteen pence in credit, your forecast balance is Six thousand, five hundred, and sixty five pounds and sixteen pence in credit'** *clerk is ready to read it out again. If the customer seems to have taken note of it, s/he anticipates customer's*

> *next request and enter 'movement of recent items' screen code –*
> *most customers want this information after a balance.*

Customer.   **'6435, and 6565'**

Clerk.   **'That's right . . . can I help you with anything else?'**

Customer.   **'No that's all, thanks, goodbye.'**

Clerk.   **'Thank you for calling, Goodbye'** *presses button on phone*
to clear line, enters first screen code, checks telephone display,
any calls waiting? if so s/he must be ready to greet next
customer, if not clerk begins next transfer she had saved up
from earlier.

The amount of emotional and technical micro-self management involved in even this, one of the most straight-forward calls, is considerable, especially if we consider that this whole process, from start to finish, *will last only between 40 and 60 seconds* (possibly half the time it took you to read this description of the call). To perform the actions that both customers (current and previous) required within this time frame, the clerk exercises various forms of micro self-discipline.

First, the extract is illustrative of the discipline of managing one's workday. Keying-in work (transferring money) had been saved from an earlier busier period so that the clerk could maximise the number of calls taken by avoiding using 'wrap-up'. Second, the clerk exercises considerable computer literacy and speed to key-in information on another customer's account in the imperceptible (to the customer) spaces in the current customer's dialogue. Third, the clerk holds and manipulates several different pieces of information, procedures and tasks simultaneously. The information the current customer gives and the procedures involved in giving an account balance are held and used in addition to the information and procedures from a previous customer's account. The previous interaction as in this case is often the responsible task of transferring money between two accounts. Fourth, and finally, the clerk interprets and manages the emotional aspect of the encounter. By controlling the emotional tone of their voice the pressure the clerk is under is masked from the customer. The customer is responded to as if they hold the clerk's full attention and not as if the clerk is working on another customer's account. Also the customer is managed or directed to give the clerk only the necessary information. In effect the clerk takes control of the call but in a way that does not leave the customer feeling manipulated. The clerk interprets the customer's emotional tone and can use this to work out if some non-direct task focused talk might be engaged in to create a little more space to finish the transfer. Further it is important for the clerk to manage their own emotional responses, to guard against the communication of any frustration, haste, curiosity, surprise, envy or pity as well as to guard against emotional de-personalisation of the service being communicated to the customer.

To successfully achieve or surpass targets, the clerk continually applies these and other techniques of emotional and technical micro-self discipline throughout an eight-hour day on the telephones. In very busy periods the clerk will use these skills at a frantic pace to shave vital seconds off a call, so as to get back in the queue quickly: thus enabling the next call to be taken and the targets to be brought that little bit closer. At such times a clerk is ever vigilant about the length of time a call is taking and is always self-surveilling to see how fast they are typing and moving between screens.

A result of successfully learning and applying these forms of micro self-discipline is a fragmented, fast paced, and pressured job, that requires both 'hard' technical competence in the manipulation of the computer system and knowledge of procedure, and 'soft' emotional labour in the form of direct customer contact, management of tone and emotion. In the experiences of clerks at the call centre, aspects of the 'hard' technical and 'soft' emotional/personal elements of the job conflicted. Clerks named and affirmed this conflict by constructing in their conversations an *antagonism* between the department manager's privileging of quantified targets as the over-riding measure of employee performance and the clerks' privileging of notions of 'customer service' and quality of service. As one clerk explained:

> At first when the figures were first given out there was a lot of animosity about it, because I mean for the first ten months we worked here we didn't have a target, you just come in, did your work, so there wasn't any pressure on to do a certain amount any day which I feel . . . I must admit I enjoyed more because the quality of service you can give is a lot better when you've not got the pressure on that today you've got to do 81 and you've only done 50 and you've only got one hour to go, you know its a case of getting everybody off the phone, and I think that side of it, you're then taking away the quality issue, erm . . . so that was like my argument not, I mean, Gary would come back and say 'yeah but you can do that' and I would say 'I don't dispute I can do it, I know I can do it, but what quality am I going to be giving?', that side of it . . . I did think it was a minus really, I thought they was going backwards not forwards.

By drawing upon a discourse of 'customer service' clerks constructed the meaning of their labour as *distinct from* the meanings promoted by the departmental manager and as *opposing* these meanings. 'Customer service' was understood by clerks as an *alternative* to the privileging of targets: an alternative that enabled clerks to construct their labour/themselves as performing socially relevant activity.[3] For instance, Kevin, a clerk who was initially temporarily employed drew upon the language of 'helping people' to explain his decision to work in the call centre rather than pursue his previously planned career choice of counselling. For this clerk, both occupations had at their root the social/moral relationship of helping the public. The intimacy of customers' voices reproduced in stereo through clerks' headsets, and the immediate satisfaction of customers' transactional or informational requests could be used by clerks to affirm this sense of performing a helpful and socially necessary job. Further, though call centre customers may well experience and communicate aspects of the service as frustrating, the quote below demonstrates how clerks could still reinterpret such encounters to affirm their valued constructions of helping the customer:

> If you've had a customer on and erm . . . I mean I had one not last week, the week before, who was rude to me and like I said to him like 'I don't feel there's any need to be rude', you know, and then he said, 'I'm not being rude, do you want me to be rude? I'll be rude', and something like that I would say nine times out of ten I guarantee they're going to complain . . . I spent like five minutes trying to help him, I tried to ring him back, he wouldn't let me ring him back, then he was complaining about the phone bill . . . You know all that type of thing.

As illustrated here a key aspect for creating relations with customers as 'service', rather than for instance as 'commodity', was time. In the example above, though the encounter was personally upsetting for the clerk, she could still present herself as trying to help the customer because of the extra-ordinary amount of time she spent on the call: 'I spent like five minutes trying to help him'. In the context of strictly monitored and policed call times, five minutes was an unusually long amount of time for clerks to be talking to one customer. Here again the 'hard' managerial privileging of targets was understood by clerks to conflict with the need to take time to help and provide a service for the customer. Within this conflict clerks used discourses of 'customer service' to critique the managerial privileging of targets, a position succinctly summarised by call centre clerk Sharon.

> If you pick up the phone 100 times a day and cut them off that's okay with Gary [department manager] . . . I'm at odds with Gary over targets . . . it's not good customer service . . . I've got a target of 40 calls but I don't care – I do the job as I think it should be done . . . we're here to help people.'

I use the remainder of this chapter to explore available representations from within organisational studies for making sense of clerks privileging of this 'oppositional' discourse of 'customer service'. In particular I focus upon the likely effects of alternative representations – the likely 'social relations' (Smith, 1990a:168) and 'courses of action' (ibid:162) that these representations encourage. My central concern is to argue that available representations of customer service (and many other aspects of organisational life) may pathologise others. Relations of distance and denouncement are engendered by texts in which academic 'experts' judge and criticise others' engagement with organisational realities and discourses while remaining themselves comfortably isolated from the fray (see also hooks, 1989; Opie, 1992; Seidman, 1992; Wray-Bliss, 1999).

Customer Service: As Enterprising Managerial Control

In this section I explore the effects of representing clerks' 'customer service' discourse as a practice that reinforces managerial control over the call-centre labour process. I draw upon du Gay and Salaman's (1992) work *'The Cult(ure) of the Customer'* as illustrative of a literature that enables this representation. I argue that through drawing upon such literature the discourse of 'customer service' may be represented not as an alternative or oppositional practice but rather as central to the wider managerial re-imagining and re-structuring of commercial life around the enterprising figure of the 'sovereign customer'.

In their review of contemporary organisational theory and practice, du Gay and Salaman argue that the cult(ure) of the customer 'is fundamental to current management paradigms' (1992:616). They continue:

> Recent emphasis on a clearly defined notion of the customer as represent-ing the key dynamic of market relations has become a central feature of work reorganisation, and critically, of attempts by managers and their advisers to delineate and intervene into the organisation of paid work (ibid).

du Gay and Salaman – in common with a number of other Organisational Studies and Labour Process authors (e.g. McKinlay and Taylor, 1998; Sewell and Wilkinson, 1992; Willmott, 1993; Willmott and Wray-Bliss, 1996) – have argued that attempts by management to 'delineate and intervene' into the organisation of the labour process are increasingly focusing upon employ-ees' attitudes or subjective understanding and experience of their labour (du Gay and Salaman, 1992:621). In particular it has been argued that management is attempting to govern the 'soul' of the employee (Rose, 1990) in such a way that paid employment becomes a means of individual fulfilment and enterprising self-actualisation. So understood, modern management practices may be represented as desiring to create an affinity between an ethic of the self and a capitalist work ethic. According to du Gay and Salaman this affinity between (or is it colonisation of?) the employees' private self and(/by?) the work self is achieved by re-aligning and re-imagining both 'public' and 'private', commercial and non-commercial, around the 'moral centre of the enterprising universe': the figure of the 'consumer-customer' (1992:622).

Drawing upon this thesis clerks' use of a discourse of 'customer service' could be represented as another successful translation of enterprise culture into the 'subjective understandings and identities' (du Gay and Salaman, 1992:621) of a group of employees. For instance, I have already argued that the discourse of 'customer service', which privileges the needs and rights of the customer, was the principal means by which clerks represented their work and themselves. Further, clerks' use of this discourse could easily be understood as an enterprising ethical discourse, focusing upon the customer as the 'moral centre' of their work practices. Remember, for instance, Kevin's explanation of his decision to stay at the bank rather than to go into counselling, and Sharon's statement that 'I do the job as I think it *should* be done . . . we're here to *help* people'.

By drawing upon du Gay and Salaman's writings, instead of representing 'customer service' as an oppositional discourse, clerks' construction of the meaning of their work and themselves may be understood as a further example of the saturation or colonisation of employees' subjectivities by the wider managerial culture of enterprise. In this way the 'alternative' discourse of 'customer service' is understood as no alternative. It is a managerial discourse that strengthens enterprising managerial control.

What are the likely effects of such a representation of the clerk's use of a discourse of 'customer service'? A beneficial effect of drawing upon literatures that problematise the cult(ure) of the customer, is that we, as readers of this representation, may become sensitised to the potentially problematic implications of this seductive and widespread discourse. This critical sensitivity when applied to the call centre clerks' situation alerts us to several possible unintended consequences of clerks' use of this discourse to resist management, three of which I consider below.

First, by privileging 'customer relations' over 'industrial relations' clerks may be understood to be following a less established path of resistance to management control with less developed support structures, such as legally recognised and, to some extent, protected trade unions. Further, by privileging a discourse that is outside more traditional industrial relation concerns (of, for example, pay or employment rights) clerks may be interpreted as potentially contributing to a decline in the political visibility and viability of unions. Thus, for instance, despite the pressures and stresses that working at the call centre engendered, for eight out of the nine months I was working there, there was no local union representative and many clerks expressed little overt interest in one.

Second, the focus upon customers' needs may also mitigate against clerks engaging in more traditional and overt forms of resistance. Feelings of responsibility to the customer may, for instance, inhibit clerks from engaging in forms of resistance (such as striking or work-to-rule) that derive their political power precisely through *disrupting* 'normal' service provision.

Third, the focus on 'customer needs' could be understood to potentially accommodate clerks into providing the emotional labour (Hochschild, 1983) required of tele-service workers. So understood, clerks' focus upon 'customer service' could be regarded not as an *alternative* to speed and targets but as an essential *mediation* between on the one hand management's focus upon speed and on the other hand customers' requirements of a personalised and attentive telephone service. The focus upon 'customer service' could be understood to function to accommodate clerks into softening management's' objectification and commodification of the customer by providing the human face (voice) of the bank. Mobilising such a strategy enables work to be performed at target pace and without alienating customers.

As a way of sensitising us to the potential unintended effects of clerks' use of a discourse of 'customer service' to resist the department managers' privileging of speed and targets, literatures such as du Gay and Salaman's are useful. Such studies can, for instance, be read as improving the chances of workers exercising their political agency by highlighting some of the risks of particular discourses. However, a focus upon and privileging of the problematic effects (and theory) of managerial technologies and discourses over their contestation, reinterpretation and transformation in practice (see also e.g. Sewell and Wilkinson, 1992; Willmott, 1993; Willmott and Wray-Bliss, 1996) may also be understood to risk reproducing problematic effects.

One risk of drawing upon theoretical critiques of managerial technologies or ideologies such as du Gay and Salaman's is that we may reproduce the lack of consideration of workers' political agency within these texts in our own empirical representations and thus our and others' understandings of the workplace. For instance, if I was to exclusively or principally draw upon concepts from du Gay and Salaman's article I might be forgiven for representing the discourse of 'customer service' as *necessarily* reinforcing managerial control. For example the authors (1996:622) argue that: 'enterprise has remorselessly reconceptualized and remodelled almost everything in its path. Ostensibly different "spheres of existence" have fallen prey to its "totalizing" and "individualizing" economic rationality.'

In this representation of enterprise culture, few people or areas of our life seem to be able to escape from its 'totalizing' influence. 'from the hospital to the railway station, from the classroom to the museum, the nation finds itself translated. "Patients", "parents", "passengers" and 'pupils" are re-imagined as "customers"' (ibid:622).

Further, even when people elude its grip on their consciousness or maintain a distance from its narrative, du Gay and Salaman argue that enterprise is still being reproduced through 'their involvement in the everyday practices within which enterprise is inscribed' (ibid: 630).

To represent enterprising managerial control as *necessarily* inscribed in the discourse of 'customer service' risks representing clerks as lacking the agency to re-shape this discourse for non-managerially posited ends. By representing clerks as subordinate to a managerially controlled 'customer service' discourse, our texts risk becoming complicit in making this subordination a reality. Further, we position those who engage with such a discourse as necessarily colonised by enterprise and therefore deluded if they think otherwise. This conveniently legitimises traditional (positivist) academic social relations *vis à vis* the researched – relations whose roots seem to intertwine with the roots of colonialism where the researched/colonised are:

> a subject race, dominated by a race [of academic experts?] that knows them and what is good for them better than they could possibly know themselves (Said, 1978:35)

Customer Service: As Clerks' Collaboration in Their Own (Gendered) Oppression .

In this section I explore the effects of representing clerks' use of a discourse of 'customer service' as a partial, though ultimately ineffectual, form of resistance to managerial commodification of the call centre labour process. To facilitate this I draw upon Knights and Collinson's (1987) 'Disciplining the shopfloor' as illustrative of conceptual approaches that enable us to explore employees as active agents involved in the construction of their own gendered identities and understandings of work (see also Collinson, 1994; Knights, 1990; Knights, 1997; Knights and Willmott, 1989, cf. Collinson, 1992).

Knights and Collinson's (1987) article represents the events leading up to shopfloor workers' acceptance of (or acquiescence to) redundancy from their employing organisation 'Slavs'. The authors present the male workers as drawing upon masculine discourses (1987:460) to construct and affirm a 'gendered subjectivity' (ibid:459) that emphasised their independence from management and the honest and practical nature of the workers' physical labour and selves (ibid:466).

The authors represent this masculine identity as differentially conditioning the workers' responses to two managerially promoted discourses: a 'soft' psychological discourse and a 'hard' accountancy discourse. The 'soft' psychological discourse emphasising 'open-communication' and 'co-operation', promoted through the medium of a glossy company magazine, was openly resisted and ridiculed by the men. Knights and Collinson argue that this discourse, rather than securing the workers' co-operation as intended, only served to 'solidify oppositional shopfloor cultural understandings of what was valuable in life and work' (1987:466). The explanation given by Knights and Collinson for this opposition and resistance is that the messages of 'co-operation' and 'communication' drawn upon by this managerial discourse conflicted with the workers' daily experience of the manipulative nature of managerial control and routine construction of workers as dispensable commodities. Further it was argued that the men's privileging of 'straight talking' and 'honesty' central to the men's' masculine identity enabled them to resist the pressures for identification contained within what they experienced as management's use of a dishonest and manipulative psychological discourse.

If the workers' sense of identity facilitated their resistance to the 'soft' psychological discourse it had, according to the authors, precisely the opposite effect when workers were confronted with a 'hard' accounting discourse contained within the redundancy audit. Though the audit was questionable as a 'true and fair' representation of the plant's finances and served to rationalise making the men redundant, Knights and Collinson represent the workers as politically passive in the face of this discourse and to the prospect of their own redundancies that it contained (ibid: 469, 474). The explanation given by the authors is that the accountancy discourse coincided with, and reinforced, the men's masculine sense of their labour and self. The discourse privileged a hard numerical, apparently objective, form of representation which both affirmed the men's own sense of the problematic financial position of the company and resonated with their masculine privileging of direct, honest and straight-talking forms of speech. Furthermore, Knights and Collinson argue that the men's masculine identity privileged ideas of independence from the organisation which was a 'subjective position that could not acknowledge the reality of labour's actual *dependence* on the company since this would deny the very autonomy which was the foundation of shopfloor dignity' (ibid:472).

Drawing upon Knights and Collinson's (1987) text as a resource for understanding and representing the labour process makes available a particular way of understanding clerks use of the discourse of 'customer service'. As with the workers at Slavs, call centre clerks could be understood as drawing upon 'gendered' images and concepts to construct a valued sense of their identity and opposition to management. The male workers at Slavs were presented as constructing a *masculine* 'gendered subjectivity' that drew upon discourses of independence and physical/practical labour. The predominantly female call centre clerks could be understood to construct a *feminine* 'gendered subjectivity' that centred upon ideas of 'care', 'service', and 'responsibility'. Further, as in the example of Slavs, this sense of identity could be understood to enable clerks to resist identifying with or accepting a managerially promoted (*masculine*) discourse of 'targets', 'quantity' and 'commodification' that conflicted with the clerks' valued sense of self and work. A positive effect of representing clerks through such arguments is that a possibility of understanding and exploring 'customer service' as a manifestation of *resistance* is opened-up. In Marxist terms, clerks' use of a discourse of 'customer service' may be represented as their resistance to *self-alienation* (Marx, 1844 in Simon, 1994; Wray-Bliss and

Parker, 1998). Despite the rigid discipline, the stigmatisation of 'manual' labour, 'the precariousness of economic reward' and the 'perpetual job insecurity", Knights and Collinson's text approach enables us to understand the men they studied as able to derive dignity and satisfaction from, and even to celebrate, their labour (ibid:466). Similarly, call centre clerks can be understood as relating to their work in a way that enabled them to experience it as a manifestation of their care for, and desire to help the customer and thus as a worthwhile and valuable activity. Further this understanding of, and relationship to, their labour was in explicit opposition to how the work was commodified and routinised within the managerial discourse of targets. Clerks' use of the 'customer service' discourse may thus be represented as resistance to a managerially promoted 'alienating' way of experiencing self and labour.

Having opened-up possibilities of understanding the call centre clerks and the workers at Slavs as resisting the oppressive effects of self-alienation, Knights and Collinson's work may also be understood to risk marginalising the importance of this form of resistance. Although they highlight the sense of dignity, integrity and freedom Slav workers had constructed around their labour, the authors then represent this valued subjective experience of labour and self as 'illusionary' (ibid:474). Workers had the 'illusion that they are autonomous from, and superior in dignity to, management' (ibid:472) and their valued sense of self could be dismissed as 'purely at the level of subjective positioning' (ibid:472). Knights and Collinson may be understood to marginalise further the political significance of this 'purely subjective positioning' by contrasting it with what they call 'real resistance'

> despite the shopfloor's scepticism about the content of the journal in general, expressed in their re-naming it 'Goebbel's Gazette', when the time came for *real resistance* to the proposed redundancies, the Associated Union of Engineering Workers (A.U.E.W) was unable to generate workforce opposition . . . resistance was absent despite the widespread rejection of management explanations (1987:465, emphasis original).

The explanation the authors give for the 'absence' of resistance to redundancy was that the men's sense of independence and valuing of straight talking and honest communication rendered them 'overwhelmingly disadvantaged in resisting financial discipline' (ibid:475). Further, not only does the men's valued construction of self and labour render them 'politically docile' (ibid:474) in the face of their own redundancies, but such a representation allows us to understand workers to actively 'collaborate in' (ibid:471) and 'voluntarily extend the power of' their own subordination (ibid:459). Applying these arguments to the call centre, clerks' constructions of the meaning of their labour in ways they experienced as valuable and worthwhile may be similarly represented. Clerks' 'customer service' may be understood as offering them only the illusion of dignity and integrity and as rendering them particularly susceptible to forms of managerial discipline couched in terms that resonate with the clerks' 'caring' subjective positioning.

Drawing upon Knights and Collinson to represent call centre clerks may be understood to reproduce similar subordinating effects as drawing upon du Gay and Salaman. That is, call centre management apparently only have to present their demands in a 'customer service' vocabulary to secure a *politically docile* workforce who *actively collaborate* in their own subordination. Literatures like Knights and Collinson's (1987) article enables us to imagine the call centre workplace as an arena where 'clever', 'enterprising', male managers use discourses of 'customer service' to manipulate 'poor' women employees 'trapped' in a caring, service orientated, subjectivity. Such a representation, is unfortunately not a particularly uncommon portrayal of (women) workers' agency in organisational theory (see Collins and Wray-Bliss, 2000 for a review and critique of women's subordination in malestream Labour Process Theory texts). The kinds of social relations between researcher and researched that such representations engender are suggested in Knights and Collinson's conclusions. Rather than, for instance, exploring with the researched the accuracy, meanings, or implications of the text, the authors privilege outside 'experts' as the only group of people capable of making sense or use of their research.

> Its [refering to the authors own research] only potential then must lie with the audience of academic accountants who, in recognising the enormous disciplinary power of accounting knowledge, may give more attention to the moral and political consequences of their practice (1987:474).

Customer Service: As a Moral Challenge to Organisation

Here I draw upon Bauman's (1989, 1993) writings as illustrative of literatures that enable clerks' use of a discourse of 'customer service' to be explained as a moral/political discourse, a discourse that is potentially radically unsettling for organisation.

For Bauman, the 'decisive defining feature' of all organisation is the rendering of its members' actions predictable (1989:213). Organisations exist by creating a 'precarious regularity' (ibid) of human behaviour. To achieve this precarious regularity, organisations must suppress or otherwise limit unpredictable action on the part of its members. According to Bauman the most disruptive, unpredictable force that organisational members may draw upon to resist organisational pressures for conformity and predictability is *morality* (1989, 1993). Organisations have been concerned throughout modernity to suppress or otherwise mitigate against members' evaluation of organisational demands according to their own independent moral standards (1993).[4]

The modern organisation has developed numerous strategies to fulfil this task (see Bauman, 1989). These include subjecting organisational members' behaviour to instrumental or procedural rather than moral criteria (Bauman, 1989:213). Distancing the individual from the effects of their actions renders moral evaluation of these effects much more difficult. Distancing may be bureaucratic: by dividing work into discrete and separate tasks, none of which appear to coalesce into a task or action significant enough to warrant moral evaluation. And distancing may be psychological: by dividing up other individuals into discreet traits or roles (e.g. customer, employee) who appear to warrant our interest only in particular and specific ways (e.g. provision of a quality service or abiding by employment law) rather than demanding our more fundamental moral concern. Finally, organisations may deflect our moral responsibility by establishing chains of authority, where there is always somebody above who takes the operational responsibility, and to whom organisational members may also abdicate their moral responsibility (Bauman, 1989; see also Milgram, 1974).

The result of an organisation successfully deflecting its members morality would be the maintenance of the 'precarious regularity' and uniformity of behaviour on which it relies. The price of failing to suppress morality is the potential for organisational members to challenge what are for Bauman the very foundations of organisational control (Bauman 1989). Drawing upon these ideas, clerks' use of a discourse of 'customer service' may be represented as their construction of call centre labour as morally infused: as ordered around morally charged notions such as care, responsibility, and service. Further, in so constructing themselves/their labour, the effect can be to destabilise the precarious *amoral* regularity of organisational control. I explore this representation and its effects further below.

By understanding clerks to be constructing their labour as morally charged, they may be represented as resisting the colonisation of organisational activity by '*instrumental* or *procedural* criteria of evaluation' (Bauman, 1989:213). The clerks do not accept management's definition of service as 'speed' and resist the construction of their labour as merely applying standardised techniques to achieve a fast turnaround of customer calls (remember Pam's 'I know I can do it, but what quality am I going to be giving?' and Sharon's 'I've got a target of 40 calls but I don't care . . . we're here to help people').

Clerks may be represented as resisting the further bureaucratisation and (sub)division of their work, where seemingly inconsequential tasks never seem to add up to anything worthy enough of ethical consideration (Bauman, 1989). In their use of the 'customer service' discourse, clerks may be understood to reject the rationale, and resent the practice, of separating the more routine tasks from the more time consuming and potentially rewarding work of answering customers' queries. Currently, management like this more involved work to be passed on to other departments so as not to disrupt the single-minded pursuit of targets. Yet the clerks vigorously rejected the image of themselves as 'glorified switchboard operators' that this practice contributes to. As call centre clerk Steve recounted 'they [customers] say "aren't I through to the switchboard? Can't I put you through?" you know what I mean, that grinds away at you'.

Further, clerks' emphasis upon their wider (social and moral) responsibility to the customer may be represented as in direct conflict with the commodification of the customer within the statistical control and surveillance systems on the department. Through these mechanisms the customer is reduced to a call (or less, a statistic), one of between 95 and 115 that must be clocked-up by each clerk each shift. The uniqueness of individual customers' social, financial, or informational needs are dissolved into statistics concerning average length of calls. Clerks' discourse of 'customer service' may be represented as a (moral) respect for customers' difference in opposition to management's standardisation and quantification of performance. Where management could be understood to morally *de-face* (Bauman, 1993) the customer both physically (by closing face-to-face branches and organising administration of customer service at remote centralised call centres) and symbolically (by constructing the customer as a commodity or statistic), clerks may be represented as trying to bring this face back into clearer focus. In the discourse of 'customer service' the 'customer' may be understood as a *person* who is *also* a customer, and a person to whom clerks relate socially and morally.

This 'moral' representation of clerks' use of a 'customer service' discourse enables several effects for understanding and relating to clerks. Drawing upon Bauman, with his privileging of the ethical *impulse* and *emotionality* over *rationality* and rules, opens-up possibilities for understanding moral identifications as the *heart* of politics (Bauman, 1993). We can use this understanding to represent resistance not as a product of intellectualised or academic knowledge of oppression but rather, or perhaps also, as a result of being emotionally involved, of *feeling* the need to resist. To represent it another way, *ethics may be understood as the heart of politics.*

In this way call centre clerks, through constructing and drawing upon the moral discourse of 'customer service', can be interpreted as rejecting and resisting the amorality of organisation. A crucial construction of clerks' ethical discourse is their lack of identification with managerial privileging of depersonalised targets and identification with moral values of care, help, responsibility and service. Values that Bauman represents as threatening the precarious regularity of organisation (Bauman 1989). For example, clerks' current demands for better 'customer service', more time to deal with queries, etc, conflicts with the organisation's current commercial agenda and would likely threaten the organisation's financial standing *vis à vis* other call centre organisations. Clerks can thus be represented as using a 'customer service' discourse to construct for themselves a sense of their moral responsibility that could form the heart of a radical political challenge to the current direction, if not foundations, of the call centre.[5] To effect this representation of the radical potential of customer service more generally in our texts and minds might demand of organisational researchers that we step outside of our historical malestream privileging of 'masculine' confrontational discourses as the only basis of resistance and reflect, for example, upon the experiences of peace campaigners and much of the women's movement where values such as compassion, care and peace have long constituted the ethical core of a radical politics (Barrett, 1980; Firestone, 1980; Griffin, 1984). Rather than seeing values such as service as 'weak' we can reflect upon the fact that 'compassion can become the starting point of revolution against systems of inhumanity sustained by myth' (Berger, 1963:184).

By drawing upon conceptual resources that enable clerks' engagement with a discourse of 'customer service' to be represented as informing a potentially radical politics, their agency is less easily written-off, or written-out of, our texts and minds. Instead clerks can be represented as actively involved in a process of reimagining customer service as morally/ethically charged, and as linked to a potentially transformative politics. Such representations open-up possibilities for different social relations between researcher and researched, where the researched rather than being known and thereby objectified in the text, may instead retain potentiality and the ability to step outside of, and disrupt, our containing 'authoritative' pronouncements/denouncements. As Opie (1992:59) writes, one way to diminish textual appropriation of the researched is to pay 'attention to the paradoxical, the contradictory, the marginal, and by the foregrounding (not suppression) of these elements'. A sense of the researched's potentiality and uncontainability, reproduced as in here through exploring the link between ethics and politics, figures strongly in Rothschild and Miethe's (1994) study of whistleblowers. Rather than closing off incentives for our shared engagement with the researched by marginalising whistleblowers agency as 'known' and 'limited', their text nicely illustrates how relations of deep interest in the researched may be encouraged through representing the *potentiality* and unknowable *possibility* inherent in the agency of those they study.

> Virtually all political behaviour and social movements are rooted in values, in people's sense of right and wrong. Political opposition develops when there is a values-based challenge to elite's ways of running things. Whistleblowers are no different than other types of political protestors in that they are opposing existing practices, and at the base of their opposition are alternative values or ethics. The only difference is

that whistleblowers begin their opposition at the organisational level and only gradually (and sometimes) work their way up to the national level. However, many social movements (e.g. the civil rights movement) follow a similar historical progression: they frequently begin by attacking local conditions and only later connect these local injustices to a national pattern that they seek to change. So it is with whistleblowers (Rothschild and Miethe, 1994:256).

Conclusions: Customer Service and Academics

I have been concerned in this chapter to explore social–political effects of plausible representations of a discourse of 'customer service'. Following Jodelet (1991), Opie (1992), Said (1978) and Smith (1990a), I have argued that our texts inscribe or encourage particular social relations. And further, that we need to make central to our consideration and production of texts the likely social relations that they legitimise. Specifically, I have highlighted how three different representations of call centre clerks' use of 'customer service' legitimise differential subordinating or enabling effects for how we understand and may relate to those clerks. Organisational studies literatures have been used to highlight how 'customer service' may variously be represented as: (1) colonisation of clerks' labour by a discourse of enterprise; (2) resistance to self-alienation resulting in unwitting self-subordinating via gendered subjectivity, and; (3) clerks' moralisation of their selves and labour that may radically challenge the precarious amoralism of organisation.

As the production of just these three accounts should begin to suggest, a multitude of further plausible representations, drawing upon varied conceptual resources, hearing other voices in the organisation, and legitimising other social relations and understandings are possible. We do not, and cannot, definitely know therefore what 'customer service' is or what it will become at the hands of those who use it, resist it, transform it. Like Smith (1990b:24) 'I take it as axiomatic that, for any set of actual events, there is always more than one version'. To produce texts that give the impression that this is not so, texts that apparently contain, limit, or know the present and have some privileged access to the future (of for instance 'customer service') is, to put our 'professional integrity' at risk. For

the competence of sociology ends where the future begins . . . thinking of the landscape still hidden behind the horizon, we imagine it as similar to what we see around; we expect 'more of the same'. We do not know, of course, how well founded our expectations are . . . claiming otherwise he [sic] puts his professional integrity at risk (Bauman, 1988:89).

And yet, academic texts in our fields are routinely constructed, are *expected* to be constructed, in a way that authorises the singular representation which they normally contain (Edwards and Potter, 1992; Opie, 1992; Said, 1978; Smith, 1990a; Van Maanen, 1988). Had I constructed this chapter differently, for instance, and concentrated upon working-up just one of the above accounts of customer service using standard authorising and corroborating devices then any one of the three representations explored here could likely have become a (fairly) convincing and seemingly authoritative narrative. By being so authorised the differentially subordinating and empowering relations between researcher/reader and researched that these texts encourage would be similarly strengthened. For (at least) the first two of the three representations of customer service explored here, I have argued that this would mean the text: (1) authorising relations of superiority/inferiority, with the clerks being represented as possessing inferior understandings of customer service *vis à vis* managers and/or academics, and; (2) as a result of clerks supposedly 'inferior understandings', encouraging us to view the clerks as being necessarily colonised by a discourse of 'customer service'.[6]

To do this, to use our privileged access to socially authorised texts to represent others as 'inferior' and 'lacking agency' is to do a grievous *disservice* to those we research. Rather than accept (as readers), or collude with (as writers), the reproduction of these relations we should give primary consideration to the 'service' we are likely giving in our texts to our 'customers' the researched. Though our texts are normally written in ways and reproduced in forms that practically exclude the researched from reading them, I call the researched our 'customers' here because we explicitly or tacitly cite their experiences and lives as justification for the production of our critiques. It seems to me that if we benefit from implicit authorisation and legitimation of our critiques from the lives of those we research, then we owe them a responsibility. An expression of our 'service' for these 'customers' would be to make central consideration of 'whether or not our work will be used to reinforce and perpetuate [their] domination' (hooks, 1989). I have suggested here, through the examples of texts like du Gay and Salaman (1992) and Knights and Collinson (1987) that relations of distance from, and judgement of, the researched do reinforce domination (on this point see also Seidman, 1992; Stanley and Wise, 1983; Wray-Bliss, 1999). To undermine this and begin to construct our texts in ways that are accountable to those we represent we need to:

> break down the shibboleths of disengagement and objectivity . . . be involved both with the 'research subject' and with changing those conditions that seek to silence and marginalize (Tierney, 1993:5 in Lincoln, 1995:282).

If it takes a discourse of 'customer service' to help shift us from relating to the researched as *objects* of our study to viewing them as *people* to whom we are responsible and accountable, then I would suggest that this is one positive step toward unsettling the often subordinating authority of 'expert' academic texts, like this chapter and this book.

Notes

1   Thank you to Gill Aitken, Helen Collins, the editors of this current volume, and participants at the workshop 'Working Together?: Knowledge and Management in the Information Society', Keele, 16–17 June 2000, for their comments on this chapter.
2   The call centre research used in this paper is developed from original research for my PhD thesis (Wray-Bliss, 1998). Some of the research used in the thesis, and here, has also figured in Wray-Bliss and Willmott, 1999.
3   Interpreting workers to be using ideas and concepts of 'customer service' to imbue their labour with value and meaning and oppose managerial definitions of work is not unknown in studies of service organisations (see e.g. Hochschild, 1983). For example O'Connell Davidson in her study of telephone clerks in a privatised utility argued that:

> Because clerks at NU saw the organisation as fulfilling a *socially useful function*, the strengthened emphasis on profit at the expense of service was also deeply resented and *contributed to the intensity of opposition to management's plans* (1994:95, emphasis added).

4   I draw upon Bauman's conceptualisation of morality here to represent call centre clerks use of discourses of customer service, but I do not find the ideas to be unproblematic. In particular, I understand Bauman's conceptualisation of morality as 'impulse', as inherently personal, as pre-social, and as resisting rational codification, to render the idea (and existence) of morality very slippery to grasp – though I also think that this might have been Bauman's intention, that is, to present a morality that is opaque to (academic) attempts to know it and thus contain it. As the editors have noted, I retain some of this ambiguity regarding what morality 'is' in my use of Bauman's work here, and I do not try and straighten this ambiguity out in this endnote. Instead, I recommend readers try Bauman's (1993) *Post-modern Ethics* for themselves.
5   Though I draw upon Bauman's work here as illustrative of writings that enable us to represent clerk's use of a discourse of customer service as the moral basis of a potentially radical politics, I find Bauman's work at other times to be unjustifiably dismissive and patronising of people's resistance in contemporary society. For instance:

> the momentary explosions of solidarity action which may result do not alter the essential traits of the postmodern relationships: their fragmentariness and discontinuity, narrowness of focus and purpose, shallowness of contact.' (Bauman 1996:34–5)

6   Even for the third representation, drawing upon Bauman's writings to represent clerks as engaged in a potentially radical challenge to organisation, serious questions should be asked concerning the appropriateness of representing, yet again, women workers through another expert male voice. In particular, we might question whether such practice can be understood as what hooks (1989) calls a politics of domination (see also Collins and Wray-Bliss 2000).

References

Barrett, M. (1980) *Women's Oppression Today: Problems in Marxist Feminist Analysis*, London: Verso.

Bauman, Z. (1988) *Freedom*, Milton Keynes: Open University Press.

Bauman, Z. (1989) *Modernity and the Holocaust*, Oxford: Polity Press.

Bauman, Z. (1993) *Post-modern Ethics*, Oxford: Blackwell.

Bauman, Z. (1996) 'From Pilgrim to Tourist – or a Short History of Identity', in Hall, S. and Gay, P. (eds), *Questions of Cultural Identity*, 18–36, London: Sage.

Berger, P. (1963) *Invitation to Sociology: A Humanist Perspective*, Harmondsworth: Penguin.

Collins, H. and Wray-Bliss, E. (2000) 'Women's Consciousness, Man's World: (Un)learning Patriarchy and LPT', paper for *18th Annual International Labour Process Conference* 25–27 April 2000. University of Strathclyde, Scotland.

Collinson, D. (1992) *Managing the Shopfloor*, Berlin: De Gruyter.

Collinson, D. (1994) 'Strategies of Resistance: Power, Knowledge and Subjectivity in the Workplace', in Jermier, J., Knights, D. and Nord, W. (eds), *Resistance and Power in Organizations: Agency, Subjectivity and the Labour Process*, 25–68, London: Routledge.

du Gay, P. and Salaman, G. (1992) 'The Cult(ure) of the Customer', *Journal of Management Studies*, 29:5, 615–33.

Edwards, D. and Potter, J. (1992) *Discursive Psychology*, London: Sage.

Firestone, S. (1980) *The Dialectic of Sex: The Case for Feminist Revolution*, London: The Women's Press Ltd.

Griffin, S. (1984) *Woman and Nature: The Roaring Inside Her*, London: The Women's Press Ltd.

hooks, b. (1989) *Talking Back: Thinking Feminist, Thinking Black*, London: Sheba Feminist Publishers.

Hochschild, A. (1983) *The Managed Heart: The Commercialization of Human Feeling*, Berkley, CA: University of California Press.

Jodelet, D. (1991) *Madness and Social Representations* (trans. T. Pownall; ed. G. Duveen), London: Routledge.

Knights, D. (1990) 'Subjectivity, power and the labour process', in Knights, D. and Willmott, H. (eds), *Labour Process Theory*, London: Macmillan.

Knights, D. (1997) 'Organization Theory in the Age of Deconstruction: Dualism, Gender and Postmodernism Revisited', *Organization Studies*, 18:1, 1–19.

Knights, D. and Collinson, D. (1987) 'Disciplining the Shopfloor: A Comparison of the Disciplinary Effects of Managerial Psychology and Financial Accounting', *Accounting, Organisation and Society*, 12:5, 457–77.

Knights, D. and Willmott, H. (1989) 'Power and Subjectivity at Work: From Degradation to Subjugation in Social Relations', *Sociology*, 23:4, 535–58.

Lincoln, Y. (1995) 'Emerging Criteria for Quality in Qualitative and Interpretive Research' *Qualitative Inquiry*, 1:3, 275–89.

McKinlay, A. and Taylor, P. (1998) 'Through the Looking Glass: Foucault and the Politics of Production', in McKinlay, A. and Starkey, K. (eds), *Foucault, Management and Organization Theory*, 173–90, London: Sage.

Marx, K. (1844) 'Alienated Labour', in Simon, L. (ed.) (1994) *Karl Marx: Selected Writings*, Cambridge: Hacket Publishing Company.

Milgram, S. (1974) *Obedience to authority: An experimental view*, London: Tavistock.

O'Connell Davidson, J. (1994) 'The sources and limits of resistance in a privatized utility', in Jermier, J., Knights, D. and Nord, W. (eds), *Resistance and power in organizations*, 69–101, London: Routledge.

Opie, A. (1992) 'Qualitative Research, Appropriation of the 'Other' and Empowerment', *Feminist Review*, 40:52–69.

Rose, N. (1990) *Governing the Soul: The Shaping of the Private Self*, London: Routledge.

Rothschild, J. and Miethe, T. (1994) 'Whistleblowing as resistance in modern work organisations', in Jermier, J., Knights, D. and Nord, W. (eds), *Resistance and Power in Organisations: Agency, Subjectivity and the Labour Process*, 252–73, London: Routledge.

Said, E. (1978) *Orientalism: Western Conceptions of the Orient*, Harmondsworth: Penguin Books.

Seidman, S. (1992) 'Postmodern Social Theory as Narrative with a Moral Intent', in Seidman, S. and Wagner, D. (eds), *Postmodernism and Social Theory*, 47–81, Oxford: Basil Blackwell.

Sewell, G. and Wilkinson, B. (1992) 'Empowerment or Emasculation? A Tale of Shopfloor Surveillance in a Total Quality Organisation', in Blyton, P. and Turnbull, P. (eds), *Human Resource Management: Conflicts and Contradictions*, London: Sage.

Simon, L. (ed.) (1994) *Karl Marx: Selected Writings*, Cambridge: Hacket Publishing Company.

Smith, D. (1990a) 'Femininity as Discourse', in Smith, D., *Texts, Facts, and Femininity: Exploring the Relations of Ruling*, 159–208, London: Routledge.

Smith, D. (1990b) 'K is Mentally Ill: The Anatomy of a Factual Account', in Smith, D. *Texts, Facts, and Femininity: Exploring the Relations of Ruling*, 12–51, London: Routledge.

Spivak, G. (Harasym, S. ed.) (1990) *The Post-Colonial Critic: Interviews, Strategies, Dialogues*, London: Routledge.

Stanley, L. and Wise, S. (1983) *Breaking Out: Feminist Consciousness and Feminist Research*, London: Routledge.

Tierney, W. (1993) 'Introduction', in McLaughlin, D. and Tierney, W. (eds), *Naming Silenced Lives: Personal Narratives and the Process of Educational Change*, New York: Routledge.

Van Maanen, J. (1988) *Tales of the Field: On Writing Ethnography*, Chicago: The University of Chicago Press.

Willmott, H. (1993) 'Strength is Ignorance, Slavery is Freedom: Managing Culture in Modern Organisations', *Journal of Management Studies*, 30:4, 512–52.

Willmott, H. and Wray-Bliss, E. (1996) 'Process Reengineering, Information Technology and the Transformation of Accountability: The Remaindering of the Human Resource?', in Orlikowski, W., Walsham, G., Jones, M. and Degross, J. (eds), *Information Technology and Changes in Organizational Work*, London: Chapman and Hall.

Wray-Bliss, E. (1998) 'The Ethics and Politics of Representing Workers: An Ethnography of Telephone Banking Clerks', PhD thesis, School of Management, UMIST.

Wray-Bliss, E. (1999) 'Abstract Ethics, Embodied Ethics: The Strange Marriage of Foucault and Positivism in LPT', paper presented at *The First International Critical Management Studies Conference*, UMIST.

Wray-Bliss, E. and Parker, M. (1998) 'Marxism, Capitalism and Ethics', in Parker, M. (ed.), *Ethics and Organizations*, 30–52, London: Sage.

Wray-Bliss, E. and Willmott, H. (1999) 'Battling with the Gods: Workers, Management and the Deities of Post-industrial Management Culture', in Goodman, R. (ed.), *Modern Organizations and Emerging Conundrums*, Oxford: Lexington Books.

Wylie, I. (1997) 'The Human Answering Machine', *The Guardian*, 26 July, 2–3.

4

Juggling Justice and Care: Gendered Customer Service in the Contemporary Airline Industry

Melissa Tyler and Steve Taylor

Introduction

Whatever you say, sir. You're right and I'm an asshole
(McDonald's employee, cited in Leidner, 1993:192)

During the last twenty years or so, the airline industry has been shaped by managerial initiatives that have endeavoured to deliver 'quality' service. In this chapter, we focus on some of the gendered consequences of these, arguing that recent managerial responses to competitive pressures have resulted in a customer service ethos defined largely by subjective commitment to the organisation and its customers that, in turn, has intensified demands for the performance of emotional labour. Our contention is that these developments impact upon female employees in particular, who tend to be concentrated in 'front line' service roles that often require a high degree of emotional investment (Ashforth and Humphrey, 1993; Bettencourt and Gwinner, 1996; Leidner, 1999). Furthermore, we explore the extent to which the work of airline service providers suggests that the ethos referred to above can be analytically differentiated in line with a distinction that has shaped recent debates on ethics and moral development, namely between an 'ethic of justice' and an 'ethic of care' (Gilligan, 1982; Kohlberg, 1981). We examine this theme in the first part of the chapter which explores the relationship between justice, care and the ethos of customer service.

Contemporary managerial discourses on customer service seem to be located in an objectivist conception of 'generalised others' that forms the basis of an 'ethic of justice'. We explore this in the second part of the chapter in relation to 'quality' customer service and emotional labour in the airline industry. Here, we focus largely on the way in which what management defines as quality customer service resonates with the 'ethic of justice'

60

outlined earlier. We then go on to equate a more individualised emphasis on 'concrete others' with the actual provision of service from the perspective of service workers, who are required to anticipate and respond to the specific needs of customers in terms of an 'ethic of care'. We reflect critically on customer service from this latter perspective in relation to the gendered expectations that govern customer service relationships. These are embedded within the need, on the one hand, for service providers to mediate between managerially defined customer service discourse on the rights of customers to 'quality' service and, on the other, to respond to various performance indicators established and enforced by management. Our analysis suggests that the work of service providers in the contemporary airline industry and, very likely, elsewhere involves mediating between the two conceptions of ethics outlined here; a mediation process that can have a detrimental effect on an individual service provider's subjective sense of self – a theme we explore in the final section of the chapter.

Throughout the chapter, we explore the extent to which the effectiveness of recent managerial imperatives can be related to the way in which they are embedded within the gendered norms that shape the tri-partite relationship between employees, managers and customers (Leidner, 1993). In particular, we focus on the ways in which front line service providers themselves – in this case, telephone sales agents and flight attendants – must negotiate this relationship. We argue that this negotiation is grounded largely in the need to mediate between managerially defined service *expectations* (on the part of managers and customers) and the actual *provision* of customer service from the perspective of service providers themselves. We explore the former as they are embedded within gendered expectations of 'quality' service interaction and the latter (the actual provision of service) in relation to managerial demands for increased levels of productive output. Taking into account the implications of this tension, particularly for the subjective experience of customer service work, our focus is primarily on the consequences for service workers of the requirement to undertake 'human work' (inter-subjective, caring, attentive and so on) in an increasingly instrumentalised way.

Justice, Care and The Ethos of Customer Service

Much of the recent prescriptive literature on customer service emphasises both justice and rights as the ethical prerequisites of 'quality' customer interaction. At the heart of management discourse on 'quality' customer service seems to be what has come to be known in contemporary debates on ethics and moral development as an 'ethic of justice'. As Judith Squires (1999:141) notes, the latter can be seen as an articulation of moral objectivism based on the conviction that there is some permanent, ahistorical framework that can be appealed to in determining what is universally 'right'. This can be identified, in the language of customer service at least, in the somewhat cliched dictum 'the customer is always right'. The most notable representative of moral objectivism, Immanuel Kant, argued for a universal framework within which to ground moral claims and rejected any attempt to locate morality in experience. On the contrary, Kant sought to establish the existence of a universal and objective moral law – a 'categorical imperative' – that could be applied to all rational, human beings. Essentially, this conception of ethics is grounded in a form of rationalism requiring that 'in order for the agent to escape egoism, and attain objectivity, he or she must adopt a universal point of view that is the same for all rational agents' (Young, 1990:100). The emphasis on detachment from context or the 'ideal of impartiality' in moral objectivism demands, then, that 'one abstracts from particular experiences, feelings, desires and commitments and adopts a detached and dispassionate view from nowhere' (Squires, 1999:142).

A more recent manifestation of this universalistic form of moral reasoning can be found in the (not uncontentious) work of Lawrence Kohlberg (1981)[1] who developed a psychological, rather than a philosophical, theory of moral development. Based on his empirical research into moral reasoning, Kohlberg asserted that the ability to apply moral judgement evolves through various stages of development, culminating in the capacity to perceive moral issues objectively. For Kohlberg (echoing Kant), achieving this stage of moral reasoning involves actually creating the world as moral, rather than merely comprehending it as such.[2] It is this emphasis on moral objectivism and an ideal of impartiality that has provided both the philosophical context for the development of an 'ethic of justice' perspective on moral reasoning and also much of the momentum for a feminist critique of objectivist conceptions of ethics and justice.

Several feminists, most notably Carol Gilligan (1982), have argued that women tend to adopt a different approach to moral reasoning than that espoused by Kohlberg, one that refrains from privileging an objectivist, ethic of justice and emphasises instead 'notions of care and empathy, of thinking of the interests and well-being of others' (Okin, 1989:15). Gilligan, in particular, has argued that a more accurate representation of women's approach to moral reasoning is a contextual morality, or an 'ethic of care'. In her (equally contentious – see Assiter, 1996:97–9) critique of Kohlberg's emphasis on the moral superiority of an 'ethic of justice', Gilligan claims that it is women's interconnection with other subjects that shapes their moral judgement.

She bases this assertion on her analysis of three studies (one involving 25 college students; one involving 29 women considering abortion in the first trimester of pregnancy; and another based on interviews with 144 men and women focusing on rights and responsibilities). Each study included the same set of questions about self and morality, and experiences of conflict and choice (see Gilligan, 1982:2–4). On the basis of this research, Gilligan argues that it is possible to distinguish between two ethical orientations: an ethic of justice and an ethic of care. The former, Gilligan argues, can be associated with a masculine emphasis on moral rights, whereas the latter more closely relates to a feminine concern with ethical responsibilities requiring, as it does, a more sophisticated engagement with relational context than is the case with regard to an ethic of justice. As Benhabib (1992:146) notes, Gilligan challenges the 'justice bias of universalist moral theories' and the Kantian-derived assumption that the ultimate level of moral development is signified by the ability to apply universal moral principles to concrete social relations. Rather, Gilligan's approach is pre-mised upon the conviction that:

> the importance of separation and autonomy in men's lives often leads them to focus the discussion of morality around issues of justice, fairness, rules and rights, whereas the importance of family and friends in women's lives leads them to emphasize people's wants, needs, interests, and aspirations (Tong, 1989:162).

In considering the origins of women's disposition towards an ethic of care, however, Gilligan also emphasises that:

> a sense of vulnerability . . . impedes . . . women from taking a stand . . . which stems from her lack of power and consequent inability to do something in the world . . . The women's reluctance to judge stems . . . from their uncertainty about their right to make moral statements or, perhaps, the price for them that such judgement seems to entail (1997:554).

This latter statement suggests, as both Tronto (1993) and Squires (1999) have noted, that the different moral voice to which Gilligan refers might be a function of a subordinate structural position that is not necessarily exclusive to women and which might be better identified with a subordinate social status. Following Gilligan, Tronto claims that there is nothing inherent in women that associates them with an ethics of care rather than with reason and justice, with the particular rather than the universal. Rather, as Squires (1999:147) also emphasises, 'historical circumstances led to the containment of both women and moral sentiments within the domestic sphere. It was then only one short step to naturalize this by claiming women to be essentially caring'. What this approach to Gilligan's work emphasises then is the extent to which women's propensity to an ethics of care is not natural, but *naturalised*.

Underpinning debates on the origins of women's alleged disposition towards an ethic of care is Gilligan's conception of the relationship between ethics and subjectivity. Gilligan emphasised that all of the women in her research had a subjective understanding of the self different from that associated with the men in Kohlberg's analysis. Whereas men, she argued, tend to see the self as an autonomous and separate being, women tend to view selfhood as interdependent; the existence of which depends on others. Gilligan identified at least four implications of this difference for the ways in which men and women engage in moral reasoning. These are, first, that women tend to stress a moral agent's continuing relationship with others, whereas men tend to stress abstract rights; second, when making a moral decision, women tend to take more account than men of its effects on all concerned; third, women are usually more willing than men to accept explanations for inappropriate behaviour on the part of moral agents and finally, whereas men tend to abstract moral decisions from their particular context, women are more likely to locate moral choices specifically within a particular social location. As Tong (1989:164) notes, Gilligan's reflections led her to develop the idea that, whereas for Kohlberg the moral self is 'an individual legislating absolute laws for everyone without exception', a more feminine conception of the moral agent is of a communicative or co-operative self that exists and acts only in relation to others. What Gilligan's account emphasises in this respect, is that women's moral development involves evolving initially from an egocentric self to an overly altruistic or self-sacrificial one, into a position in which the interests of others are perceived as being as valid as those of the self. This process of moral development is understood to culminate in what she terms a 'self-with-others' conception of subjectivity, according to which the ethical needs of the self are understood to be convergent with those of others, and vice versa.

This particular theme in Gilligan's work has been developed further by Seyla Benhabib (1992), whose main focus is a reconceptualisation of reason in the light of communitarian, feminist and post-modernist criticisms of the legacy of Enlightenment rationality. She argues that each of these perspectives has contributed to the emergence of an intellectual climate that is sceptical of the moral and political ideas of modernity and particularly its emphasis on the moral superiority of the concept of selfhood, privileged by Kant and subsequently Kohlberg, that Benhabib terms the 'unencumbered self'. Benhabib argues that the two ethics of justice and care, identified by Kohlberg and Gilligan respectively, relate to two fundamentally different philosophies of subjectivity. For Benhabib, an ethic of justice is shaped, at least in part, by a generalised concept of others as a homogenised mass, distinct from oneself. An ethic of care, however, is grounded in the recognition of what Benhabib refers to as 'concrete others'; individuals with irreducible social differences and ethical needs. Whereas the standpoint of the generalised other 'requires us to view each and every individual as a rational being entitled to the same rights and duties we would want to ascribe to ourselves' (Benhabib, 1992:158), that of the concrete other 'requires us to view each and every rational being as an

individual with a concrete history, identity and affective-emotional constitution' (1992:159).

Where Benhabib (1992:163) develops Gilligan's distinction between the
two conceptions of subjectivity is in her conviction that a system that
polarises commonality and individuality 'becomes incoherent and cannot
individuate amongst selves'. Adapting Habermas's discourse ethics, Benhabib argues that we should strive to develop an ethical framework capable
of acknowledging that 'every generalised other is also a concrete other'
(1992:165). For Benhabib, this reversal of moral objectivism implies that 'to
stand in such an ethical relationship means we as concrete individuals
know what is expected of us in virtue of the kind of social bonds which tie
us to the other' (1992:10).

It is important to note here that consideration of the relationship between
these two perspectives on ethics, particularly in relation to gender difference, has generated a great deal of controversy and a huge body of literature
within which there seems to be little consensus (Barry, 1995; Benhabib, 1992;
Collins, 1991; Lister, 1997; Okin, 1989; Tronto, 1993). Our intention here is
certainly not to review this literature – this would entail another chapter –
but, rather, to consider the extent to which the various ideas it has generated
over the last two decades or so can be applied to a critical account of the
relationship between gender and customer service. Presumptions about the
feminine disposition towards an ethic of care, in contrast to the masculine
propensity towards an ethic of justice do seem, to us at least, to resonate
with commonly held beliefs about the gendered nature of work. Indeed,
much of the research into gender, caring and the organisation of work has
emphasised the extent to which women tend to be recruited specifically
because it is assumed they are particularly skilled in caring for others
(Adkins, 1995; James, 1989; Morgan and Knights, 1991; Pringle, 1989; see
Tyler and Taylor, 1998). These presumptions also provide, for our purposes,
a useful analytical basis for a critical account of the gendered nature of
customer service in contemporary work organisations, particularly in terms
of how the two ethics are understood to relate to each other.

In what follows, we attempt to develop the idea that an ethic of justice
and an ethic of care operate in a tense interplay that requires, in the case of
customer service work, service providers to negotiate this relationship and
to mediate the tensions it creates, resulting in demands for emotional labour
and considerable levels of work stress (Hochschild, 1983). Indeed, Benhabib's commitment to an ethical system driven by knowledge of 'what is
expected of us in virtue of the kind of social bonds which tie us together'
seems to echo Hochschild's (1979:568) conception of the gendered nature of
emotional labour as based on 'shared understanding of perceived entitle-
ment . . . measured by a prior sense of what is reasonably owed, given the
sort of bond involved'. Our concern then, is that the kind of social bonds to
which Benhabib refers become gendered, instrumental commodities in

customer service interactions. This results, we would argue, in what Squires (1999:152) has termed a naturalised 'moral division of labour, in which one group of people adopt one ethic and another group the other', one that seems to concentrate women in service work on the basis of what tends to be perceived by employers as their 'special capacity' for caring.

'Quality' Customer Service and Emotional Labour in the Airline Industry

Within contemporary western economies, characterised by intensified competition and de-humanisation (Bauman, 1993), the way in which a service is delivered has come to be perceived as central to organisational success. As a result, those employees who operate as 'front line' service providers have become the focus of considerable managerial intervention. Recent empirical accounts of management initiatives in various service sector organisations have focused on managerial attempts to mobilise the subjective commitment of employees to the delivery of quality customer service (Jones *et al.*, 1997; Knights and McCabe, 1998; Rosenthal *et al.*, 1997). Managerial programmes that aim to shape the feeling management of service employees during their interaction with customers often emphasize the importance of 'quality service' and 'customer satisfaction' within an increasingly competitive business environment (Jones *et al.*, 1997; Rosenthal *et al.*, 1997; Taylor 1997). Within parts of the service sector, quality of customer service is perceived as a, if not *the*, key differentiation strategy by management (Fuller and Smith, 1991; Hughes and Tadic, 1998; Leidner, 1993).

More theoretical analyses have emphasised the extent to which so-called 'new style management' has aimed to secure subjective commitment to the organisation by fostering notions of normative commonality. This means that, as employees, we are 'told that it is "right" to desire to be entrepreneurial, and also to become more emotionally involved' (Hatcher, 1999:10). With this in mind, Hancock (1997:93) has argued that contemporary management 'seeks to colonize the potentiality for subjective rational autonomy, through the propagation of a mystical and symbolic dependency upon the personified organizational lifeworld'. Central to this colonisation seems to have been a perpetual emphasis on familial and community–based discourses within recent management initiatives, according to which emotional commitment 'gains hold as an ethical comportment' (Hatcher, 1999:11) (often, it must be noted, as a substitute for contractual rights on the part of employees).

As suggested above, the airline industry is no exception to this and has been shaped, in recent years, by managerial programmes aimed at maximising 'service quality' and 'customer satisfaction' by engaging employees in a range of initiatives designed to encourage identification with the organisation. Such strategies have been identified within the airline industry (Anthony, 1994; Boyd and Bain, 1998; Colling, 1995) where cultural management initiatives – such as the oft-cited programme at British Airways (Anthony, 1994; Legge, 1998) – have been designed to secure employee commitment to the values enshrined in the company mission statement, notably to 'quality' customer service.

With this in mind, we conducted ethnographic research into two aspects of the airline industry: the telephone sales of airline services by telephone sales agents (TSAs)[3] representing a major British airline ('Flightpath') and airline service delivery by flight attendants[4] within the same airline and one other, both of which are 'key players' in an intensely competitive market. The research was conducted between 1994 and 1996, during which time both airlines implemented 'quality management' programmes that focused on service as the key to success in the highly competitive and largely undifferentiated airline industry. As we try to highlight in the following sections, managerial discourses emphasising the centrality of service quality were evident in every aspect of the airline industry we studied.

Defining 'quality service' within the airline industry – an ethic of justice?

An essential characteristic of a managerial focus upon customer satisfaction seems to be the perception on the part of senior management that there is a requirement to actively manage the delivery of quality service (Fuller and Smith, 1991; Jones et al., 1997). Active management of service delivery that involves employee–customer interaction clearly has implications for the feeling management of employees. However, within both of the cases under consideration here, and this is also noted elsewhere (Jones et al., 1997; Rosenthal et al., 1997), the delivery of service quality, and the feeling management this can involve, should (according to management) be achieved through the empowerment of workers rather than through managerial prescription. Here, the presumption seems to be that managerial initiatives should strive not to prescribe the implementation of a particular service ethos, but to liberate an essential disposition to serve on the part of individual employees as rational, autonomous subjects. Hence, the mobilisation of employee commitment to an organisational aim of quality service was found to be a crucial element in the quality management programmes at both of the airlines studied.

At Flightpath, this was epitomised in a mission statement that aimed to 'excel in anticipating and quickly responding to customer needs and competitor activity'. Flightpath as a whole, and the telephone sales centre in particular, achieved huge commercial success within the research period. Telephone sales management attributed this to a 'culture change' sweeping through the organisation, 'empowering' TSAs and enabling them to deliver quality customer service 'spontaneously' and 'naturally'.

Similarly, airline management have always seen the nature of interaction between flight attendants and customers as central to customer perceptions of quality service (Hochschild, 1983; Mills, 1998) so that an emphasis on the need to 'liberate' an essential disposition to serve also characterised management prescriptions on the work of flight attendants. Our research into the work of flight attendants has emphasised the importance of 'quality service' and 'customer satisfaction' (Tyler, 1997). One particular flight attendant recruitment advertisement emphasised the extent to which 'our cabin crew are free to make the spontaneous decisions that create a special in-flight atmosphere'. Clear attempts were made by management to stress the importance of flight attendant autonomy, spontaneity and 'natural personality', for the attainment of 'customer satisfaction'. Thus, competitive pressures within the airline industry have resulted in managerial initiatives which attempt to 'manage' the 'natural' delivery of quality customer service during employee–customer interactions, often with reference to generalised statements about 'quality of service', 'a commitment to excellence', 'a determination to provide the very best' and so on. What such initiatives tend to emphasise are the rights of all customers to quality service and the responsibilities of service providers to deliver that quality of service, regardless of the context of the interaction.

In most of the written documentation that we analysed, reference was made to 'a responsibility to customers to be the best'. In other words, underpinning management initiatives privileging service seemed to be a conception of customers as 'generalised others' yet to which customer service employees would have to relate as 'concrete others'. This is because, as Mills and Murgatroyd (1991:22–4) have noted, organisational rules and rights are (often designed to be) generally so abstract that it is virtually impossible to implement them in concrete situations without considerable adaptation on the part of individual employees. This served to locate customers within a management discourse, governed by a collective yet instrumental rationality, that emphasises (at a discursive level) universal customer rights to 'quality' social interaction according to a service ethos akin to the 'ethic of justice' perspective discussed above.

In terms of the implementation of these values, and their translation into actual service provision, airline management seemed to assume that service providers (described in recruitment literature as 'caring, customer-focused people') are able to liberate a natural, pre-determined propensity to 'care' and to implement these generic terms as they apply to the actual needs of customers as concrete individuals. As one flight attendant recruitment advertisement put it, 'you will . . . have all the personal qualities needed to deliver world-class customer service'. This latter point, our research emphasised, seems to be reflected in the extent to which gendered assumptions about the importance of employee–customer interactions for capital accumulation, within an intensely competitive commercial environment, are embedded within managerial selection, training, supervision and evaluation of employees within the industry.

Our analysis emphasised the extent to which management processes at Flightpath are underpinned by gendered assumptions about the 'natural' skills and capacities of women and men embedded within them. In particular, women are positioned as possessing the 'soft skills', as Peters and Waterman (1982:11) put it, deemed necessary for achieving 'excellent' interaction with customers. This was observed within the selection and training of both TSAs and flight attendants. Selection panels in TSA recruitment argued that they attempted to select 'personalities' who will 'naturally' deliver quality service. The 'personalities' selected by airline management were overwhelmingly female. When questioned, selectors (overwhelmingly male) articulated their gendered assumptions. As this particular Section Team Leader (STL) put it:

> The vast, vast majority of the agents we select are women . . . it's not as if we don't get men applying for the job . . . they just seem to fit it better, they're better at it . . . we are looking for people who can chat to people, interact, build rapport. What we find is that women can do this more, they're definitely more natural when they do it anyway. It doesn't sound as forced, perhaps they're used to doing it all the time anyway . . . women are naturally good at that sort of thing. I think they have a higher tolerance level than men . . . I suppose we do, yes, if we're honest about it, select women sometimes because they are women rather than anything they've particularly shown in the interview.

In this description, we can identify many of the subjective qualities outlined earlier that, according to Gilligan (1982), underpin an ethics of care – an emphasis on relations with others shaped by continuity between the ethical needs of the self and those of others (manifest as 'building rapport') and a consideration of the needs of others (in the need for high levels of tolerance). Once selected, agents are expected to deploy their 'natural' personality within employee–customer interactions, regardless of the emotional stance which customers may adopt towards them.

Because, as we suggested earlier, such qualities are naturalised rather than natural, these gendered beliefs and the way in which they are inscribed within the training, supervision and evaluation of TSAs represent demands for gendered emotional labour during employee–customer interaction. TSAs are, to some extent, trained in the techniques of emotional labour. They are instructed to respond to the perceived feelings and expressions of customers in a manner that upholds the commercial interests of Flightpath, and through a general ethos of customer service that embodies gendered assumptions about social interaction:

> If a man's having a go at you . . . he might even be embarrassing you . . . don't get ruffled, you've got to keep your cool. Remember that you are trying to offer him something and get him to pay for the privilege. He can really talk to you how he wants. Your job is to deal with it . . . just take a few deep breaths and let the irritation cool down . . . think to yourself he's not worth it.

Despite this kind of prescription, TSAs, telephone sales management and members of the training section stressed that the training programme was only a framework for the delivery of quality service, within which employees were expected to use discretion. TSAs argued that they frequently, with the encouragement of management, interact with customers in their own personal or 'natural' manner. As indicated earlier, this is known as 'building rapport'. However, the individualised surveillance and remuneration systems encourage 'positive divergences' while aiming to eliminate 'negative divergences' from managerial prescription within agent–customer interaction (Taylor, 1998). Unless TSAs' spontaneous feelings can be utilised as 'positive discretion' (ie, to deliver 'quality' service as defined by management), many employees are coerced into deploying emotional labour, given the knowledge that they can be supervised at any time – through targeting systems, direct observation, known and remote monitoring. With management also explicitly stating that consistent TSA failure to meet monthly targets would result in dismissal, what we are witnessing here is the mobilisation of powerful managerial resources in the demand for emotional labour. This occurs within what seems to be an 'ethic of justice' conception of customer service, yet which is premised on the assumption that service providers have to interact with customers as concrete individuals and will deploy what are assumed to be their gender-specific 'soft skills' in doing so.

One of the ways in which this ethos manifests itself in relation to gender is that the majority of female and male TSAs interviewed agreed that the few male TSAs within the telephone sales centre studied were actually supervised and evaluated according to different criteria. Females tended to be judged according to both 'hard' *and* 'soft' standards (that is, in relation to both quantifiable levels of productive output and the nature of their interaction with customers; that is, with the level of service they provided and with their ability to translate management discourse on 'quality' service into customer service provision), whereas for male TSAs the nature of the service interaction was largely overlooked if the agent was considered a 'good seller' (ie, consistently surpassed revenue and productivity ('hard') targets).

Gendered assumptions about service also shaped the selection of flight attendants whose work is deemed to involve, perhaps more so than TSAs, 'caring', physically and emotionally, for others. A regular (male) business traveller outlined these skills in relation to the work of flight attendants:

A good flight attendant, or hostess . . . should be organized and attentive, she should ideally be helpful and knowledgeable, she should be well-prepared and trained, and should be sincere, . . . She should be percep-tive and be able to work alongside her colleagues to ensure that all passengers' needs are taken care of . . . She should be able to anticipate the needs of her passengers and go beyond their expectations . . . He or she should be firm and self-confident, and be able . . . to think for themselves and so plan ahead [note the use of the female pronoun until being 'firm and self-confident' is introduced].

Elsewhere, we have emphasised the extent to which women are seen as being capable of carrying out service work that is deemed to involve being 'organised', 'attentive' and so on, by virtue of their sexual difference from men (Tyler and Taylor, 1998). Consequently, the skills involved in airline service provision tend not to be recognised as skills by many of those who provide and consume the service, but are seen as 'common-sense' ways of being a woman; that is, of anticipating the needs and [exceeding the] expectations of others. In a similar vein to the TSAs, flight attendants were encouraged and expected to exercise discretion when interacting with customers – to take what was referred to in training literature as 'the Secret Second Step – anticipating the needs of others'. This means that despite management discourse on customer rights and quality service, customer service providers have to conceptualise customers as what Benhabib (1992:159) terms 'concrete others' – individuals 'with a concrete history, identity and affective-emotional constitution'. Service providers attempt to mediate the tensions between managerial imperatives and customer ex-pectations, and to negotiate the, often contradictory, relationship between managerially defined discourses on service and the realities of service provision on a day-to-day level. This means that service providers tend to have little choice but to interact with customers in a way that is more akin to an ethics of care, than to an ethics of justice that emphasises customer rights to quality, in their delivery of service.

Delivering 'quality service' within the airline industry – an ethic of care?

Within the delivery of customer service at both airlines studied, in the work of TSAs and also flight attendants, employees work within something of a 'duties discourse' it could be argued, within which employee obligations are promoted over their rights. In particular, the 'ethics of justice' approach that we have associated with management prescriptions on customer service emphasises the obligations of service providers to implement generic values of 'quality', 'excellence' and so on while simultaneously eroding their own rights as employees through the introduction of various initiatives designed to ensure productive output. Hence, the mobilisation of powerful managerial resources results in a demand for emotional labour driven by the structural constraints imposed on service providers. As one particular female TSA commented:

> You can't let yourself be impolite towards a customer or feel angry with them . . . As we are always told, they pay our wages . . . I suppose it's something that I learnt to do since I came here . . . you're taught to think about the customers, to think about what they're like and to try and get on with them whatever they're like.

Many other TSAs expressed similar sentiments, emphasising the gendered expectations that shaped interaction with customers as 'concrete others':

> They expect us to put up with a lot more from customers than the blokes . . . if someone is having a go . . . and we get some real dirty bastards . . . especially on American calls when it's the middle of the night over there . . . you're just expected to put up with it . . . because 'you never know, you might get a sale'. It's seen as normal behaviour, men just having a laugh . . . one supervisor said to me . . . 'just because it's not your sense of humour, it doesn't mean you have to get offended by someone else's' . . . they tell us 'you've got to have a thick skin, you can't let it affect you, get rid of the feeling' . . . I suppose it's bound to affect how you respond in your social life, your tolerance levels.

What this suggests is that, although airline management and passengers are accustomed to a service ethos grounded in generalised conceptions of justice, the actual provision of customer service, from the perspective of service providers themselves, necessitates that they operate within a model more akin to Gilligan's 'ethics of care' framework, one that (somewhat ironically) requires that they often do *not* treat individual customers as 'rational beings entitled to the same rights and duties'. In practice, this seems to involve service providers mediating between an 'ethics of justice' and an 'ethics of care'; between a dominant (managerial) discourse of quality and rights and the concrete responsibilities of service providers on a day-to-day level requiring a more inter-subjective engagement with an 'ethic of care'.

Echoing Leidner (1993), we would argue that the power of the gendered managerial demands manifest as an 'ethic of justice' perspective must be related to the ways in which customer service interaction is located within the structurally induced and inequitable employment relationship. This reflects Gilligan's conviction that women's location within an ethics of care can be attributed to structural location and not to any pre-determined caring disposition. On the contrary, many of our respondents emphasised the high levels of emotional labour and alienation engendered by the need to work within an ethics of justice (manifest as a concern with 'quality' customer service on the part of management) that assumes service provider engagement with an ethics of care according to which customers are conceived of as 'concrete others'.

Further to this, TSAs and flight attendants, like many other front-line service providers, operate in an organisational environment in which familiarity with service routines, corporate marketing and so on engender fairly well defined service expectations among customers. When these are not met, front-line service providers constitute a ready target. As Leidner notes, in this respect, service workers without the authority to alter policies or work routines in any significant way can, from a management point of view, provide a useful buffer zone for absorbing and diffusing the hostility of dissatisfied customers that might otherwise be directed against the organisation as a whole. In this sense, then, customers engage with service providers as 'concrete others', yet in a highly individualised and instru-mental way that renders them responsible for the organisation as a whole. This latter point is suggested by the following account of the subjective experience of customer dissatisfaction:

> Whether they're mad at you or mad at some other thing, they're gonna direct it on you, it's gonna be focused on you – 'Why haven't, why is this going wrong, why haven't *you* done this?' Because they aren't gonna turn and look at a wall and say, 'I hate this place, why isn't the service good?' They're gonna take it out on you. So it is personal. And you know, you try to tell yourself it's not personal . . . You feel like shouting back at these people 'This is not my fault' (McDonald's employee cited in Leidner, 1993:131–2).

On this basis, our concern is that which Benhabib (following Habermas) advocates as a need 'to mediate between the standpoints of the generalized other and the concrete other' in order to appreciate what she terms 'the standpoint of collective concrete others' (Benhabib, 1992:11–12). This is precisely the strategy underpinning recent managerial initiatives aimed at ensuring 'quality' service while maintaining employee efficiency. As out-lined above, her adaptation of Habermas's communicative ethics results in Benhabib arguing that the privileging of universalistic theories of justice and morality should be altered to take account of the standpoint of concrete others. Our analysis indicates that this is exactly what service providers are involved in when they attempt to implement management initiatives concerned with the efficient delivery of quality service. Returning to Gilligan's conception of the relationship between self and others within an ethic of care outlined earlier, it seems that striving to deliver quality customer service indeed involves stressing the service provider's continu-ing relationship with others; taking account of the affects of a particular decision on the needs of all concerned; accepting explanations for inappropriate behaviour, and locating moral choices within their specific social circumstances.

Within this framework, 'quality' customer service can be understood to originate precisely from the 'standpoint of collective concrete others' to which Benhabib refers. The service providers discussed above seemed to be aiming to achieve this while, simultaneously, striving to satisfy a range of hard and soft productivity targets and standards. The mediation between an ethic of justice and an ethic of care as the basis for 'quality' customer service within a competitive, commercial environment can then be understood, we would argue, as an instrumentalisation of the ethos to which Benhabib (1992) in particular is committed. The overall effect of this is that service providers become alienated from themselves and others, working within an ethical framework laid down by 'moral experts' (managers) in the 'community' (work organisation) to which they belong. Our concern is not only that contemporary management initiatives emphasising quality customer service are associated with an essentialist conception of a feminine propensity to engage with an ethic of care (rather than with promoting ethical subjectivity more generally), or with the detrimental effects of this on a service provider's sense of self, but also that concepts and ideas associated with critical social science (in this particular case, Benhabib's development of Habermas's discourse ethics) can be seen to be reflected so clearly in contemporary managerial discourse aimed at enhancing productive output.

Conclusions

In sum, our central argument has been that dominant managerial discourses on customer service stress the need (if service encounters are to be productive) for employees to mediate between an ethic of justice and an ethic of care. These discourses are gendered in so far as they assume the natural propensity of women to put the principles associated with an ethic of care into practice. Crucially, in our view, it is the instrumentalisation of this ethic that is potentially alienating. It also inverts the commitment of critical theorists such as Benhabib to an 'ethical subjectivity' grounded in recognition of the collective needs of concrete others, largely because subjective autonomy is crucial to the development of such an ethical subjectivity. Such autonomy is precisely what is denied through instrumentalisation.

We have also argued that the gendered discourses and managerial prescriptions identified here are particularly powerful because they are embedded within control processes that are manifestations of structural constraints imposed by both the capital–labour relation and of 'settled ways of thinking' about gender difference (Connell, 1995).

Our analysis has also sought to emphasise that the delivery of 'quality service' which inevitably draws upon employee capacities for feeling management, is considered particularly important to capital accumulation by management within companies that are world leaders in the airline industry. We are not suggesting that this is the only differentiation strategy being pursued within an increasingly competitive industry. However, we have sought to demonstrate how management within our research sites have embedded discourses of 'quality service' – that we have located within an objectivist, 'ethic of justice' – in their selection, training, supervision and evaluation processes. Inherent to the quality management programmes established within both aspects of the airline industry studied is an expectation that service employees will work beyond managerial prescription when interacting with customers and delivering quality service and engage, in a highly gendered way, with 'an ethic of care'.

Throughout, we have argued that management, within all of our research sites, assume that women workers in particular can accomplish this 'discretionary' or mediating aspect of the job, by utilising skills that they supposedly possess by virtue of their sexual difference from men; capacities deemed to derive from women's natural propensity to locate themselves within an 'ethic of care'. However, quality management programmes that aim to emphasise the significance, and tap the presumed potential, of this gendered discretion simultaneously involve heightened surveillance and control of the labour process in an attempt to eradicate 'negative divergences' from managerial prescriptions. This erodes rather than expands employee autonomy, intensifying demands for the production of gendered emotional labour based on the reality that customer service providers are required, literally, to work through a contradiction between a managerial conception of customers as 'generalised others' and the necessity to interact with customers as 'concrete others' in the implementation of quality customer service programmes. Our account has also sought to highlight, then, the extent to which the development of mechanisms enabling thoroughgoing supervision and evaluation involves particularly female service providers in attempting to implement 'quality' programmes by mediating between an ethics of justice and an ethics of care while, simultaneously, striving to meet productivity targets and comply with supervision and appraisal systems according to which their own rights as employees, as well as their status as autonomous subjects, are increasingly eroded.

Notes

1   Kohlberg has been criticised for being prescriptive, ideological and patriarchal (see Squires, 1999).
2   Kohlberg (1981) estimates that only 5 per cent of the population reach this final stage of moral development.

3   TSA employment involves receiving, and dealing with, calls from people who are interested in purchasing or reserving Flightpath services. Agents work within a large open-plan office (a 'community'). One Sales Team Supervisor (STS) manages TSAs. A team of eight supervisors is responsible to one Sales Team Leader (STL). There were five STLs working in the office at the time of the research. These are, as a team, responsible to the Unit Manager of the telephone sales centre studied. S/he is then accountable to the head of Telephone Sales, UK. Everyone within the centre is on performance-related pay, from the TSAs to the Unit Manager. The research at Flightpath, undertaken by Taylor, consisted of undertaking non-participant observation and semi-structured interviews, focusing on TSA recruitment and training, the nature of the labour process and the way in which the introduction of a quality management programme had affected the work situation. Particular attention was paid to the operationalisation of managerial prescription, supervision and evaluation of the TSA labour process. Much of the two weeks of observation was spent sitting with TSAs and 'listening in' to their telephone interaction with customers and observing sales team meetings. The observational research also involved attending the final training session and award ceremony for successful trainees, the Flightpath Telephone Sales Annual Conference and observing general TSA–management interaction.

4   The empirical research into the work of flight attendants, undertaken by Tyler, was split into three main phases. The first stage involved undertaking observational research into the recruitment, training and supervision of flight attendants. This initial phase of the research also involved undertaking observational flights in various classes of travel (ten in total). The second phase of the fieldwork involved semi-structured interviews with airline personnel and passengers; with applicants to airlines; with trainee and experienced flight attendants, including those who were involved in the recruitment, training and supervision of other flight attendants, and with passengers. The third stage entailed a content analysis of airline documentation, ranging from company mission statements, recruitment and training literature to advertising and marketing materials depicting female flight attendants obtained from some 48 airlines (out of 64 which were contacted). See also Taylor and Tyler (2000).

References

Adkins, L. (1995) *Gendered Work: Sexuality, Family and The Labour Market*, Milton Keynes: Open University Press.

Anthony, P. (1994) *Managing Culture*, Milton Keynes: Open University Press.

Ashforth, B. E. and Humphrey, R. H. (1993) 'Emotional Labour in Service Roles: The Influence of Identity', *Academy of Management Review*, 18:1, 88–115.

Assiter, A. (1996) *Enlightened Women*, London: Routledge.

Barry, B. (1995) *Justice as Impartiality*, Oxford: Clarendon Press.

Bauman, Z. (1993) *Postmodern Ethics*, Oxford: Oxford University Press.

Benhabib, S. (1992) *Situating The Self: Gender, Community and Postmodernism in Contemporary Ethics*, Cambridge: Polity.

Bettencourt, L. and Gwinner, K. (1996) 'Customization of The Service Experience: The Role of The Frontline Employee', *International Journal of Service Industry Management*, 7:2, 3–20.

Boyd, C. and Bain, P. (1998) 'Once I Get You Up There, Where the Air is Rarified: Health, Safety and the Working Conditions of Cabin Crews', *New Technology, Work and Employment*, 13:1, 16–28.

Colling, T. (1995) 'Experiencing Turbulence: British Airways' management of human resources', *Human Resource Management Journal*, 5:5, 18–32.

Collins, P. H. (1991) *Black Feminist Thought: Knowledge, Consciousness and the Politics of Empowerment*, London: Routledge.

Connell, R. W. (1995) *Masculinities*, Cambridge: Polity.

Fuller, L. and Smith, V. (1991) 'Consumers Reports: Management by Customers in a Changing Economy', *Work, Employment and Society*, 5:1, 1–16.

Gilligan, C. (1982) *In A Different Voice*, Cambridge, MA: Harvard University Press.

Gilligan, C. (1997) 'In A Different Voice: Women's Conceptions of Self and of Morality', in Meyers, D. T. (ed.), *Feminist Social Thought*, 549–82, London: Routledge.

Hancock, P. (1997) 'Citizenship or Vassalage? Organizational Membership in the Age of Unreason', *Organization*, 4:1, 93–111.

Hatcher, C. (1999) 'Practices of the Heart: Constituting The Identities of Managers', paper presented at the 1st International Critical Management Studies conference, Manchester, UK.

Hochschild, A. R. (1979) 'Emotion Work, Feeling Rules and Social Structure', *American Journal of Sociology*, 85: 551–75.

Hochschild, A. R. (1983) *The Managed Heart: The Commercialization of Human Feeling*, Berkeley: University of California Press.

Hughes, K. D. and Tadic, V. (1998) 'Something to Deal With: Customer Sexual Harassment and Women's Retail Service Work in Canada', *Gender, Work and Organization*, 5:4, 207–19.

James, N. (1989) 'Emotional Labour: Skill and Work in the Social Regulation of Feelings', *Sociological Review*, 37:1, 15–42.

Jones, C., Taylor, G. and Nickson, D. (1997) 'Whatever it Takes? Managing "Empowered" Employees and the Service Encounter in an International Hotel Chain', *Work, Employment and Society*, 11:1, 541–54.

Knights, D. and McCabe, D. (1998) 'Dreams and Designs on Strategy: A Critical Analysis of TQM and Management Control', *Work, Employment and Society*, 12:3, 433–56.

Kohlberg, L. (1981) *The Philosophy of Moral Development*, San Francisco, CA: Harper Row.

Legge, K. (1998) 'Is HRM Ethical? Can HRM be Ethical?', in Parker, M. (ed.), *Ethics & Organizations*, 150–72, London: Sage.

Leidner, R. (1993) *Fast Food, Fast Talk: Service Work and the Routinization of Everyday Life*, Berkeley, CA: University of California Press.

Leidner, R. (1999) 'Emotional Labour in Service Work', *Annals of The American Academy of Political and Social Sciences*, 561: 81–95.

Lister, R. (1997) *Citizenship: Feminist Perspectives*, London: Macmillan.

Mills, A. (1998) 'Cockpits, Hangars, Boys and Galleys: Corporate Masculinities and the Development of British Airways', *Gender, Work and Organization*, 5:3, 172–88.

Mills, A. J. and Murgatroyd, S. (1991) *Organizational Rules: A Framework for Understanding Organizational Action*, Philadelphia: Open University Press.

Morgan, G. and Knights, D. (1991) 'Gendering Jobs: Corporate Strategy, Managerial Control and the Dynamics of Job Segregation', *Work, Employment and Society*, 5:2, 181–200.

Okin, S. M. (1989) *Gender, Justice and The Family*, New York: Basic Books.

Peters, T. and Waterman, R. (1982) *In Search of Excellence*. New York: Harper Row.

Pringle, R. (1989) *Secretaries Talk: Sexuality, Power and Work*, London: Verso.

Rosenthal, P., Hill, S. and Peccei, R. (1997) 'Checking Out Service: Evaluating excellence, HRM and TQM in Retailing', *Work, Employment and Society*, 11:3, 481–503.

Squires, J. (1999) *Gender in Political Theory*, Cambridge: Polity.

Taylor, S. (1997) 'Empowerment or Degradation? Total Quality Management and the Service Sector', in Brown, R. K. (ed.), *The Changing Shape of Work*, London: Macmillan.

Taylor, S. (1998) 'Emotional Labour and the New Workplace', in Thompson, P. and C. Warhurst (eds), *Workplaces of the Future*, London: Macmillan.

Taylor, S. and Tyler, M. (2000) 'Emotional Labour and Sexual Difference in the Airline Industry', *Work, Employment and Society*, 14:1, 77–96.

Tong, R. (1989) *Feminist Thought*, London: Unwin Hyman.

Tronto, J. (1993) *Moral Boundaries: The Political Argument for an Ethic of Care*, New York: Routledge.

Tyler, M. (1997) 'Women's Work as the Labour of Sexual Difference: Female Employment in the Airline Industry', unpublished PhD thesis, University of Derby.

Tyler, M. and Abbott, P. (1998) 'Chocs Away: Weight Watching in The Contemporary Airline Industry', *Sociology*, 32:3, 433–50.

Tyler, M. and Taylor, S. (1998) 'The Exchange of Aesthetics: Women's Work and The Gift', *Gender, Work and Organization*, 5:3, 165–71.

Young, I. M. (1990) *Justice and The Politics of Difference*, Princeton, NJ: Princeton University Press.

5

The Contradictions of Service Work: Call Centre as Customer-Oriented Bureaucracy

Marek Korczynski[1]

Two Images of Service Work

There are two main contrasting images of contemporary service work. This introductory section will briefly outline these images before the following section puts forward the argument that the contradictions of customer service work are best captured through the analytical lens of the customer-oriented bureaucracy. Here, Taylorism is tailored, emotions are rationalised, and the customer becomes 'our friend the enemy' (Benson, 1986). Then, following a brief discussion of research methods and sites, the chapter turns to examine the organisation and experience of call centre work in these contradictory terms.

The first image of service work is a positive one and stems from a group of management writers who form the new service management school. If we are to believe these writers, the contemporary service firm is increasingly becoming a terrain in which workers, customers and management all emerge as winners. In the words of a training manual in a firm studied in this chapter, this is the *'win:win:win'* scenario. While it is acknowledged that in the past many services were often managed in a command and control, Taylorised manner (Levitt, 1972), it is argued that there is now a new terrain of competition in service work. Here, customers' evaluation of the nature of the service *interaction*, rather than just of the separate product being delivered, becomes central to their evaluation of the overall service experience and hence also to their decision whether to give the firm repeat business. To illustrate this point Zemke and Schaaf (1989:4) write that 'a 1987 Gallup Poll asked 1,045 people what makes them decide not to return to a given restaurant. Number one on the list of reasons, identified by fully 83 percent of the respondents, was poor service. Not food quality, not ambience, not price. Poor service'. A number of management writers have also highlighted this as a common factor across many types of service work and have drawn up instruments to help managers measure and improve customers' evaluation of the service interaction (Bitner *et al.*, 1990; Carlzon, 1987; Parasuraman *et al.*, 1991).

Customers appear to want empathy from service workers, a genuine commitment to giving good service and a feeling that they are being treated as an individual rather than the next customer in the line. The implication of this new terrain of competition is that the old production-line approach to managing service work is no longer seen as appropriate. As Bowen and Lawler (1995) put it, the question that service managers have to face is: 'empowerment or production line?'. The answer new service management literature unequivocally delivers is that production line belongs to the past, and that to deliver the sort of qualities of service that customers want requires an 'empowerment' approach to service work. Schlesinger and Heskett (1992) agree that only by treating workers in a more humane way, by 'de-industrialising the service sector', can managers expect workers to give good quality service to customers. As long as firms can hire the right sort of people with the right customer-focused attitude and treat their workers well then their customers will receive good service. Heskett *et al.* (1997) have summarised research which shows that customers' perception of the quality of service is significantly correlated with service workers' perception of the climate of their firm. The more favourably service workers view the firm and how management treats them, the more favourable are customer perceptions of the service delivered by these same workers. This, then, is the circle completed for the 'win:win:win' fairy tale: customers win because they receive qualitatively superior service, workers win because they become empowered to act on their firmly held customer service values, and are freed from the old industrial tyranny, and managers win because customers keep coming back to the firm

In stark contrast to this optimistic imagery, Ritzer (1996; 1998) and Hochschild (1983) have portrayed contemporary service work as fake, invasive, demeaning and highly routinised. Hochschild has argued that management's need for emotional labour from service workers means that more and more of the worker's self is being taken over by the firm. The title of her book, *The Managed Heart*, brings out well the increasingly invasive nature of management control in service work. This has deeply worrying consequences (p. 198):

> When the product – the thing to be engineered, mass-produced, and subjected to speed-up and slowdown – is a smile, a mood, a feeling, or a relationship, it comes to belong more to the organisation and less to the self. And so . . . more people privately wonder, without tracing the question to its deepest social root: What do I really feel?

Ritzer has argued, in direct contrast to the new service management school, that the production-line approach to organising service work, far from being buried as a relic of the past, is alive and thriving. He sees the organisation of contemporary work as informed by the intensification, not replacement, of the bureaucratic logic of rationalisation. It is most plainly manifest in the way McDonald's organises service work with its application of Taylorist principles to the fast food restaurant. Ritzer argues that there is an ongoing general McDonaldisation of society. As such, his is not an argument restricted to service work. However, given that his paradigmatic case, McDonald's, 'to which the argument continually returns' (Smart, 1999:8), is a service firm it seems fair to assume that his arguments should have particular resonance within service work. Indeed, Ritzer (1998:60) argues that 'the process of McDonaldisation is leading to the creation of more and more McJobs. *The service sector*, especially at its lower end, is producing an enormous number of jobs, most of them requiring little or no skill'. He also notes that the 'service worker . . . has come to dominate McDonaldised systems' (1998:63). Within these increasingly widespread McDonaldised jobs, the worker is treated as a 'mechanical nut' (1996:139) and a 'human robot' (1998:60).

The Customer-Oriented Bureaucracy and Call Centre Work

What then are we to make of these two contrasting images of service work? The new service management school is right in heralding important changes in service work through the rise of the logic of customer-orientation. Ritzer is correct in speaking of the important logic of rationalisation. Both are right, yet both are wrong for each sees only a part of the nature of front line service work. When the two logics of customer-orientation and rationalisation are seen as co-existing in service organisations, the full, deeply contradictory, nature of front line (ie, customer-contact) work comes into focus. As such, contemporary service firms can be fruitfully analysed against the model of the *customer-oriented bureaucracy* (Korczynski, 2001).

There are a number of ways of thinking about the dual logics present in the customer-oriented bureaucracy. It can be seen as an updating of Max Weber's sociology of organisations and societies. Writing in the early years of the twentieth century, Weber saw the rise of rational-legal authority in which organisational members obeyed rules because they appeared to be built upon rational principles. The bureaucracy was the organisational manifestation of this form of authority. This is the element that Ritzer focuses upon in his McDonaldisation thesis. However, a broader view of Weber's overall project suggests the following question – if Weber were alive in the early years of this century, would he see another key basis of authority in organisations and societies? My answer is that it is that he may agree with a wide range of commentators who position the customer or the consumer as a central figure of authority in contemporary Western societies. The key idea is that there has been a fundamental shift in the structuring principle of society from production to consumption. Consumption comes to be a key aspect informing people's identities (du Gay, 1996; Gabriel and Lang, 1995). The idea of the customer-oriented bureaucracy acknowledges the rise of the customer as a figure of authority, but suggests that it joins rather than supplants the bureaucratic logic particularly in the sphere of production that is front-line work. Like Weber's concept of bureaucracy, the customer-oriented bureaucracy is put forward as a theoretical model. Essentially, it is a model to help analysis and understanding. It is not meant to suggest that in reality all service organisations share all of the characteristics of the model. The customer-oriented bureaucracy is a theoretical abstraction, based on identifying two dominant logics in front-line work and showing the implications of their dual presence across various aspects of organisations. If it is a useful model it will 'illuminate' (Mills, 1959) the management and experience of front-line work.

There is another way to think about the customer-oriented bureaucracy that particularly brings out its contradictions. One of the dimensions of customer contact work is that production and consumption are *simultaneous*. This is an important observation given the starkly different principles that writers have ascribed to the two spheres of production and consumption. For Bell (1976), *The Cultural Contradictions of Capitalism* lay in the clash between the discipline, rationality and asceticism required in production and the indiscipline, irrationality, and hedonism of consumption. Similarly, Bauman (1988; 1992) argues that in the sphere of production, work life is something rigorous to be endured – a burden that is only acceptable because it allows for the pursuit of pleasure in consumption. Although Bauman now sees a way in which the differing principles in the two spheres can inform rather than clash with each other, the key point is that there are very different principles ascribed to production and to consumption. Indeed, it is only by implicitly placing a buffer between production and consumption that Bauman can argue the two can inform each other. When production meets consumption directly it is Bell's idea of contradiction that is likely to be the more pertinent.

The central features of the customer-oriented bureaucracy are given in Figure 5.1. In each of the key dimensions listed the increasing status and role of customers means a significant shift in the nature of the organisation, away from the uncontested dominance of the bureaucratic paradigm. Within the bureaucratic model there was one simple dominant logic of rationality and efficiency, which pervaded the organisation. In this sense, Weber's ideal type of bureaucracy was free from contradictions. The customer-oriented bureaucracy, however, is infused with two logics – that of the customer orientation, alongside that of rationality and efficiency. These two logics frequently stand in contradiction to each other. The logic

Dimension

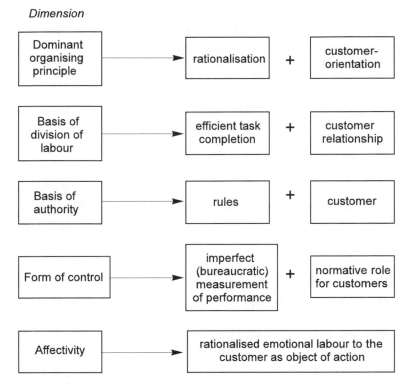

Figure 5.1   **Features of the customer-oriented bureaucracy**

of variability and unpredictability alongside the logic of routinisation, the logic of the personal and emotional alongside the logic of the impersonal rationality. As such, the customer-oriented bureaucracy has a number of *essential* contradictions – contradictions that are necessarily part of the organisational form.

The customer-oriented bureaucracy ideal type, by presenting the two dominant logics of contemporary service work as co-present within firms, can aid understanding of a wide range of service settings. It is particularly appropriate in examining the nature of call centre work. The dramatic rise of the call centre as key mode of employment in many advanced economies has been noted and documented by a number of recent studies (Batt, 1998; Frenkel *et al.*, 1998; Kinnie *et al.*, 1998; Taylor, 1998). Recent estimates suggest that within two years, *1.3 per cent of Europe's working population will be employed in call centres* (Datamonitor, 1998). These same estimates have catalogued an annual growth of 100,000 jobs per year in call centre jobs in Europe. The dual logics of efficiency and the customer underlie the dramatic growth in this mode of service employment. Call centres are attractive to firms for two main reasons (Datamonitor, 1998). First, they allow a dramatic reduction in costs per customer transaction compared to face-to-face transaction, carried out for instance in the high street bank branch. This is the logic of efficiency pushing the development of call centres. Second, they also enable firms to deliver what they consider to be higher and more consistent levels of customer service, for instance through allowing customers to make transactions outside of normal business hours. This is the logic of customer-orientation pushing the development of call centres.

To examine the nature of call centre work in terms of the customer-oriented bureaucracy this chapter presents findings from research carried out in five call centres in Australia, Japan and the USA. The following section outlines the research methods underlying these data and details some of the key characteristics of the call centres that were studied.

Research Sites and Research Methods

The research was part of a larger project into the nature of the work organisation of different types of front-line work internationally. Some of the findings of the wider project are reported in Frenkel *et al.* (1999). Qualitative research was undertaken in five firms using call centres. Each of the centres employed between 60 and 160 workers and received incoming calls. All call centres were relatively new service delivery channels for the large established firms of which they were a part. Four centres were in the financial services and one (TELO) in the telecommunications industry. Three call centres – here labelled AUS-BK, AUS-FIN and TELO[2] – were located in Australia. USA-BK was located in the USA, and J-FIN was based in Japan. Each of the centres dealt with high volume inbound calls from individual customers with individual accounts. In Keltner and Finegold's (1998) schema of market segmentation in service delivery these call centres were located in the 'mass customisation' segment. For instance, TELO was in the residential segment of the telecommunications firm, dealing with calls of less complexity and less value than the small business and large business operations (Keefe and Batt, 1997).

Within each site two researchers were present full-time for a minimum of three weeks. The research involved extensive semi-structured interviews with all managers and supervisors. We also interviewed a random sample of workers, segmenting by gender, length of experience, age, employment status (full-time/part-time), and management evaluation of performance level (low/high performer). Typically, management attempted to guide us to interview 'model' workers, but our research strategy allowed us to circumvent this. We interviewed union representatives where relevant.[3]

In addition, the research involved a range of observations and examination of documents. Tables 5.1 and 5.2 gives an overview of the research undertaken in the five sites.

Table 5.1 Interviews and observations undertaken, and documents examined in the call centres

Site	No. of interviews with managers/ supervisors/ union reps	No. of interviews with workers	No. of observations of labour process	No. of other observations	No. of documents examined
TELO	30	13	7	31	86
AUS-FIN	30	16	19	17	112
AUS-BK	56	24	26	58	92
USA-BK	39	14	6	15	60
J-FIN	33	12	32	21	70

Table 5.2 Total number of employees, number of respondents and response rate in each of the call centres

Setting	Total number of employees	Number of survey respondents	Response rate (%)
Total	1079	665	75
TELO			
Site A	82	69	84
Site B	123	73	59
Site C	160	87	54
Site D	78	61	78
AUS-BK	84	74	88
AUS-FIN			
Site E[a]	121	67	100
Site F	110	69	63
USA-BK			
Site G[a]	133	68	100
Site II[a]	127	53	100
J-FIN	61	44	72

Notes: [a]Due to the disagreement of management with full workforce coverage, sampling was conducted at this site. Approximately half of the staff members were chosen at random and were invited to participate in the survey. Unlike those of the other sites, the response rate for this site is based on the number of employees chosen instead of on the total workforce.

In addition to qualitative research, we also surveyed a representative sample of the workforce in the five centres plus five other centres run by the same firms. Most respondents were female, had a relatively short tenure on the current job, and were less than 30 years old.

The Contradictions of Call Centre Work

In this section the nature of work in the five call centres studied is examined in terms of the five organisational dimensions featured in Figure 5.1. The emphasis here is upon management actions and the *structure* of the work. This sets the context in which to appreciate the contradictory pleasures and pains in the *experience* of call centre work in the five sites, which is covered subsequently.

Dominant organising principle

Within the management literature on the new service workplace the dominant organising principle of the firm is taken to be customer-orientation, in other words, an acknowledgement of the sovereignty of customers and consequent framing of the organisation to deal with the necessarily idiosyncratic nature of individual customers' expectations and behaviour (Riddle, 1990). As Zemke and Schaaf (1989:16) put it, 'the service manager's task is to support diversity of response between the customer and the organisation, especially between the customer and the frontline contact people'. Within the customer-oriented bureaucracy ideal type, however, there are the dual dominant organising principles – the logic of customer-orientation *and* the bureaucratic logic of rationalisation. There is '*Tailorism*' and *Taylorism*.

From research in all the five sites, these dual logics were clearly evident. On the one hand, there was evidence that the call centre workers were being given increasing discretion to deal with customers whose idiosyncrasies the firms aimed to cope with. As one worker put it, 'over the last two years we have a little more scope to change customers' types of accounts, cross-selling, and do business referrals to other parts of the bank. We can also waive fees up to a certain amount . . . so you can be creative in the way you deal with customers, compromise with them'. On the other hand, there was still considerable evidence of efforts to routinise the behaviour of customers and workers. There were two main ways in which firms sought to routinise the behaviour of customers. One was through the use of Automated Voice Recording systems which presented customers with pre-set options and forced them to navigate a planned path through the sections of the firm. The other was through the training given to the call centre workers in the importance of 'controlling' the conversation with customers. Despite the discussions of the increased scope of customer sovereignty common to a number of literatures, there was a deafening silence in the rhetoric and symbols of customer sovereignty within the call centres. A central explanation of this lies in the importance management attached to limiting the variability of customers by ensuring that call centre workers could control and direct the service interactions. Any rhetoric of customer sovereignty would clearly work against such efforts. In each site management had designed training courses in how workers could effectively control conversations with customers, effectively forcing customers into certain routinised areas and paths in the conversation. This was further reinforced in the control system, with supervisors monitoring calls and evaluating them partly in terms of how well the workers were able to control the calls (see also Wray-Bliss, in this volume).

The dual dominating principles were also apparent in the management emphasis on achieving and measuring, both qualitative and quantitative goals, or what Taylor and Tyler (2000) call 'hard' and 'soft' goals. The qualitative goals related to ensuring that the customers' subjective and qualitative evaluation of the service interaction was a positive one. This aim was frequently alluded to by supervisors and managers in performance evaluation sessions, and was measured by proxy through supervisors monitoring calls and adducing whether the customers would have favourably evaluated the call. This was evidence of the importance of the new terrain of competition in service work and evidence of the logic of customer-orientation infusing organisational practices. The quantitative goals related to ensuring that workers dealt with customers *efficiently*. Goals were set, and measures taken, relating to the number of calls taken per day by workers, the time they spent on each call, and the amount of time they took in doing follow-up work to calls. These are the quantitative goals of the bureaucratic imperative of efficiency.

At USA-BK management shifted from one predominant logic to another over time. Managers stated that in the recent months they had started 'paying more attention to the numbers', the quantitative measures of efficiency. The senior manager stated that 'efficiency is now an issue'. A team manager admitted that the centre workers 'are constantly hearing numbers. It's exasperating not only to the reps [centre workers] but also to management. *It's almost as if we have double standards*'. This awareness of contradiction within management came from the contrast between the recent 'numbers' focus and the previous emphasis on the customising logic, allowing greater latitude for workers in the way they dealt with customers, and in the time they took to do this. The managers' awareness of the waxing and waning of their recent actions between the two logics was such that a central aspect of a management meeting concerned the need to find a 'balance' between their twin imperatives. This waxing and waning of management initiatives between dual logics is likely to be a dynamic played out in many service workplaces.

In another example, this time at AUS-FIN, the different logics led to tensions within management. At this site, senior management attempts to use a white-collar time and motion system entitled 'Clerical Work Measurement' had been recently dropped. The call centre manager had refused to use it because 'cutting talk time cuts *service*'. Here senior management advocated routinisation only to be vetoed by the middle manager's championing of the logic of customer-orientation. But it would be incorrect to view this as part of a story of the end of Taylorism in call centre work. There were still set targets of call-length to be achieved for calls which management sought to categorise into distinctive types. The workers were expected to key into the computer the type of call taken and this data combined with the automatic recording of the length of the call would be assessed against the target length for the specific type of call. Taylorism was tailored. In addition, the bureaucratic imperative was clearly present in the hopes of the effects of the new IT systems being designed in two of the sites. At AUS-FIN, it was anticipated that the new expert system being developed would effectively de-skill the work, allowing newly hired staff to become 'fully productive' in a matter of a few weeks. Similarly, one manager at AUS-BK suggested that the new IT system would make the job of the call centre worker a 'no brainer'. Both the logic of customer-orientation and logic of the bureaucracy were present in the call centres and this underpinned the tensions within management and within the work itself.

Basis of division of labour

Within the bureaucratic paradigm, efficient task completion is the primary basis of the division of labour (Jones, 1996). Within this logic, the customer appears as something to 'process' to enable the efficient completion of tasks within the bureaucracy (Prottas, 1979). The new service management literature suggests that the new terrain of competition demands that the *creation and maintenance of a customer relationship* becomes the primary basis for the division of labour. The analytical lens of the customer-oriented bureaucracy posits that this argument holds only a partial truth because it obscures the continuing importance of the bureaucratic logic within service firms. There are *dual* bases of the division of labour – efficient task completion *and* the customer relationship.

The dual bases of the division of labour were most exquisitely seen in the attempts by management to structure 'pseudo-relationships' (Gutek, 1995) with customers in the five call centres. The workers were instructed to give out their first name to customers, but *not* encouraged to direct customers to call them back specifically (rather than call back the centre as a whole). Management were opposed to the development of relationships between specific workers and specific customers because they saw this as working against their aims associated with efficient task completion. If customers waited for a specific worker to be available, rather than the next available call centre agent, the customer would necessarily have to wait longer in the queue. For management, customers waiting a long time in the queue were synonymous with inefficiency in their operations. Further, one of the great advantages to service management of call centres is that the technology of call centres allows a maximising in the efficiency of the use of the workers' time. In individual high street branches, for instance, there are often slack periods when there are few customers to serve, but there are still staff on duty. In call centres, however, the directing of calls immediately to the next available agent means that tasks are completed more efficiently, with slack time virtually abolished except on night shifts. For the service workers this means a considerable intensification of effort. Management saw relationships as inefficient and so sought to create pseudo-relationships. In addition, the call centre workers could quickly bring up a range of information on each customer, allowing them to simulate an ongoing knowledge of the particular individual.

Basis of authority/form of control

The management literature heralding the new service firm suggests a major change in the nature of authority and control. As Peccei and Rosenthal (1997) summarise, the argument is that 'the traditional command and control style of management practised within the firm is not conducive to gaining competitive advantage through customer service'. For the empowerment model to work there must be cultural control in which the workers become self-disciplined (Edwards *et al.*, 1998). This suggests a shifting in the locus of control. Hence the management literature has highlighted the importance of the recruitment process, stressing the need to select service workers with the appropriate values. Again the argument of the management literature holds only a partial truth. In heralding the new, there is an unwarranted dismissal of the bureaucratic past. Within the customer-oriented bureaucracy ideal type, authority is seen as vested in both rational-legal rules *and* the customer. Within the system of control, there is a *supplementing* of traditional bureaucratic methods of output and process measurement with cultural forms of control in which norms are based around the customer (Korczynski *et al.*, 2001).

The supplementing of output and behaviour measures with cultural control based around norms of customer empathy was exactly the characterisation of the nature of control in the research sites. Information technology-supported performance measures were pervasive, covering the number of calls taken, average length of calls, total time logged into the phone network, time spent in between calls, form and number of transactions completed, with such data generated in real time. As one centre worker put it, 'you get measured on how many times you scratch your shoulder'. These measures were necessarily imperfect however, in that they did not generate meaningful data on the quality of the service interaction which was deemed to be a key outcome by management. Only customers held this information and while management undertook systematic customer satisfaction surveys these surveys were unable to relate the experiences of specific customers to specific workers and hence could not be used for control purposes. As a proxy for measures of customer perception of the service interaction management undertook monitoring of approximately five calls per worker per week. Management assessed worker behaviour in calls against set criteria that they supposed related to customer satisfaction with the service interaction. While this call monitoring was an important part of the regime of control in the sites it was highly labour-intensive for supervisors and hence only covered a very small percentage of a worker's weekly calls.

Behaviour and output measures were supplemented with cultural control. Workers were recruited on the basis of customer empathy, they were further socialised into it and call monitoring continued to assess their delivery of such empathy. Important vehicles for socialisation were customer service training sessions. A central motif of these sessions was the promotion of self-control, with the self of workers defined in terms of their identity as, and identification with, customers (see also Sturdy, 2000). During the first half-day observation of training at AUS-FIN, the trainer continually asked questions in which workers were asked to think of themselves in their roles as customers, and the trainer set up role plays in which workers took the part of customers. Indeed in this whole session the only time when workers were able to speak from their identity and role as workers/producers was when the trainer asked them to relate their previous customer service experience. As the trainer said to the newly recruited workers, 'putting yourself in the customer's shoes is the most important thing'.

The clearest potential contradiction of management promoting customers as a supplementary basis of authority – that of the workers acting to satisfy customers at the expense of organisational goals – was also manifest in the research sites. Indeed, this phenomenon reached crisis point for management at AUS-BK. At this site there had been a number of major errors in bank statements and account details sent out to customers. Consequently, dissatisfied customers, with whom the centre workers felt considerable empathy, were phoning in with non-standard requests for clarification and help. The workers reacted by taking the management rhetoric of 'ownership of customer calls' to heart by doing meticulous supplementary work to calls and then phoning back individual customers to reassure them that their problem had been solved. This meant that the standard amount of time spent on each customer call grew dramatically, leading to a very large rise in the number of other customers left waiting in the telephone queue. It was a key (bureaucratic) management goal that the wait in the telephone queue should be kept as short as possible. Hence, workers were working diligently to solve customer problems, but in so doing were working against a key organisational goal.

Affectivity

When customer perception of service quality was not a central part of the terrain of competition, management could be satisfied with *impersonal* expression by workers as long as tasks were efficiently completed. With the rise of the new terrain of competition, workers are given an increased ability to express their personality at work (Lovelock, 1995). In this sense, the new service firm offers workers freedom from the straitjacket of impersonality that characterised the 'street level bureaucrat' (Prottas, 1979). However, the customer-oriented bureaucracy ideal type suggests this analysis is too one-sided. The continuing bureaucratic imperative of rationality and efficiency means that it is not a question of allowing an autonomous expression of emotion and personality by service workers. Rather, what firms require is *rationalised emotional labour* where workers are expected to display emotions, but only in as much as they do not conflict with bureaucratic aims of rationality and efficiency.

Rationalised emotional labour is an appropriate label to characterise management aims in the call centres. One of the key aims for management was that workers should feel empathy for customers and act out of that empathy. In all of the sites, management stated that recruitment criteria had moved towards a prioritising of customer service experience and evidence of customer focus and empathy. As a human resources strategy document at USA-BK noted, 'it is easier to train to knowledge and skills, and hire to self-images, traits and motives because they tend to be more difficult to develop or train'. At this site, the ideal candidate was described as possessing 'a positive, service-driven attitude'. A manager at AUS-BK stated that when recruiting they looked for the 'attitude to want to service customers'. Similarly, at AUS-FIN, the recruitment manager stated that 'the motivation to service customers . . . and customer sensitivity' were key criteria in recruiting. As also noted above, the focus in recruitment on customer empathy was carried through in what management expected workers to deliver in practice in their interactions with customers. 'How do you think the customer would have felt when you said that?' was the familiar refrain in call monitoring sessions between supervisors and workers.

But the form of emotional labour expected of workers by management was tightly circumscribed. Management wanted an *efficient* display of emotions. While it was stressed that workers should be 'friendly', they were told that they should not 'natter on', in the words of a trainer at TELO. Indeed at AUS-FIN, one manager suggested that 'poorer performers maybe are too friendly with the customers'. Workers had targets (of varying formality in the call centres) of completing a number of calls in a day. Becoming too friendly, and talking for longer would jeopardise these aims. Similarly, it was an important management aim that call centre workers should maintain control of the interaction with customers and being too friendly would jeopardise this aim. So in call monitoring sessions, supervisors not only assessed workers in terms of empathy but also in terms of their ability to efficiently bring a call to a close. The remarks of a manager at AUS-BK speak to the fragility of this social order: 'our measures don't give the reps time to chat with customers which may actually improve the quality of the call, but it's a fine line – we can't have them chatting all day'.

The Pleasures and Pains of Call Centre Work

The above analysis of management aims and the structure of call centre work in terms of the dual logics of the customer-oriented bureaucracy not only gives the lie to the partial picture put forward by the new service management literature, it also allows for an understanding of the pleasures and the pains in the experience of working in call centres. Given the essentially contradictory nature of call centre work it is often the pleasures of the work that beget the pains which in turn beget further and different pleasures. The existence of essential contradictions not only suggests deep tensions within the work environment which may lead to a negative work experience, it also suggests opportunities for workers as active agents to contest and reframe organisational life in creative ways that suit them, catching management entangled in the ambiguity of the situation.

The existence of both sharp pleasures and sharp pains was evident in the five centres studied. On the one hand, data generated by our questionnaire survey suggested high levels of overall job satisfaction among the workers. Asked 'all in all, how satisfied are with your job?', 73 per cent of the 610 respondents reported that they were either satisfied or very satisfied.[4] On the other hand, in all but one of the centres, management expressed concern about the continuing high levels of turnover (see also Wallace, 1999, who studied a number of the same call centres). Workers, it seems, were so satisfied with the job that they were leaving in considerable numbers. The questionnaire survey included questions examining turnover intention. Asked, 'how much do you agree or disagree with the statement "I would turn down a job at comparable pay and prospects in another company to stay with this company"', 51 per cent of respondents reported that they either disagreed somewhat or disagreed strongly with the statement.[5] Similarly, data from the questionnaire survey also suggested a significant experience of job stress among the respondents. Asked 'thinking of the past three months or so, how often has your job made you feel used up at the end of a workday?', 69 per cent of respondents reported that they felt this way sometimes, often or very often.[6] The data also suggested that *the pleasures and pains were felt by the same workers*, with 69 per cent of the respondents who reported feeling used up at the end of a workday also reporting that they were either satisfied or very satisfied with the job overall. Similarly, of the respondents who were either very/satisfied with their job overall, 63 per cent reported a turnover intention.[7]

One of the main pleasures of the job for the call centre workers that came through strongly in the research was the sense of satisfaction that was gained from 'helping people'.[8] As part of the semi-structured interviews, we asked call centre workers what the most satisfying aspect of their job was. In interview after interview in all of the sites, the message was the same:

> When you satisfy a customer and get recognition from the customer.
> I like talking to people all day.
> The best part is the customers, the things you can do for them, rapport with them.
> One of the plusses of job is speaking with people
> I love what I do – working with people.
> I love this job, because I like dealing with people, resolving issues. I feel very happy when I've resolved an issue.

These were real pleasures for many of the workers, who had been recruited precisely because of their positive attitudes towards dealing with customers. These pleasures, however, also begat their own pains. As one worker at USA-BK put it: 'the job can be rewarding from customer praise – although they can get grumpy'. The customer empathy held by workers underlay a significant experience of pain when the fragile social order of the workplace broke down and customers turned against the call centre workers. Abusive and irate customers were a systematic part of the social relations of the call centres. This can be surmised as arising ultimately from the transition from the enchantment to disillusionment that is endemic in consumption within capitalism (Korczynski, 2001). Although relatively rare compared to the satisfied customers who expressed gratitude, the abusive customers left their mark. The fragile social order between workers, managers and customers was built around customers being seen as worthy of empathy, and then workers acting out of such empathy. This was broken down when customers by being irate, abusive and aggressive acted in a way that not only made it difficult to feel empathy towards them but that also disoriented and caused pain to workers:

> One nasty call can ruin the whole day.
> Irate callers can really affect you. People can be very rude.
> Abusive calls are very hard not to take personally. Once or twice I've been in tears. I'm shocked at how aggressive people are over the phone.

> Sometimes the customer is rude, they will say 'fuck off' if you've given them a high quote. These comments are rare but they stick. They affect us all, they rebound round the whole team . . . I once had three in a day, and I was like 'put me back on the phone and I'll kill'.

The contradictions of the dual logics of the customer-oriented bureaucracy within the call centres underlay another important pleasure experienced within the workplace. A strong message that came through from the interview research was that 'the people here are great'. Collegial relations were highly rated and highly prized. The questionnaire survey asked, 'how satisfied are you with the people you work with?'. Of the 609 respondents, 83 per cent reported that they were very/satisfied.[9] A similar picture emerged from the interviews conducted, as the following selection of quotations from the call centre workers demonstrates:

> People are great – great camaraderie; we need it with job being so stressful.
> Everyone feels as if they're in the same boat and understands what everyone else is going through.
> There is high level of socialising between staff – it relieves pressure.
> I feel very welcomed here. More like a family. We are close. You can talk about anything – it helps a lot. We discuss the calls – get it off your chest.
> I heard it was a good department, especially the camaraderie of staff.

Placed within the contradictory structure and pressures of call centre work[10] as outlined above, workers sought refuge with, and support from, each other. And so from the pain came another real pleasure. The peer support was also manifest in the spontaneous 'communities of coping' which workers formed in order to give each other support in response to phone calls from irate customers (for more details on communities of coping see Korczynski, 2000a). It was also manifest in the way in which workers by and large accepted rather than challenged the strong rhetoric of 'teamwork' that was present in the call centres. 'Teams' in the call centre environment were effectively 'pseudo-teams' (Frenkel *et al.*, 1999), administrative units of workers over which one supervisor had authority. Management, however, were keen to use the terminology of 'teams' given its obvious unitarist implications (Fox, 1974). Despite the clash between the rhetoric of teamwork and the reality of largely individualised work, the call centre workers did not reject this language for they were able to use it to reinforce the strong positive peer relations on the office floor. The questionnaire survey asked, 'how much do you feel that you are part of your work team'. Eightyone per cent of respondents reported that they felt this way either a great deal or a fair amount.[11]

There was other evidence of workers actively carving out arenas of pleasure within the contradictory structure of call centre work. Some workers pointed out that it was possible on occasions to go beyond the 'pseudo-relationship' with customers. This was particularly the case at TELO where it was common for each worker to have one or two 'regulars' who would phone up to speak to specific workers. This could the source of considerable satisfaction to workers. At one training session, one worker recounted the story of 'her regular', how they had developed a mutual understanding, and how the worker had helped the customer overcome a problem of payment. The story ended with a recounting of how genuinely touched the worker had been by the customer's expression of gratitude to her. Others at this training session echoed this:

> Good to yarn sometimes.
> One customer wants to thank me face to face.
> One customer sent me blankets.
> Got a cake once. It's really good to help people out.

The creation of genuine relationships rather than pseudo ones also informed workers desire to go beyond policies and procedures. As one worker commented: 'if you follow the book probably there's not much problem solving. For example, if a customer's father died, you bend/break the rules to provide good service, to be a good human being as well'.

On the other hand, the contradictions of creating pseudo-relationships with people you do not know were also manifest. At TELO, some male customers were clearly too convinced of the relationship-nature of the interaction with female workers. As one female worker put it, 'you get asked out on a date, so many times'. This and the threat of nuisance calls directed to specific workers made the workers at this site very wary of giving out their name to customers. Management compromised that the workers should use their first names over the phone, and if they had to send written correspondence they could use the name of their supervisor.

The nature of the labour process was an important aspect of work in which some workers felt able to carve out arenas of satisfaction, but in which others felt the dead weight of the logic of routinisation. A minority of interviewees expressed the idea that within the structures of their work, there was considerable scope for self-definition and autonomy:

> I'm my own boss. Dealing with the customers, as long as you follow the guidelines. Talking to people encourages initiative and autonomy – I like that. You can't predict the calls, but it doesn't worry me . . . I actually learn from the difficult calls. It's sort of a challenge – throw me a curve ball.

For these workers, the 'customer-oriented' aspect of the nature of call centre work overweighed the bureaucratic routinising logic. For many other interviewees however, the routinising logic was too strong. The experience of the work as highly routine and non-challenging was a major source of dissatisfaction in the call centres:

> It's becoming monotonous. I want something more stimulating.
> The worst part of the job is the repetition.
> It is a bit routine.
> Sometimes you feel like battery hens.
> It is a monotonous job.
> There is a simmering discontent of staff because it's just so boring. I hate it here, but you've got to pay the mortgage.
> Supervisor: Morale is excellent for such a tedious job.

The ambiguity in the nature of the work, with a rising scope for discretion and variety existing beside a high degree of routinisation was reflected in the questionnaire survey data, with 51 per cent of respondents reporting that they were satisfied with the nature of the work.[12]

This analysis of call centre work as exemplifying contradictory tendencies which underlie the pleasures and pains experienced by the workers contrasts with the win:win:win fairytale propounded by the new service management literature. This section ends with an example of what the call centre workers, themselves, thought of the fairytale.

A researcher observed a training session at TELO on service and sales skills, entitled, 'WIN:WIN:WIN'. The trainer had been running the session for 20 minutes, when dissent began to come to the fore:

> Customer Service Representative (CSR):
> I disagree with win:win:win strongly.
> CSR: I agree.
> CSR: It's wrong.
> Trainer: Why?
> CSR: Not every customer is going to win e.g. meter-checking.
> Trainer: It depends on how you educate them.
> CSR: You know that they're not happy.
> Trainer: It's up to you to explain it to the customer.
> CSR: There will be customers who will complain regardless.
> Trainer: That's still a win to us.
> CSR: No, because they're not happy.
> Trainer: You should look at your general approach, then they are going to win from the relationship you are building with them, rather than the solution.
> CSR: If the customer is not happy, it's very hard to build a relationship.
> CSR: Some customers don't want a relationship with a company.
> CSR: That's right. Just a service with a bill.
> CSR: Some customers expect free service.

| Trainer: | Win:win:win with as many customers as possible. |
| CSR: | It's a bad way of expressing it. |

The first point to take from this interchange is that the front-line workers were clearly deeply uncomfortable with the win:win:win concept. This was not slight, subtle, or ironic dissent. The expression of dissent began with the blunt and unequivocal statement, 'I disagree with win:win:win strongly'. The analysis put forward in this chapter locates the call centre worker within a myriad of potential contradictions. Little surprise then that the win:win:win fairytale is given short shrift when the material circumstances of the work clash so clearly with this management rhetoric. The dissent is also notable because the challenges made are based on an advocacy of offended *customer* interests. The workers in the training session do not put forward objections based on the argument that *workers* themselves frequently do not 'win'. Rather it is that customers frequently do not win that is the expressed rationale for the challenges made. Such a challenge has a considerable degree of legitimacy within the logics of the customer-oriented bureaucracy. It is an example of the way in which the potentially contradictory logics at work can often create spaces for active subjects to contest and reframe the nature of their working lives.[13]

Conclusion

While the readers of *Sloan Management Review* and the *Harvard Business Review* are variously seduced and pandered to by the win:win:win story of the new service management literature, this story finds little welcome among the front-line workers of the contemporary service firm. This chapter has not agreed, however, with Ritzer's arguments concerning the simple intensification of rationalisation in service work. It has taken a rather different view of Weber's overall project, and considered the impact within production organisations of the rise of the consumer as a figure of authority. It has argued that contemporary service work is most usefully analysed through the lens of the customer-oriented bureaucracy in which there are dual, and potentially contradictory, logics. Rationality and efficiency exist alongside customer-orientation. Call centre work was chosen as a particularly clear example of the customer-oriented bureaucracy in practice. The chapter detailed research into the structure and experience of call centre work in five sites in Australia, the USA, and Japan. The structure of the work was shown to be consistently informed by the dual logics. Rationalised emotional labour was demanded in the context of pseudo-relationships in which efficient task completion was paramount. Bureaucratic measurement of the process of work was strengthened alongside the systematic development of norms of customer empathy. Although management constantly sought to maintain a 'balance' in these logics, inevitably there were fractures in the fragile social order.

The concept of the customer-oriented bureaucracy implies potentially both more spaces and more explicit tensions in the experience of service work than when it was dominated by the bureaucratic logic. This was reflected in the research into the experience of the call centre workers that was detailed in the previous section. On the one hand, many expressed a level of satisfaction with their job, while at the same time expressing an intention to leave their job. The pleasures and pains of the job were entwined, with one begetting the other. A key pleasure for workers was the ability to satisfy customers, to solve their problems. But customer empathy was also the source of an important pain imparted by irate and abusive customers, and suffered not infrequently. And yet this pain also in part underlay another of the main pleasures of the job – the camaraderie experienced with colleagues in the face of adversity.

The research presented here shows clear parallels between the call centre and the customer-oriented bureaucracy. This is both too bold and too narrow a statement, however. It is too bold in the sense that there can be call centres with significantly different logics at play. For instance, some may entail highly qualified quasi-professional work. Here logics of knowledge-intensiveness and professionalism will be present in determining the structure and experience of work. In addition, some call centres may be purely sales, rather than service, based. Here a different, entrepreneurial logic of work organisation is likely to be important.[14] But, the statement is also too narrow in the sense that there are many other forms of front-line work that can be illuminated through the lens of the customer-oriented bureaucracy. The work of the nurse, the care assistant, the retail worker, the bank teller, the restaurant worker, the hotel worker, the bar-worker can all be analysed usefully against the ideal type of the customer-oriented bureaucracy. The service society is a deeply contradictory one.

Notes

1   Thanks to Karen Shire, May Tam, Steve Frenkel and Leigh Donoghue who were part of the research project that collected the data reported in this chapter. The project was funded by the Australian Research Council and Andersen Consulting. Thanks to Laurie Cohen, Pete Ackers, Andrew Sturdy, Irena Grugulis and Damian Hodgson for comments on an earlier draft of this chapter.

   A word on the development of this chapter is necessary. Elsewhere, I have contributed to an article with colleagues which conceptualised call centres as a form of 'mass-customised bureaucracy' (Frenkel *et al.*, 1998). Reflecting on this earlier article I considered that the ideas in it needed to be theorised at a rather more abstract level and needed to be developed with reference to the specific nature of contemporary service work. This chapter represents an attempt to develop those earlier ideas with these two criteria in mind.

2   In addition to the extensive qualitative research in one centre in TELO, a small amount of qualitative research was done in another centre in this firm, and the survey research covered four call centres in total in this firm.

3   See Korczynski (2000b) for a discussion of the impact of unions on the organisation of the call centre work.

4   This gave a mean score of 3.81 (with 1 = very dissatisfied, and 5 = very satisfied).

5   Mean = 3.16 (1 = agree strongly, and 5 = disagree strongly; n = 609).

6   This gave a mean score of 3.03 (1= never, and 5= very often; n= 607).

7   That is, they disagreed somewhat/strongly with the statement 'I would turn down a job at comparable pay and prospects in another company to stay with this company'.

8   The questionnaire survey asked respondents: 'when you think of your working life, how important are good relations with customers to you?'. Of the 607 respondents reported, 91 per cent this was either important or very important to them (mean = 4.36; 1 = not important at all, and 5 = very important).

9   Mean = 4.14 (1 = very dissatisfied, and 5 = very satisfied).

10 Also note that as part of contradictory pressures of call centre work, workers often felt caught between mutually incompatible requests from customers and management. Asked, 'in providing customer service how often do you receive incompatible requests from customers and management?', 63 per cent of respondents reported that this happened sometimes, often or very often (mean = 2.87; 1 = never, and 5 = very often; n = 598).

11 Mean = 4.27 (1 = not at all, and 5 = a great deal; n = 507).

12 Respondents were asked, 'how satisfied are you with the nature of my work (e.g. Variety, challenge, opportunities to learn)?'. Mean was 3.28 (1 = very dissatisfied, and 5 = very satisfied; n = 611).

13 See Korczynski *et al.* (2001) for an extended discussion of the use of the norms of customer empathy in control in the call centres, and the spaces that this created for *legitimate* challenge and dissent (cf. Wray-Bliss, in this volume).

14 See Frenkel *et al.* (1999) for a systematic comparison of the organisation of sales work, and the organisation of service work.

References

Batt, R. (1998) 'Strategy in Context', Paper presented at 'Understanding the Service Workplace' Conference at The Wharton School, University of Pennsylvania, October 1998.

Bauman, Z. (1988) *Freedom*, Milton Keynes: Open University Press.

Bauman, Z. (1992) *Intimations of Postmodernity*, London: Routledge.

Bell, D. (1976) *The Cultural Contradictions of Capitalism*, London: Heinemann.

Benson, S. (1986) *Counter Cultures*, Chicago: University of Illinois Press.

Bitner, J., Booms B. and Tetreault M. (1990) 'The Service Encounter: Diagnosing Favourable and Unfavourable Incidents', *Journal of Marketing*, 54 (Jan), 71–84.

Bowen, D. and Lawler III, E., (1995) 'Organising for Service: Empowerment or Production Line?', in Glynn, W. and Barnes, J. (eds), *Understanding Services Management*, 269–94, New York: John Wiley.

Carlzon, J. (1987) *Moments of Truth*, Cambridge, MA: Ballinger.

Datamonitor (1998) *Call Centres in Europe*, London: Datamonitor.

du Gay, P. (1996) *Consumption and Identity at Work*, London: Sage.

Edwards, P., Collinson, M. and Rees, C. (1998) 'The Determinants of Employee Responses to TQM: Six Case Studies', *Organisational Studies*, 19:3, 449–75.

Fox, A. (1974) *Beyond Contract: Work, Power and Trust Relations*, London: Faber & Faber.

Frenkel, S., Tam, M., Korczynski, M. and Shire, K. (1998) 'Beyond Bureaucracy? Work Organization in Call Centres', *International Journal of Human Resource Management*, 9:6, 957–79.

Frenkel, S., Korczynski, M., Shire, K. and Tam, M. (1999) *On the Front Line*, Ithaca, NY: Cornell University Press.

Gabriel, Y. and Lang, T. (1995) *The Unmanageable Consumer: Contemporary Consumption and its Fragmentations*, London: Sage.

Gutek, B. A. (1995) *The Dynamics of Service*, San Francisco: Jossey-Bass.

Heskett, J., Sasser, W. and Schlesinger, L. (1997) *The Service Profit Chain*, New York: The Free Press.

Hochschild, A. (1983) *The Managed Heart*, Berkeley: University of California Press.

Jones, F. (1996) *Understanding Organizations*, Toronto: Copp Clark.

Keefe, J. and Batt, R. (1997) 'United States', in Katz, H. (ed.), *Telecommunications: Restructuring Work and Employment Relations Worldwide*, 31–88, Ithaca, NY: Cornell University Press.

Keltner, B. and Finegold, D. (1998) 'Segment Strategies and Service Productivity: Evidence from the U.S. and Europe', paper presented at 'Understanding the Service Workplace' Conference at The Wharton School, University of Pennsylvania, October 1998.

Kinnie, N., Hutchinson, S. and Purcell, J. (1998) 'Fun and Surveillance: The Paradox of High Commitment Management in Call Centres', paper presented at 'Understanding the Service Workplace' Conference at The Wharton School, University of Pennsylvania, October 1998.

Korczynski, M. (2000a) 'Customer Abuse: The Meaning, The Coping and The Consequences', paper presented at EGOS Colloquium, Helsinki.

Korczynski, M. (2000b) 'What a Difference a Union Makes', in Fernie, S. (ed.), *Call Centres: Employment Relations in the New Service Work*, Manchester: Manchester University Press.

Korczynski, M. (2001) *Human Resource Management in Service Work*, Basingstoke: Macmillan/Palgrave.

Korczynski, M., Shire, K., Frenkel, S. and Tam, M. (2001) 'Service Work in Consumer Capitalism: Customers, Control and Contradictions', *Work, Employment and Society* (forthcoming).

Levitt, T. (1972) 'Production-Line Approach to Service', *Harvard Business Review*, Sept/Oct, 41–52.

Lovelock, C. (1995) 'Managing Services: The Human Factor', in Glynn, W. and Barnes, J. (eds), *Understanding Services Management*, 220–43, New York: John Wiley.

Mills, C. Wright (1959) *The Sociological Imagination*, New York: Oxford University Press.

Parasuraman, A., Berry, L. and Zeithaml, V. (1991) 'Understanding Customer Expectations of Service', *Sloan Management Review*, 32:3, 39–48.

Peccei, R. and Rosenthal, P. (1997). 'The Antecedents of Employee Commitment to Customer Service', *International Journal of Human Resource Management*, 8, 66–86.

Prottas, J. M. (1979) *People-Processing*, Lexington, MA: Lexington Books.

Riddle, D. (1990) 'Key Strategic Decisions for Service Firms', in Bowan, D., Chase, R. and Cummings, T. (eds), *Service Management Effectiveness: Balancing Strategy, Organisation and Human Resources, Operations and Marketing*, San Francisco: Jossey-Bass.

Ritzer, G. (1996) *The McDonaldization of Society*, London/Thousand Oaks, CA: Sage.

Ritzer, G. (1998) *The McDonaldization Thesis: Explorations and Extensions*, London/ Thousand Oaks, CA: Sage.

Schlesinger, L. A. and Heskett, J. L. (1992) 'De-Industrialising the Service Sector: A New Model for Service Firms', in Swartz, T., Bowen, D. and Brown, S. (eds), *Advances in Services Marketing and Management: Research and Practice*, 159–76, Greenwich CT: JAI Press.

Smart, B. (ed.) (1999) *Resisting McDonaldization*, London: Sage.

Sturdy, A. J. (2000) 'Training in Service – Importing and Imparting Customer Service Culture as an Interactive Process', *International Journal of HRM*, 11:6, 1082–103.

Taylor, S. (1998) 'Emotional Labour and the New Workplace', in Warhurst, C. and Thompson, P. (eds), *The Future of Work*, London: Macmillan.

Taylor, S. and Tyler, M. (2000) 'Emotional Labour and Sexual Difference in the Airline Industry', *Work, Employment and Society*, 14:1, 77–95.

Wallace, C. (1999) '*The Sacrificial Strategy*', Working paper, Australian Graduate School of Management, University of New South Wales.

Zemke, R. and Schaaf, D. (1989) *The Service Edge: 101 Companies that Profit from Customer Care*, New York: NAL Books.

6

From Person- To System-Oriented Service

George Ritzer and Todd Stillman

A dramatic change in the way we consume has been underway since at least the middle of the twentieth century – far more people are consuming with much greater frequency. In fact, for many, consumption has become *the* defining feature of contemporary life. It can also be argued that consumption has come to equal, if not eclipse, production in society (Baudrillard, 1999; Debord, 1990). Customer service has a unique place in this transformation because it exists on the boundary between the spheres of production and consumption. Thus, a focus on customer service can help link an understanding of mass production to an understanding of mass consumption. In turn, this linkage can help to sharpen our theories of production, service and their interrelationship (see also du Gay, this volume).

In this chapter, we use a sociological perspective to conceptualise a homely observation – *satisfactory customer service seems increasingly hard to find*. While large corporations can draw on mass production techniques to offer a wide array of products at lower costs, when the same techniques are applied to service the demands of consumers are often not met. The source of the problem is the effort required to provide cost-effective service in an era of mass consumption. Corporate managers tend to try and solve this by using solutions, chiefly those involving increasing rationalisation, borrowed from the sphere of production. Rationalisation aims to make service as efficient, predictable, calculable and controllable as possible. However, the rationalisation of service processes brings to the fore drawbacks ('irrationalities') that have been hitherto largely hidden behind factory gates. Not only are these problems more visible to more people, but customers tend to be less tolerant of them than workers, who need to keep their jobs. If customers find the problems intolerable, they can, in many cases, move to another service provider. For this reason, management have sought to adapt to consumer needs and expectations, but, importantly, in the process they cannot sacrifice rationality and cost efficiency.

The chapter explores this tension through a discussion of an apparent trend away from person-oriented service to system-oriented service. Within the latter, routinised human interactions in service are being substituted for many consumers by information systems towards 'virtual' or 'self' service via the Internet and telephone for example. After outlining a number of ideal types of service, we locate these emerging forms within the context of consumer anxieties in 'risk societies'. Three examples of 'service' over the Internet – *Amazon, FedEx* and *Ameritrade* – are briefly examined, concluding with an open question over the sustainability of service that is increasingly based on disembedded systems. First however, we situate our approach to the changing character of customer service in reference to the labour process debate.

Customer Service from a Consumer Perspective

Consistent with the productivist bias of many sociological approaches of the time and of Marxism, relations of production dominate Braverman's (1974) labour process theory. The manner in which management controls, coerces and exploits workers and how this leads to deskilling and dehumanisation is set out. Such control developed first in manual trades before being extended to, and perpetuated in, white collar jobs and a service economy. Braverman emphasises the effect that the focus on efficiency, mechanisation and Taylorism have on the changing workplace, how they satisfy managers' needs for a controllable and malleable workforce and how they enable them to maximise output while minimising labour costs. Braverman's disciples have revised and extended these insights, arguing for the continuing salience of deskilling (despite the ascendancy of an 'information economy') and detailing new forms of labour control like Total Quality Management (Warhurst and Thompson, 1998). In doing so, the labour process approach has provided a solid understanding of the social consequences of capitalist management in a variety of workplace settings, including those providing customer service.

Where the labour process approach has been less useful though, is on the issue of how the management and control of work affects *customers*. Sociological analyses of the labour process have tended to stress the impact of coercive and controlling aspects of service on employees rather than on consumers. More generally, such one-sidedness has led to the comparative neglect of the changing role of consumption in social life. Where consumption has been examined, as in Gartman's work on consumer culture and the automobile industry, it has illuminated the effects of consumer tastes on the labour process – 'consumer demand for a diversity of changing products that culturally legitimate the workplace rigors of capitalism have driven employers to search for labor control methods that go beyond the minute division of labor and centralization of discretion postulated by Braverman (Gartman, 1999:109). The effects of efficiency, mechanisation and Taylorization on consumption and consumers have then, gone largely unexplored in the labour process approach.

In an argument that runs parallel to Braverman's, but extends it to consumers and consumption, Ritzer (1998:2000) draws on Weber's theory of rationalisation to make the case that the service industry, among many others, has become increasingly *McDonaldised*. This approach stresses the way in which the imperatives of instrumentally rational production and service penetrate the places where people consume. It underscores the effects of efficiency on the workplace, as Braverman does, but, because of the special place of service between the realms of production and consumption, the argument is extended to consumers who are also affected by the rationalisation of consumer settings. The defining characteristics of *McDonaldisation* (efficiency, calculability, predictability and control through non-human technology) involve customers in the rationalisation of service: by getting them to move through lines more quickly and to order large quantities of mediocre food at what appear to be low prices; by standardising orders; by scripting interactions; and, by developing norms of unpaid labour such as disposing of their own litter. Rationalised consumer 'labour' can be as alienating as the labour of paid employees. Despite benefits for management, rationalisation has the negative consequence, at least at times, of being off-putting to consumers who may just walk away.

Ritzer (1999) has also shown how management seek to deal with this tension by using spectacle, simulation and other techniques of *re-enchantment* to make rationalised settings more appealing to consumers and to obscure the rationalisation that lies at their core. Such a calculated marriage of rationalisation and enchantment is not confined to the obvious settings of theme parks like Disney World and Las Vegas casinos, but extends across the entirety of the 'new means of consumption'. Many chain restaurants, for example, adopt a theme or attempt to simulate another place or era in order to become more attractive to diners. Such themes effectively mask the rationalised production and service protocols that are typical of chain restaurants (c.f. Nickson *et al.*, this volume). As a result, the 'depthless' surface of a themed restaurant – its lack of authentic emotion and genuine meaning – fetishistically masks the relations of production that contribute to its veneer. A good example of such a masking process can be found in the enforced smiles and scripted interactions of counter employees at McDonald's. The intent to create an illusion of a happy team working the counter and toiling in the open kitchen denies the reality of the low-wage, high stress work that results in a high turnover rate for McDonald's employees. For many consumers, the manufacture of themed enchantment improves the overall impression made by a consumer space and conceals the rationalised processes that come together to produce such a themed environment. Although consumer settings remain highly rationalised, such calculated effects capitalise on the consumer's desire for escape, novelty and variety to obscure and temper the disenchanting effects of rationalisation.

From Person-Oriented to System-Oriented Customer Service

This section follows the logic of the *McDonaldisation* thesis, but attempts to extend this beyond the fast food industry and other material service venues into the non-material realm of 'virtual' service. We make the case that customer service is becoming more and more rationalised through the replacement of humans with non-human technology. We term this hyper-rationalised customer service *'system-oriented'* which is contrasted with the more traditional *'person-oriented'* service.

As consumption has become more pervasive, person-oriented customer service, centred on attentive and individualised treatment, has increasingly been restricted to elite consumers. Given economies of scale in the realm of consumption, most businesses have neither the time nor the personnel to dedicate to the craft of customer service. Person-oriented service involves face-to-face inter-subjective relations between service provider and customer and this continues to exist in less rationalised economic settings such as independent bookstores. Here, an ideal-typical sales clerk would make it his/her business to find out over time what kinds of books you like and make recommendations based on this knowledge. If you are a frequent customer, the clerk might remember to ask how you liked the book or have another recommendation ready on the next visit. The service is personalised, the interaction is personal and the entire exchange is rooted in shared understandings of what each participant looks for in a small, independent bookshop.

The craft work of such customer service entails at least two qualities that are at odds with the process of *McDonaldisation*. On the one hand, personal customer service requires experience and dedication. The service provider must have the know-how and willingness to help a consumer, qualities that require specialised knowledge and a particular temperament. On the other, personal service requires patience. It means that the service provider must be willing to understand a customer's needs and then have the time to fulfil these needs. So person-oriented customer service tends to be time consuming, skilled and relatively expensive labour and therefore incommensurate with the priorities and profit-expectations of large-scale *McDonaldised* organisations.

As a direct result of the colonisation of consumption by large corporations with aspirations to profit greatly from mass consumption, most customer service jobs have been deskilled, transformed into *McJobs* (Ritzer, 1998:59–70). These require little training and little skill to perform them. The keys on the cash register at a McDonald's restaurant, for example, are labelled with pictographs so the counterperson need not memorise the price of the menu items. *McJobs* have several advantages for managers. They allow for flexibility in personnel decisions because they do not require a large investment in training and employees can be used interchangeably.

They contribute to the standardisation of both product and service because they minimise the latitude of human discretion. And, because they use little skill, they demand modest pay. Workers, however, benefit very little from *McWork*. Compensation for *McJobs* is typically the minimum wage and there are few benefits like health insurance. Further, workers are unable to augment their own social capital in *McJobs*, ensuring slim prospects of future job mobility.

Through the use of non-human technology, system-oriented customer service pushes the deskilling of work to new heights and ultimately leads to the replacement of more workers by technology. Thus, system-oriented customer service uses such things as computers, signage, conveyor belts and bar codes to control workers further and ultimately to do work that has in the past been performed by human beings. System-oriented customer service replaces the inter-subjective dimensions of person-oriented custo-mer service with instrumentally rational processes. First, interactions with customers are scripted and strictly controlled through both training and monitoring. Second, in system-oriented customer service, the human elements are to as great a degree as possible replaced by non-human technologies. Third, the emphasis is placed on cost-effective, standardised service. An exemplar of an extreme form of system-oriented customer service, what we call *systemised service* below, is a touch-tone telephone service system where orders and inquiries are fielded by computers. (Press 1 for balance inquiry and payment information; press 2 to report a card lost or stolen, and so on.). The primary benefit of touch-tone systems is that they eliminate labour and training costs for customer service providers. But such systems have drawbacks for consumers. Users of these systems face the challenge of locating information to answer their own questions. This can involve a lengthy trial-and-error process that never quite responds to the consumers' demands. And, there is the frustration of knowing that there is not, and may never be, a human being on the line to help with the process or to provide the needed answers.

Implied in the preceding discussion are two continua. The first runs the gamut from person-oriented (the system is run by and for people) and system-oriented (the system is run by and for the organisation providing the service). The second continuum deals with a range from service encounters that involve human relationships (social) to those in which human relationships have been reduced or eliminated (non-social). When one cross-cuts the person-oriented/system-oriented and social/non-social continua, one emerges with four ideal-typical service relationships (see Figure 6.1) – *neighbourly service, artisanal service, McDonaldised service* and *systemised service*. We will argue that there is not only a long-term trend from the first two to the latter two, but that among the latter pair, McDonaldised service will, to a large degree, eventually give way to system service.

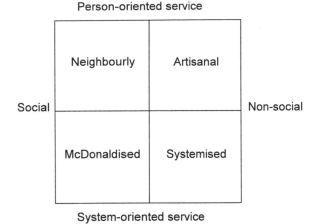

Figure 6.1   Types of service

Neighbourly service is both person-oriented and highly social in nature. It is generally part of a localised exchange that takes place between actors who know each other from serial interactions and repeat purchases; it is distinguished by its local, face-to-face character. The act of consumption is a social process and it takes place in the context of a broader and longer-term social relationship. Unlike artisanal service (see below), neighbourly service does not necessarily require a high degree of skill on the part of those providing it. The customer service in local consumer settings is highly inter-subjective and can extend beyond economic imperatives to encompass the norms of social interaction that govern the life-world. A good example of this type of service can be found in a corner news stand where the newsperson would be likely to remember to ask about your vacation when you pick up your regular paper. The consumer is as likely to ask about the newsperson's family or health. Rationalised providers of similar services (e.g. the coin-operated newspaper box) threaten the neighbourly type of service.

Artisanal service requires special skills on the part of a service provider and the service is ideally tailored to the individual customer. This form of the service has the potential to be rationalised, but is often preserved by elites who are willing and able to pay it. Like neighbourly service, it is personal, face-to-face and likely to take place in the context of a larger set of social relationships. However, unlike neighbourly service, it may well be non-social in character. That is, there is no need for the relationship between artisan and customer to be face-to-face; all that matters is that the artisan provide the desired product or service. Indeed, the nature of artisans may lead them to keep social interaction to a minimum, but that does not prevent them from providing the desired product.

Giddens writes that systems of technical expertise help to deal with the risks associated with disembedded forms of social relations. Reliance on expert systems to make sure drinking water or one's car is safe, for example, entails the need for trust that is endemic to all of modern life. When trust is habituated, reliance on expert systems is less a matter of accepting risk than not registering it, a taken-for-granted condition termed confidence. Few people turn their thoughts to the competency of design engineers when they get behind the wheel of a car (although the recent debacle involving Ford Explorers and Firestone tyres may help to change that). In short, trust in expert systems is an article of faith (Giddens, 1990:28–9). However, the intersection of risk and trust becomes more relevant when social actors make decisions. The question in these instances is simply how much trust is someone willing to place in an expert system? What becomes important here, Giddens argues, is how well face-to-face social relations buttress blind trust in expert systems. To some degree, trust remains conditional on face-to-face social relations that can help re-embed expert systems in social interaction. Thus, the micro-foundations of time–space distanciation are interpersonal relations. There could be no distanciation in the absence of trust engendered by face-to-face social relations. For this reason, every decent-sized bureaucracy has spokespeople and a public relations department.

Giddens' theories map on to consumer society and customer service with illuminating results. Modern consumption increasingly involves disembedded systems – long commodity chains link the producers of raw materials to manufacturers–distributors–retailers–consumers. These chains often extend across the globe, especially since much agricultural production and manufacturing of consumer goods today takes place in 'Third World' countries. Long commodity chains, however, are more likely to fall under the heading of confidence rather than risk for consumers who have become habituated to the predictability of most of consumer goods. Only when gasoline prices escalate or lettuce suddenly disappears from store shelves do many people think very much about commodity chains. However, the experience of the emerging, effervescent and differentiated marketplace would seem to be a primary source of risk for consumers.

As the pace of change in the sphere of consumption quickens, as simulacra of place and time become more pervasive, as goods become more abundant, a kind of vertigo develops among consumers. Consumption settings may enchant people through an array of spectacular techniques and promise a safe, sanitised and standardised experience that is calculated to stimulate with minimal discomfort. However, the cumulative effect of the means of consumption differs from the calculated effect of individual department stores, sports arenas and websites. The broader consumer archipelago is a complicated and variable bazaar that can disorient customers as a consequence of its manifold seductive powers. Today's consumer then is confronted with a set of navigational challenges, risky calculations and perplexing choices. Thus, what Giddens terms the juggernaut of modernity is as apt a description of consumer experience as any – 'a runaway engine of enormous power which, collectively as human beings, we can drive to some extent but which also threatens to rush out of our control and which could rend itself asunder' (Giddens, 1990:139).[1]

Consumer anxiety is generally associated with the question of consumer choice. Consumers face the dilemma of making sound choices in a complicated marketplace without necessarily having sufficient knowledge to make the best, or even a good, decision. First, desire is piqued at every turn in the consumer society so it becomes increasingly difficult for consumers to choose among proliferating choices. Desire for consumer goods and experiences far outrun the means of most consumers. For this reason, it may be difficult for consumers to manage the allocation of attention and resources (Schor, 1991). Second, the issue of 'caveat emptor' is heightened. In a marketplace filled with unfamiliar goods, many of which are sold over the Internet or home-shopping television networks, consumers may experience heightened uncertainty over the quality of goods and the reliability of the vendors. This is especially the case for abstract services like money management in which consumers must make an informed decision about the reliability of an expert system (see also Hodgson, in this volume). Because of the difficulties inherent in such complicated consumer transactions, consumers tend to become loyal to familiar brands and companies.

Consumers also increasingly seek aid in navigating the marketplace and in reducing its risks through customer service. When purchasing a car, for example, personal trust in a salesperson can make all the difference for a customer who knows little about how cars work. In this scheme, face-to-face service can help to reduce the risk associated with abstract systems. Customer service, then, can be conceptualised as the micro-foundational facework on which a consumer society rests. But as we have seen, face-to-face customer service is on the wane. Therein lies a paradox. With the decline of person-oriented customer service and the rise of systems-oriented service, how exactly is consumer trust to be built? In *McDonaldised* systems there are still social relationships between employees and customers that can help allay the latter's fears, but what of systemised settings where people are absent?

Trust and Enchantment Over the Internet?

We now attempt to deal with these questions by examining three examples of systemised settings found on the websites of Fedex, Amazon and Ameritrade. We try to move the risk/trust line of analysis another step forward, and to extend the insights of the re-enchantment thesis in order to consider how postmodern techniques can be used to represent abstract systems to consumers. The same techniques that are used to re-enchant rationalised settings can also be used to allay consumer apprehension and anxiety that is attendant to the experience of the newest aspects of consumer society. Here the postmodern technique of simulation can be used to project an image of order, expertise, efficiency and rationality to provide a sense of embeddedness for consumers who negotiate abstract systems.

We have already touched on techniques of re-enchantment in the context of a discussion of the effects of rationalisation. Based on the prevalence of theme parks and themed restaurants for example, it was argued that the application of a superficial theme to a consumer setting can make it more attractive to consumers – rather than merely a place to consume, the setting itself becomes an experience (Gottdiener, 1995). To the extent that consumers live in a homogenous, predictable world, this strategy makes perfect sense – consumer settings try to supply an antidote to a disenchanted world in the form of a novel spectacle.

Customer service relies on reputation and trustworthiness and this no less true in the new forms of system-service. In fields such as package delivery and money management, consumers are seeking indications that their risks will be minimised or eliminated. Will the package be delivered on time? Will I lose my savings? For these kinds of consumer acts, customer service plays an essential role in assuaging the fears of consumers by projecting an image of trustworthiness and expertise. The issue is how is this accomplished in the disembedded systemised setting where no people are present and no social interaction takes place?

FedEx: Transparency

Though most consumption continues to take place in shopping malls and other cathedrals of consumption, 'home-delivery' of special-ordered products is an important part of consumption's penetration of social life. As commodity chains extend further across space, exchange is increasingly co-ordinated by vast organisations like Federal Express and UPS that provide accelerated and reliable co-ordination commensurate with flexible and decentralised production and consumption. One of the things that Federal Express has developed is a system whereby customers can 'track' their packages on the FedEx website. This program exemplifies several of the qualities needed by systemised service to cope with both time–space distanciation and flexibility – rationality, simulation and spectacle.

First, Federal Express has reduced costs – automated customer service may cost 75 per cent less than person-oriented customer service. The tracking system is designed to handle a high volume of inquiries and to reduce personnel requirements. It employs techniques characteristic of

McDonaldisation by making customers into an extension of the system, forcing them to perform tasks that were once performed by customer service representatives. In short, it rationalises the expensive and cumbersome proposition of large-scale customer service. Second, the system serves to reduce at least the appearance of risk associated with time–space distanciation and the opacity of the expert system to which consumers entrust their parcels. For example, on the website a stylised log of a parcel's disposition is provided – it may have left Memphis and stopped in Omaha en route to Seattle (the logs can be much more involved). This account is a litany that puts a spectacular face on a complex and opaque system. Only a portion of the information it provides can be put to any practical use (has the package arrived? who signed for the package?). The rest serves as 'simulated transparency', that is, a simulation that is intended not only to be spectacular (one is to be amazed by how Fedex could possibly track every package crisscrossing its system), but also to assure customers by allowing them to 'see' (in a very abstract way) where the package is, that the expert system is operating as it should and that the package will eventually find its way to the customer's door.

Ameritrade: Information

In only a short time, online financial brokerages have become immensely popular in the USA. This might have something to do with the fact that in climates of risk, especially those involving investments, many customers prefer a 'hands-on' approach. Indeed, online trading has several advantages for customers. First, it is available around the clock. Second, it is much less expensive than using a traditional broker. Third, it enables even small investors to follow their investments closely – because the daily business pages are no longer sufficient, online traders can follow their stocks minute-by-minute throughout the day. It also has several advantages for brokerages. First, because a large number of brokers is not required, they can keep a greater share of the commissions. Second, because of low costs, online trading encourages small investors to invest, increasing the market for securities. Similarly, small investors trade more often because of low commission fees. With more customers making trades more frequently, online brokerages can realise higher profits.

There are, of course, risks for customers associated with online trading. Furthermore, there is one major disadvantage – no direct access to personal relationships and the expertise of a broker. However, although there are risks with any form of trading, the Ameritrade site provides the illusion of diminished risk by offering a spectacular flood of information about the market. This information includes annual reports of companies, up-to-the-minute stock prices, records of trading volume for entire markets and individual stocks, as well as suggestions for investment portfolios based on a customer's individualised 'risk profile'. (A risk profile is determined by having the *customer* fill-out a questionnaire on investment goals and willingness to take chances on high-yield investments.) All of this, of course, is designed to ease the mind of the online investor even in the absence of another human being to provide assurance.

Amazon.com: Expertise

Amazon.com is considered by many to be a brilliant business innovation because it takes advantage of the Internet to minimise some of the costs associated with selling books and, increasingly, many other products. The company pays no rent on a premium location nor does it keep a large inventory of books. It need not have a knowledgeable sales staff, only an assembly line of workers to process orders. There are two chief advantages over conventional bookstores of Amazon.com for consumers. They have access to a far greater selection of books and it is convenient – fast home delivery (by FedEx is an option) and the 'store' never closes. However, the systemised service offered on the website has a number of drawbacks. The books are unavailable for browsing online, so it is difficult to ascertain whether a particular book is of interest – browsers rely mainly on titles and blurbs. Further and as in the previous cases, there is no sales clerk available to ask for advice. Thus, ordering a book from Amazon.com is riskier than buying it in a local book shop or even one of the book superstores; one is far more likely to order a book that turns out to be very different from what one thought one was ordering. Amazon.com has tried to deal with this shortcoming of systemised service by, for example: linking popular books; showing photographic images of covers; and, providing reviews from major publications and other customers. Once again, these can be seen as reducing the risk of buying an inappropriate or poorly produced product.

In summary, all of the websites appear to be aiming at the same goal – replacing face-to-face customer service with systemised service that provides customers with windows into the workings of abstract systems – either the consumer bazaar, the stock market or a package delivery system. These windows are designed to reduce the consumer's perception of risk associated with dealing with websites where fellow human beings are absent. But it also adds an element of spectacle – Amazon.com for example boasts over a million titles in stock (a hundred times more than most material bookstores) and the books are delivered almost immediately, sometimes the next day.

Giddens has argued that human relationships are needed to re-embed such disembedded expert systems as those discussed above. However, the structure and the economics of web-based systems give them little or no opportunity to offer such human services. They have created spectacular ways of offering consumers services that do not involve any direct human contact or interaction. Thus, disembedded systems are simply re-embedded in yet other disembedded systems. Can this do the trick? Can people learn to feel confident about disembedded systems embedded in other disembedded systems? Judging by the early success of some of these Internet businesses, the answer seemed to be yes. But as more and more people plunge ever-more deeply into systemised service one is forced to wonder about the consequences of a life adrift in layers of disembedded systems with no possibility of ever being re-embedded in direct human social relationships. In fact, the more recent setbacks of many web-based businesses may be attributed, at least in part, to the unwillingness of consumers to give up human relationships and surrender themselves to layer upon layer of disembedded systems.

Conclusion

In this chapter, we have pointed to a general trend in the provision of customer service from a person-oriented, or face-to-face, model to a system-oriented model in which face-to-face interaction is increasingly rare. We argued that system-oriented service has a host of benefits from the perspective of *production* – it is more efficient, less costly, and more easily controlled than person-oriented service. Partly for these reasons, service providers (and developers of the technology) have been quick to see the potential for the system-oriented approach. However, the system-oriented model has drawbacks that become obvious when looked at from the point of view of the *consumer*. In an extension of Giddens's theoretical framework, we conceptualised the fundamental problem that system-oriented service must overcome – trust is rooted in face-to-face interaction. If customer service providers turn to system-oriented service, how are they to establish a trustworthy relationship with consumers? By considering the case of customer service on the Internet, we suggested that trust *could* be created by making abstract systems more knowable and transparent.

Will this alternative be as satisfactory to consumers as it is attractive to providers? We cannot yet know whether the Internet has permanently revolutionised customer service, but we suspect that consumers will become more acclimatised to it as alternative modes of service are gradually abandoned. What is unfortunate is how little say consumers have in this process (see also Fitchett and McDonagh, this volume). Those who have means can make their preferences known with their wallets and choose person-oriented service. Those who lack the means will live with the economical but faceless and dehumanising service systems. As service systems become more prevalent across a range of social spheres, a dystopian future looms on the horizon. This future has social actors suspended in layer upon layer of disembedded systems, with fewer and fewer social interactions. We grow increasingly comfortable interfacing with machines, but at what cost?

Notes

1   An important facet of this engine is the shift in the techniques of production from Fordist mass production to flexible production (Harvey, 1989; Piore and Sabel, 1984). The consequences of the post-Fordist model claimed for consumers are a wider variety of available goods and a quicker turnover of fashions. In short, the marketplace becomes increasingly complex.

References

Baudrillard, J. (1999) *The Consumer Society*, Thousand Oaks, CA: Sage.

Bauman, Z. (2000) *Liquid Modernity*, Malden, MA: Blackwell.

Beck, U. (1992) *Risk Society: Towards a New Modernity*, Thousand Oaks, CA: Sage.

Braverman, H. (1974) *Labour and Monopoly Capital: The Degradation of Work in the Twentieth Century*, New York: Monthly Review Press.

Debord, G. (1990) *The Society of the Spectacle*, London: Verso.

Gartman, D. (1999) 'Dialectics of the Labour Process, Consumer Culture, and Class Struggle: The Contradictory Development of the American Automobile Industry', in Wardell, M., Steiger, T. L. and Meiksins, P. (eds), *Rethinking the Labour Process*, Albany, NY: State University of New York Press.

Giddens, A. (1990) *The Consequences of Modernity*, Stanford, CA: Stanford University Press.

Gottdeiner, M. (1997) *The Theming America: Dreams, Visions, and Commercial Spaces*, Boulder, CO: Westview Press.

Habermas, J. (1981) *The Theory of Communicative Action. Vol. 1, Reason and Rationalisation of Society*, Boston, MA: Beacon Press.

Harvey, D. (1989) *The Condition of Postmodernity*, Malden, MA: Blackwell.

Piore, M. and Sabel, C. (1984) *The Second Industrial Divide: Possibilities for Prosperity*, New York, NY: Basic Books.

Ritzer, G. (1998) *The McDonaldization Thesis: Explorations and Extensions*, Thousand Oaks, CA: Sage.

Ritzer, G. (1999) *Enchanting a Disenchanted World: Revolutionising the New Means of Consumption*, Thousand Oaks, CA: Pine Forge Press.

Ritzer, G. (2000) *The McDonaldization of Society*, revised edn, Thousand Oaks, CA: Pine Forge Press.

Schor, J. (1991) *The Overworked American: the unexpected decline of leisure*, New York: Basic Books.

Warhurst, C. and Thompson, P. (1998) 'Hands, Hearts and Minds: Changing Work and Workers at the End of the Century', in Thompson, P. and Warhurst, C. (eds), *Workplaces of the Future*, London: Macmillan.

7

'Empowering Customers Through Education' Or Governing without Government?

Damian Hodgson

Introduction

Despite the increasing sophistication of techniques aimed at manipulating consumers in modern society, it is frequently claimed both in management and in the popular media that this is necessitated, and even counteracted, by the replacement of the gullible consumers of yesteryear by an informed, educated and streetwise breed of 'sovereign customer'. To help understand the paradox of this simultaneous 'empowerment' and 'manipulation' of the consumer, the concept of 'governmentality' (Foucault, 1991) is adopted (and adapted) in this chapter. Governmentality, described by Foucault as the study of 'the conduct of conduct', attempts to translate the 'macrophysics' of political economy into the 'microphysics' of power by examining how control is effected *through* the management of freedom. This chapter will develop these themes by drawing on research conducted in the UK on the financial services industry, a particularly interesting area of study as citizens are increasingly enrolled in this market relationship as 'consumers' of financial services. This relevance is enhanced by the widespread 'deregulation' of financial services, intended to stimulate the private sector into playing a greater role in the provision of welfare. Rather than understanding this as the 'rolling back of the State' or as cutting back on 'Big Government', this shift instead constitutes a specifically liberal (or neo-liberal) form of *'government'*, in the Foucauldian sense, through specific modes of regulation and subjection.

After a brief introduction to the recent history of financial services in the UK, the theoretical context will be established through a discussion of the twin themes of consumerism and governmentality. This will first involve an examination of the increased attention given to issues of *consumption* and the relationship between *marketing* and the changing nature of *consumerism*. Drawing on key elements of work on *governmentality*, it will be argued that consumerism may be both liberating *and* manipulative, a practice of freedom

117

which enables the further subjection and control of a population. These themes will be developed by drawing on empirical material from a two-year study of a major UK life assurance institution. Over the two years, a series of interviews were conducted with over 20 employees at different levels of the organisation, including senior management, branch managers, team managers, financial consultants and administrative assistants (see Hodgson, 2000). This will be illustrated through a consideration of the way in which neo-liberal government policy has attempted to construct a consumer relationship in the financial services industry through self-regulation, or 'government at a distance' (Miller and Rose, 1990; Rose, 1999). From this perspective, it is argued that ongoing 'consumer education' initiatives in the industry, rather than 'empowering' consumers of financial services, instead reflect the neo-liberal principle that 'in order to act freely, the subject must first be shaped, guided and moulded into one capable of responsibly exercising that freedom through systems of domination' (Dean, 1999:165).

The Consumer of Financial Services

The major transformations that have taken place in the financial services industry in recent years have accorded particular importance to the role of the consumer (see Morgan and Sturdy, 2000). The UK financial services industry, previously divided by statute into such areas as banking, insurance, credit provision, investment, and mortgages was formally 'deregulated' through a raft of legislation in 1986 including the Financial Services Act, the Social Security Act, the Building Societies Act and the 'Big Bang' in the London Stock Exchange. The key effect of the 'deregulation' was to enhance competition between the three main types of financial institutions (banks, insurance companies and building societies) by breaking down the statutory barriers to competition in the industry. This change was accompanied by the installation of a system of regulation to ensure the smooth operation of this market. As well as reflecting the Conservative programme to eliminate restrictions on competition and thus stimulate the sector as a whole, a key objective of the changes was to takes steps to tackle the oncoming 'Welfare Crisis' (Knights, 1997) that is, the argument that working populations in developed countries will soon be unable (or unwilling) to shoulder the increasing financial burden of the ageing populations. The challenge for the State since then has been to persuade people that they would need to take *personal* responsibility for financing their retirement and that this responsibility can be fulfilled by investing in the products of private financial institutions. This 'responsibilisation' of populations has been a major theme of several studies of governmentality (e.g. Burchell *et al.*, 1991; Grey, 1997; Rose, 1999), as shall be discussed below.

This project has been hampered to some extent by the fact that the financial services industry in the UK has been infamous as the location of serious consumer exploitation, major scandals and intense regulatory attention. The most notorious of these scandals, the pensions mis-selling scandal, occurred after the deregulation of pensions, a change that allowed individuals to switch from company-based occupational pensions to personal pensions which could be carried from job to job. Some years afterwards it was discovered that large numbers of clients had lost large amounts of money having been persuaded to switch to a personal pension against their 'best interests', in the process earning significant amounts of commission for life assurance salespeople and profit for their organisations. 'Severe' financial sanctions were imposed by the regulator upon a number of named financial institutions, and the industry as a whole suffered as revelations about the scale of the misconduct emerged in the press. However, despite the severe loss of trust suffered by the UK financial services industry, the media coverage has contributed to an unprecedented public awareness of the 'crisis' in UK state pension provision, such that (middle-class) individuals are now 'as concerned about their personal investments, insurance and pensions as their cars' (Knights, 1997:18). It will be argued below that this shift has been effected in part by enrolling the private sector in the marketing of 'financial services' and coupling personal finance to the powerful contemporary discourse of the sovereign consumer.

The Sovereign Consumer

The growing interest in understanding consumption has been linked by many to the emergence of consumerism as a distinguishing feature of late modern Western society and the growth in the importance of the service industry in contemporary economies (Knights and Morgan, 1993; Warde, 1991). One key difference from traditional manufacturing industry is that the 'good' provided in service industries is typically intangible, heterogeneous (Regan, 1963) and is created and exists only at 'the simultaneous moment of production and consumption which constitutes the service' (Knights and Morgan, 1994:138, from Warde, 1991). This *direct* involvement of the consumer in the production process indicates a key way in which the growth of service industries has enhanced the role that the 'consumer' now holds in contemporary business activity. The way in which this figurative 'consumer' has been depicted in recent years has thrown up a number of conceptions of the modern customer whose 'needs' and 'choices' must be catered for (see Rosenthal *et al.*, this volume). This primacy accorded to the 'sovereign consumer' is reflected in contemporary popular management wisdom, built upon a number of basic nostrums, which include a rejection of overtly disciplinary management techniques, a belief in the need for/ potential of 'empowerment', a need to bring the employee closer to the market and, crucially for this analysis, an emphasis on the importance of customer focus (Huczynski, 1993). From Peters and Waterman (1982) onwards, a whole lineage of managerialist prescriptions, including TQM and BPR, have started from the premise that 'The Customer is King' and that successful companies are first and foremost 'driven by the desire to provide service, quality and innovative problem solving in support of their customers' (Peters and Waterman, 1982:321). These key themes of 'quality' and 'service' have adopted totemic significance in the popular business consciousness (Gabriel and Lang, 1995:135), intimately linked to the idea of the omnipotent 'sovereign consumer'. As Leidner (1993) argues, customers are increasingly incorporated as a disciplinary device in modern business, as the employer–employee relationship is being replaced in many indus-tries by a triangle of influence, Employer–Employee–Consumer, with the *consumer* supplementing more traditional mechanisms of surveillance and control.

More recently, controversy over the theme of consumption has centred on sociological and anthropological debates over the role and meaning of consumption in contemporary society. Such debates beg the question; should the recent explosion of interest in consumption and shifts towards consumerism in (post-) modern societies be a cause for celebration or despair? One the one hand, writers have highlighted positive aspects of the symbolic/communicative function of consumption (Bourdieu, 1979; Douglas and Isherwood, 1979), seeing consumption as representative of the potential for practices of freedom expressed through the creative development of a 'unique selfhood' (Bauman, 1988:75). On the other hand, critical work on consumption has emphasised the relationship between consumption and capitalist control and exploitation (Baudrillard, 1988; Lasch, 1980); for such writers, this narcissistic pseudo-freedom is 'no more than the generalities of power to stamp so firmly that it is accepted as such' (Horkheimer and Adorno, 1972:154).

Much of this debate hinges upon the influence of the Marketing function in contemporary society, and the role it plays in the *manipulation* (or the *'education'*) of the modern consumer. While technologies of marketing have been subjected to a more comprehensive analysis in other quarters (Knights and Sturdy, 1997; Rose, 1990), it is important here to emphasise the role of marketing practices in the creation of 'the customer' as an object whose freedom (and duty) to choose and to consume allows it to be *governed*.

Marketing and the 'New Consumer'

The organisational and societal influence of the marketing function has become increasingly evident since the 1960s, as technologies of power developed in the fields of psychology and socio-psychology (Rose, 1999:84) have been adapted and implemented in a business context.

Marketing draws on each of these disciplines as it integrates large-scale demographic/economic surveys and focused motivational/attitudinal research to achieve a social mapping of 'desire' (see Knights and Sturdy, 1997, for a discussion). A key element in this process is the 'segmentation' (or 'sequestration') of the subject population on the basis of demographic and psychographic analysis, reflecting what Foucault (1977) terms the 'dividing practices' of régimes of power/knowledge. Both Rose (1990) and Knights and Sturdy (1997) have highlighted the development of such techniques, harnessing the advances in IT to develop and store complex databases of customer characteristics in a form amenable to sophisticated statistical analysis. It is argued that such technological developments are instrumental in organisations' increasing rejection of mass-marketing in favour of a more 'customised', 'authentic' and 'personal' approach.

'Relationship marketing' is an increasingly popular strategy involving the 'mass customisation' of products and services which are more or less tailored to match specific groups with specific 'lifestyles' (Desmond, 1998), from the Yuppies of the 1980s to the much-cited 'Mondeo Man' of current discourse. Marketing techniques such as 'Relationship marketing' and 'Lifestyling' project identities which may then be 'offered' as part of the product through targeted advertising campaigns (du Gay, 1993; Knights *et al.*, 1994). It is important to highlight that such categorisations are active constructions, that they shape, rather than reflect, reality; as Knights and Sturdy point out, 'marketing does not merely respond to individual needs or lifestyles but is proactive in constituting and modifying them so as to render the production-consumption relationship less problematic' (1997:171). Advertising then proffers such 'lifestyles', or 'constellations of consumption' (Solomon and Buchanan, 1991), as reference points, attractive 'designs for life' centred around particular brands. Drawing on debates around 'governmentality', Knights and Sturdy (1997:168) argue that marketing should, therefore, be understood as part of a set of techniques 'which allow us to construct, sustain and remodel the self'. This shift is particularly evident in the financial services sector, where, it is claimed, 'companies are increasingly adopting a strategic marketing orientation where the emphasis is on consumer "needs" (Knights *et al.*, 1994:44), in preference to the previous 'product-led, hard-sell approach' (Morgan and Sturdy, 2000). Here, marketing has played a very important role in linking personal finance products to images of attractive identities; the responsible parent making provision for school fees, the capable father providing for family happiness, the contented retired couple in idyllic cottage, the self-satisfied businessman taking early retirement, and so on.

However, this focus on the sophistication of marketing techniques risks overstating the effectiveness of such strategies. Rather than seeing consumers as powerless victims, manipulated through subtle marketing into the slavery of capitalism (cf. Marcuse, 1964), it should be emphasised that the effectiveness of marketing initiatives cannot be assumed. Reprising de Certeau (1984), Knights and Sturdy (1997:179) note, 'no matter how sophisticated and scientific the segmentation and market research, consumers may resist or fail to comply with the consumer behaviour expected . . . because subjectivity can never be wholly captured and thereby controlled'. While technologies of marketing, operating to construct the consumer as an object for analysis and manipulation, have become more complex, there is currently a counter-argument that the practices of consumers themselves have become markedly more sophisticated in recent times (e.g. Gabriel and Lang, 1995). It is argued in the first instance that traditional marketing techniques are too blunt an instrument and consumers are increasingly likely to look further than the truth claims of advertising campaigns. Furthermore, it is argued that consumers are increasingly likely to resort to proactive campaigns as part of a general ethical stance, either by certain brands (e.g. the Body Shop, Fair-Trade goods) or by boycotting other brands (e.g. recent boycotts of Shell, Nestlé). This argument is taken yet further by current marketing writers, who argue that this change requires a paradigm shift in the approach taken to marketing in the future. The authors of *The Soul of the New Consumer* assert that the next century will be dominated by the demands of 'an emerging and powerfully influential group of well-informed customers who reject mass production, mass-marketing and mass-consumption in favour of an independent, individualistic quest for authenticity in all their purchases' (Lewis and Bridger, 2000:1). In financial services, this image of the consumer 'becoming more financially literate, sophisticated and discerning (i.e. sovereign)' (Knights *et al.*, 1994:46) is all the more striking given the volume of evidence of deep-rooted customer inertia when it comes to financial products (see Morgan and Sturdy, 2000:182). Nonetheless, this image appears particularly influential in terms of both company strategy and regulatory policy in the industry.

However, this sophistication of the average consumer is not a neutral process, levelling the playing field; it moves beyond *caveat emptor* ('let the buyer beware') to directly implicate individuals in the practices of consumerism (du Gay, 1996). Transforming oneself into a 'new consumer' entails a great deal of personal investment, learning the language, the signs, the rules and the customs of marketing and consumption, developing specific personal tastes and actively seeking fulfilment through consumption. For survival, individuals must *embrace* their identity as consumer, learn to play their part in the game of production and consumption and take personal responsibility for the accomplishment of this role. At this point the boundary between 'education' and 'advertising' is more than a little porous; hence health and beauty products rely increasingly on 'educating' consumers in the dangers of invisible bacteria, insidious forms of plaque, or particularly stubborn forms of ear-wax, all of which the consumer was blissfully ignorant prior to the advertising campaign.

In the field of financial services, this 'consumerisation' of society is mobilised in support of a broader project; that of the responsibilisation of the modern citizen in neo-liberal society. Increasingly it is argued that the individual's power as a consumer is supplanting his/her power as a democratic citizen, as more and more 'civic' relationships, in education, in healthcare, and in welfare, are rewritten as 'customer' relationships. The State thus reinforces this discourse of the consumer with a moral imperative, as citizens must be educated, in schooling and through lifelong learning, to understand the importance of financial responsibility and to be equipped to make the 'correct' choice i.e. to make financial provision for illness and old age. In addition, the task of educating consumers in the importance of savings, pensions, etc has been largely devolved by the State to private organisations and their considerable advertising budgets, but now with a moral legitimation. Thus, Rose describes the transformation of the democratic citizen into the sovereign consumer as symptomatic of neo-liberal democracies; 'Individuals are now to be linked into a society through acts of socially sanctioned consumption and responsible choice' (1999:166). It is in the field of financial services therefore, that notions of modern consumerism collide most clearly with the concerns of governmentality. Governmentality is of particular relevance for our understanding of consumerism because of the perspective it allows us on liberal and neo-liberal modes of government in modern democracies that is, those modes of power which 'work *through* the freedom or capacities of the governed' (Dean, 1999:15).

Government, Governmentality and Liberalism

Although a full discussion of governmentality is beyond the ambit of this chapter (see Dean, 1999), several key concepts and issues merit some examination insofar as they shed light on our understanding of consumption and consumer education in general and financial services in particular. The concept of 'governmentality' (Foucault, 1991) has been mobilised to analyse the specific modes of government that have emerged in Western societies over the past two hundred years in line with liberal and neo-liberal discourses. 'Government' in this sense in not coterminous with 'the State'; rather it should be understood as 'any more or less calculated and rational activity undertaken by a multiplicity of authorities or agencies . . . that seeks to shape conduct by working through our desires, aspirations, interests or beliefs for definite but shifting ends' (Dean, 1999:11). One of the aims of studies of governmentality (such Barry *et al.*, 1996; Burchell *et al.*, 1991; Rose, 1990, 1999; among others) is to 'make intelligible the reconfiguration of the social as a set of quasi-markets in services and expertise at the end of the twentieth century, of the governed as customers or consumers of such services and expertise' (Dean, 1999:6). It is here, over issues of choice, freedom, discipline, control and desire, that the study of government and governmentality intersects with studies of consumerism and the role of the consumer in modern society.

In a practical sense, Dean (1999) describes the mechanisms by which neo-liberal societies supplement this traditional disciplinary power by managing the population indirectly, 'by working on the environment and the spaces within which [choice] is exercised' (Dean, 1999:159). Dean specifies two complementary technologies through which neo-liberal governmental power is exercised; *technologies of agency* and *technologies of performance*. Through *technologies of agency*, individuals, groups and organisations are encouraged to take on responsibility, through citizenship or contract, for tasks or areas of action and to reconstitute themselves as autonomous and responsible actors. At the same time, such moves are usually accompanied by *technologies of performance*, which serve as quasi-independent means of regulating such 'autonomous actors', through the establishment of regimes of standards assessed independently by a range of agencies. The growing reliance upon *self-regulation*, in the financial services industry as in many other spheres, exemplifies the operation of such technologies. The 'Know Your Customer' principle, for example, is a key element of the regime of self-regulation in financial services and states that it is the responsibility of the financial institution to become sufficiently familiar with the financial affairs of their client to avoid selling the client inappropriate policies or investments. However, as described by a branch manager in a major UK life assurance company:

> the regulators seem to say to the company 'These are the broad principles that we want you to meet, like "Know Your Client"' . . . They don't actually then go on to say what they want to be done about it. The company then goes away and puts a series of measures in place . . . Unfortunately, sometimes, the regulators then say 'Oh no, that's not actually what we wanted' because they don't make it simple'.

Thus, the *responsibility* for specifying the client knowledge to be acquired is devolved by the regulator to the institutions themselves, a clear 'technology of agency', in Dean's (1999) terms. In addition, the institutions are free to set their own compliance processes, to check internally that they are not contravening industry regulations. However, the institutions are then held *accountable* for the effectiveness of the steps that they have taken, judged by an 'independent' regulatory audit, reflecting Dean's (1999) description of 'technologies of performance'. The combined effect of these technologies is the 'autonomization plus responsibilization' (Rose, 1999:154) of the financial services institutions themselves. Quite apart from the reduced financial cost to the State of such 'self-regulation', such technologies give the impression of moral reflexivity and responsibility on the part of the companies while enrolling them (in theory) in the implementation of Government policy. Increasingly, however, attention is turning to the government of the other party in this 'market'; the 'autonomization plus responsibilization' of the consumer of financial services.

Three main points, then, emerge from the debates in the field of governmentality with particular importance for our understanding of consumerism and consumer education. One key insight of this theoretical approach is to challenge the traditional opposition of power and freedom; instead, forms of freedom should be understood to be constructed *through* the operation of power, and conversely power operates *through* the conduct of individuals 'freely' pursuing their needs and desires. The second point reflects another element fundamental to neo-liberal discourse; the assumption that the consumer is, or can/should be, both knowledgeable and free, able to make a rational choice. Thus *choice*, understood in liberal discourse as a fundamental human attribute (Burchell *et al.*, 1991) is highlighted as a powerful tool of neo-liberal modes of government, one which, as noted above, 'can be made calculable and manipulated by working on the environment and the spaces within which it is exercised' (Dean, 1999:159). In exercising choice in consumption, therefore, individuals are at the same time implicated in mechanisms which both predict and direct their choice as a means of manipulation. As individuals are conceptualised as essentially entrepreneurial with respect to their life projects, government must 'be directed to empowering the entrepreneurial subjects of choice in their quest for self-realisation' (Rose, 1999:142). This leads directly on to a third and final insight, regarding the relation between subjection and freedom in (neo-) liberal society; that 'freedom' is conditional upon the individual's willingness to exercise freedom 'responsibly'. Through a range of technologies, particularly (but not only) in the fields of advertising and marketing, strategic attempts are made to shape desires and inscribe these upon the individual consumer, to manipulate 'consumer behaviour'. Hence discipline and freedom interact; as Rose notes, 'modern individuals are not merely 'free to choose' but obliged to be free, to understand and enact their lives in terms of choices' (1999:87).

Regulation, Surveillance and the 'Failure' of Government

The cornerstone of state regulation of financial services is self-regulation, allowing the institutions to set up bespoke systems of monitoring to ensure that their staff comply with the industry rules. Surveillance in capitalist industry is certainly nothing new. Within financial services, however, the demands of compliance with the regulator play a vital role.

Financial services' institutions are required by the regulator to keep records of client details, staff conduct, transactions and outcomes and through this to monitor the enforcement of compliance regulations within their own operations. This is typically done through the maintenance of two linked databases; 'Management Information Systems' (MIS), monitoring the actions of the salesforce, and parallel, Customer Information Systems (CIS), monitoring the make-up and conduct of the company's client base. Both the MIS and the CIS are key elements in the control of the staff–customer relationship. The MIS is in many ways a typical bureaucratic system of monitoring, requiring the weekly submission of large amounts of detailed information – on clients visited, financial reviews conducted, policies discussed, information provided, regulated policies sold, regulated policies renewed, unregulated products sold, unregulated products renewed, policies cancelled, and so on – all of which is used in the monthly assessment meeting with the salesperson. The CIS, on the other hand, is instrumental in the complementary objectification of the consumer, building on new technologies of marketing and operationalising the 'segmentation' of the consumer population, as discussed above. Through the CIS, each individual client is quantified on a number of axes – income, age, occupation, marital status, dependants, etc – which forms the basis for the internal marketing, provides 'leads' for the salesforce and provides client information to direct their selling techniques.

While loudly complaining about the cost of gathering and centralising information in the MIS and the CIS, however, the financial institutions have also recognised the potential to exploit this information for commercial advantage rather than mere compliance. Insofar as the systems are enforced then, they act in a typically disciplinary fashion, to render employees visible and accountable for their conduct at work. The surveillance system is thus felt by many staff in a direct and personal way; as one salesperson graphically complained;

> every man and his dog in the company, from the senior executives who I absolutely love to bits, I think they're wonderful people, can go and tap my computer information and get it up on a computer screen no matter where they are in the country. So there's no hiding now. . .'

In practice, the compliance information appeared to be the least important aspect of the system for both management and employees. At branch level, it seemed that the only data of real importance were those that were linked to the payment of commission; the rest could be ignored or fabricated. As one salesperson explained

> I [work out] my own appointments, the prop[osals], the premium, the income and what I've earned . . . those first four, as far as I'm concerned, are a load of bollocks – if at the end of the day I haven't earned money, I'm not a happy teddy at all. I couldn't give a *toss* whether [the company] think I'm brilliant.

In effect, the combined effect of both of these technologies has been to intensify the pressure on salesforces to exploit their advantage over the 'free' consumer, in terms of their monopoly over information and representation, to the benefit of themselves and their institution.

The salespersons themselves appear deeply reluctant to acknowledge the unequal power relations central to the process. Thus, the ability to transform a 'lead' into a 'sale' is ascribed to the application of the skill of selling, based on the individual's ability to 'manage' the sales encounter to their own benefit. In conversation, there is a general recognition that the ability to 'manage' the sales encounter and manipulate the attitude and action of the client is fundamental to the sales process. The difference between activity and performance is attributed in a highly individualistic way to sales technique and determination, as one salesperson boasts:

> I was happy with my twenty quid a month, it was going to stick like glue and I was happy as a pig in shit 'cos I got something and I was out. They might have paid thirty pounds a month to the next insurance man from another company who came along the day after, and maybe sold a bit harder, so what that made me do, this system that (my old manager) told me, he said 'Just get out of the twenty pound a month ten years, it's no good – up the premium, up the term and you'll see your income take off' and that's exactly what I've done.

By experience, guile and sheer force of will, the salesperson is heroically depicted transforming minor wins into major victories, thus 'upping their ratios' and earning larger bonuses.

Despite their training in sales techniques, their monopoly over information, and their careful manipulation of the sales encounter, the sales staff in interviews repeatedly maintain the fundamental mutuality of interest between salesperson and client. Thus, one branch manager argues rather disingenuously:

> Have they been too pushy? . . . That's in nobody's interest – not the client's interest, cos they've taken out accounts that they can't maintain, not the company's interest, cos we don't make any money on it, in fact we lose money on it, and what affects us affects the other customers – if you're a company that's always selling rubbish business, that never makes any profit, and it's the profit that . . . 90% of our profit, in certain areas, is distributed back to the policy-owners. So the better business that we can sell, through better advice, the more profit we make, the more profit the customer makes, and basically everybody's happy then, yeah?

Interestingly, the relationship between the salesperson and his/her manager is seen in the same neutral, even naturalistic terms, wilfully blind to the power relations in operation between supervisor and salesperson, and between salesperson and consumer. Thus, another manager explains:

> They're doing the same as the manager's doing in this one-to-one with the rep.; they're having a one-to-one with the client saying 'Let's look at your situation, let's look at what's gone well for you financially, let's look at what you can achieve and let's look at the things you could put in place to make you a lot better . . .' and that's what life's about, isn't it'

However, this image of a fortuitous convergence of interests is contradicted by the frequent failure of regulation. In particular, the temptation of maximising sales and hence commission has frequently over-ridden the requirement that salespeople provide best advice based on the needs of the client. Thus, one salesperson sets out a typically dubious moral justification for his maximisation of sales, backed up sympathetically by his superior:

> *Salesperson*:   Alright, you sell to needs, but there's two sets of needs, there's what the client needs and there's what I need, and somewhere there's some grey area where we can be happy about that, right so [a savings policy over] ten years, twenty quid a month – even though we don't do that now – didn't answer my problems . . . it may not have answered theirs.
>
> *Supervisor*:   'You weren't doing them no favours, neither.

Aspects of exploitation become apparent in the sales encounter, not despite but *supported by* the efforts of the regulator. The matrix of information routinely gathered by the financial institutions accentuates the disparity in information between salesperson and consumer and thus enhances the manipulatory techniques employed by the sales-staff.

As a consequence of the unproblematised understanding of 'the consumer of financial services' as a knowledgeable, autonomous subject, regulation has so far centred upon devolving the responsibility for information provision (and regulatory compliance) to the financial institutions, and specifically the salesforce, leaving consumers 'free to choose' and entirely disregarding the power relations implicit in the interaction. While the operation of technologies of surveillance and the compilation of databases of information clearly has not prevented the various misconduct scandals in the industry, they have nonetheless advanced the effectiveness of the marketing and IT departments within the financial services sector. As a consequence, attention has turned from the institutions to the customers, and recent shifts in policy seem instead to be increasingly concerned with the failure of the sovereign consumer to play his/her part in this market. More recent remedies, following the logic of governmentality, are aimed to operate through the counterpart of choice, *responsibility*.

'The New Prudentialism'

As we have seen, regulatory policy so far has focused on requiring companies to monitor closely the conduct of their sales staff. Given the failures of this policy over the past decade, recent announcements have shifted the focus towards the education of *consumers*, so that they may learn to play their part in this market relationship more successfully. So although the various UK regulators have recently been unified in one body, the Financial Services Authority (FSA), and their powers to some degree strengthened, a new and complementary line of policy has been to increase the reciprocal responsibility of the consumer of financial services. One of four statutory objectives of the new regulator, alongside existing goals such as maintaining market confidence, protecting consumers, and reducing financial crime, is the novel inclusion of *consumer education* as a key objective, through the promotion of public awareness of the financial services industry (FSA, 2000).

The shift in responsibilities is significant – trust in the supervisory capacity of the regulator over the industry is to be supplemented with a faith in the power of an educated, discerning consumer, who may be relied upon to act in an economically rational manner. Hence 'the intention is to ensure customers are put in the position where they can make an effective and well-informed choice and are subsequently kept well-informed about matters relating to their investment' (FSA, 2000). To use Gabriel and Lang's metaphors (1995), the consumer is no longer to be depicted as victim; instead, the goal is to recreate consumers as activists and citizens, to serve as the constant watchdog both of the industry and of themselves.

As traditional aspects of welfare are underfunded and dismantled, material security increasingly depends upon one's willingness to accept responsibility and participate in this nexus of the private and the public; consequently, these moves can be interpreted as as much a *social* as a *financial* shift in society. O'Malley (1992) refers to this as 'the New Prudentialism': 'the use of technologies of consumption – advertising, market research, niche marketing and so on – to exacerbate anxieties about one's own future and that of one's loved ones, to encourage each of us to invest in order to master our fate by purchasing insurance designed especially for us and our individual situation' (Rose, 1999:159). In line with Beck's discussion of 'Risk Society' (Beck, 1992) writers on government such as Ewert, Defert and Castel have traced the ways in which technologies of insurance have been utilised to make risk calculable and thus to encourage the 'responsibilisation' of the subjects of insurance (see Burchell *et al.*, 1991). Through this shift in responsibility, the individual is reconstructed as an 'enterprising subject', in du Gay's terminology, as 'autonomous, self-regulating and self-actualising individual actors seeking to maximise their "quality of life"' (1996:77). Educating the consumer is therefore in large part not simply a question of information provision, but a process of subjection, whereby individuals come to think of themselves as enjoying an emancipating freedom in their financial arrangements, of taking advantage of an unprecedented choice over financial products, but equally as sober bearers of a weighty financial responsibility.

Within financial services then, there are a number of channels through which this 'education' is taking place. Thus, the UK Government of the 1980s relied upon the financial institutions themselves to trigger a boom in the industry post-deregulation through a major investment in marketing initiatives which aroused concerns over financial security in the minds of previously unconcerned individuals. At the same time, the burden of 'educating' consumers therefore fell on the marketing and sales departments of the financial institutions; indeed, as Morgan and Sturdy argue, the marketing literature's only recognition of the role organisations play in creating consumer 'needs' is 'in the apparently neutral sense of educating potential buyers' (2000:163).

In addition to such 'market-based' technologies, a range of public measures have been mooted to support the 'education' of the financial services consumer in the UK, including the integration of financial literacy in the National Curriculum for schools, and the establishment of some form of continuing lifelong learning programme of adult education. All of these initiatives are underpinned by the alignment of the *moral* case for investment/savings with the moral case for consumption *tout court* within the moralising discourse of the 'Third Way' neo-liberal philosophy of the New Labour government (McLean and Knights, 1999). As du Gay notes, the 'active, "enterprising" consumer is placed at the moral centre of (this) market-based universe. What counts as good, or "virtuous" in this universe is judged by reference to the apparent needs, desires and projected preferences of the "sovereign consumer"' (1996:77). The distinctive feature of such governmental strategies is that they work *through* 'freedom' on the basis that 'in order to act freely, the subject must first be shaped, guided and moulded into one capable of responsibly exercising that freedom' (Dean, 1999:165). Discourses of consumerism, of the ethical consumer, of customer rights, and of customer empowerment are powerful means of subjection, allied as they are to the pervasive moral discourse of self-help, self-reliance and responsibility promulgated by the range of neo-liberal Governments since the 1980s. These are discourses to which a range of agents can subscribe, from government departments to financial services companies and marketing consultancies, and through which a population may be governed. This should not be seen to exculpate customers themselves from the active role they have also played in this process; periods of relative affluence and the spread of middle-class aspirations over the recent decade are implicit in this process. Overall though, the evolution of the consumer of financial services can be seen as reflecting the moral discourse of responsibilisation among neo-liberal states, of 'government at a distance', a project whose appearance of liberalisation and of empowerment does much to obscure the operation of power and to disarm traditional forms of resistance such as that of consumers failing to be drawn into sales techniques as well as that through the 'democratic process'.

Conclusion

The preceding analysis is aimed at reflecting upon insights from the growing literature on governmentality to enhance understanding of current debates over consumerism and the customer, and, to some extent, to use issues of consumption in financial services to develop understandings of governmentality. The value of work on governmentality lies in its reformulation of understandings of power so as to problematise easy notions of freedom and empowerment, and of exploitation and determination, particularly as they may be used in relation to the modern consumer. Such work also offers a useful sensitivity to issues of responsibilisation within discourses of autonomy, and to the fine line between freedom and subjection.

The recent emphasis on educating the consumers of financial services appears a perfectly reasonable solution to the unreliability of self-regulation following the rationale of neo-liberal policy, remaining faithful to such cornerstones of liberalism as 'freedom of choice', 'market relations', 'competition' and so on. At 'best', such educational initiatives may prove to be yet another vain attempt at social engineering, which serves little purpose other than fortifying the status quo and sparing the Government more direct intervention in the free market of financial services. At worst, the shift threatens to have serious implications for both employees in the industry and consumers themselves. Although little sympathy may be immediately forthcoming for handsomely paid life assurance salespersons exploiting their position of power over clients, such employees are at the same time implicated in networks of surveillance within their organisations and subject to severe pressure for constantly improving sales. More widely, as service workers they have been at the sharp end of the growth in the 'consumer rights' movement, which has taken place in line with the emergence of Customer Focus, BPR, TQM, etc. The effect for the front-line employee in service industries is a direct increase in competitive pressure, as marketing departments boast increasingly extravagant promises of customer service which employees must then deliver, under the gaze of the 'new consumer', sure of his/her rights and more than willing to supplement the imperfect surveillance of the supervisor. At the same time, the implications for consumers themselves are equally dangerous. The burden of information promises to be considerable as responsibility is shifted from the companies themselves to the individual customer. In fulfilling his/her duty as a conscientious consumer/citizen, the consumer is implicated in the intensification of competitive pressures upon front-line staff. And at the same time, the individual's own identity is subject to careful reconstruction, as he/she becomes instrumental in a broader network of power relations and contributes to the expansion of market relations into more and more areas of contemporary society.

To an extent, the theoretical position taken here entails an agreement with both sides of the consumption debate. On one side, this means an acceptance that choice and freedom are by no means artefacts of further domination, illusions of autonomy within a reality of capitalist hegemony. At the same time, understandings of the variety of relations of power would warn against the uncritical celebration of the benefits of freedom and choice. Power relations need to be reconceptualised beyond notions of institutional power and repressive disciplinary mechanisms towards an understanding of its *productive* and *seductive* operation, and consumerism provides a very powerful illustration of this point. The fundamental approach is to encourage an immediate scepticism regarding the modes of freedom being offered, through the problematisation of the ideas of 'autonomy' and 'empowerment' implicit in modern consumerism. Much of Foucault's critique rests on the notion that power is not in itself bad but 'dangerous' and, as the changes within financial services indicate, the 'solution' to a problematic situation frequently leads to a yet more dangerous situation.

A wider issue is to underline the dangers of contemporary neo-liberal solutions. While traditional liberal discourse may be accused of a misplaced faith in the potential of the market as a solution for all social ills, neo-liberalism may be seen as even more ill-conceived in promoting a faith in markets supported by a mixture of regulation and power of the autonomous yet responsible consumer. This consumer, being both knowledgeable and responsible, both entrepreneurial and communitarian, forms the backbone of an assortment of current policies and consequently merits critical scrutiny, particularly in relation to those policies of education intended to promote this identity. More fundamentally, the intention is to question the rationale which underpins neo-liberal solutions and the specific formation of government which is becoming apparent in developed countries in the early years of the new century. At the very least, attention to debates of governmentality may bring into question beguiling promises of empowerment and freedom through consumerism.

References

Barry, A., Osborne, T. and Rose, N (1996) *Foucault and Political Reason: Liberalism, Neo-Liberalism and Rationalities of Government*, London: UCL Press.
Baudrillard, J. (1988) *The Consumer Society: Myths and Structures*, London: Sage.
Bauman, Z. (1988) *Freedom*, Milton Keynes: Open University Press.

Beck, U. (1992) *Risk Society: Towards a New Modernity*, London: Sage.

Bourdieu, P. (1979) *Outline of a Theory of Practice*, Cambridge: Cambridge University Press.

Burchell, G., Gordon, C. and Miller, P. (1991) *The Foucault Effect: Studies in Governmentality*, Chicago: Chicago University Press.

Collinson, D., Knights, D. and Collinson, M. (1990) *Managing to Discriminate*, London: Routledge.

De Certeau, M. (1984) *The Practice of Everyday Life*, Berkeley, CA: University of California Press.

Dean, M. (1999) *Governmentality: Power and Rule in Modern Society*, London: Sage.

Desmond, J. (1998) 'Marketing and Moral Indifference', in Parker, M. (ed.), *Ethics and Organizations*, London: Sage.

Douglas, M. and Isherwood, B. (1979) *The World of Goods: Towards an Anthropology of Consumption*, London: Allen Lane.

du Gay, P. (1993) 'Numbers and Souls: Retailing and the De-Differentiation of Economy and Culture', *British Journal of Sociology*, 44:4, 563–88.

du Gay, P. (1996) *Consumption and Identity at Work*, London: Sage.

Financial Services Authority (2000) *The Conduct of Business Sourcebook (draft)*

Foucault, M. (1977) *Discipline and Punish: The Birth of the Prison*, Harmondsworth: Penguin.

Foucault, M. (1991) 'Governmentality', in Burchell, G., Gordon, C. and Miller, P. (eds), *The Foucault Effect: Studies in Governmentality*, Chicago: Chicago University Press.

Gabriel, Y. and Lang, T. (1995) *The Unmanageable Consumer: Contemporary Consumption and Its Fragmentation*, London: Sage.

Grey, C. (1997) 'Suburban Subjects: Financial Services and the New Right', in Knights, D. and Tinker, T. (eds), *Financial Institutions and Social Transformations*, Basingstoke: Macmillan.

Hodgson, D. E. (2000) *Discourse, Discipline and the Subject: A Foucauldian Analysis of the UK Financial Services Industry*, London: Ashgate.

Horkheimer, M. and Adorno, T. W. (1972) *Dialectic of Enlightenment*, New York: Continuum.

Huczynski, A. (1993) *Management Gurus*, London: Routledge.

Knights, D. (1997) 'An Industry in Transition: Regulation, Restructuring and Renewal', in Knights, D. and Tinker, T. (eds), *Financial Institutions and Social Transformations*, Basingstoke: Macmillan.

Knights, D. and Morgan, G. (1991) 'Selling Oneself: Subjectivity and the Labour Process in Selling Life Insurance', in Smith, C. Knights, D. and Willmott, H. (eds), *White-Collar Work: The Non-Manual Labour Process*, London: Macmillan.

Knights, D. and Morgan, G. (1993) 'Organization Theory and Consumption in a Post-Modern Era', *Organization Studies*, 14:2, 211–34.

Knights, D. and Morgan, G. (1994) 'Organization Theory, Consumption and the Service Sector', in Hassard, J. and Parker, M. (eds), *Towards a New Theory of Organizations*, London: Routledge.

Knights, D. and Sturdy, A. (1997) 'Marketing the Soul: From the Ideology of Consumption to Consumer Subjectivity', in Knights, D. and Tinker, T. (eds), *Financial Institutions and Social Transformations*, Basingstoke: Macmillan.

Knights, D. Sturdy, A. and Morgan, G. (1994) 'The Consumer Rules? An Examination of the Rhetoric and "Reality" of Marketing in Financial Services', *European Journal of Marketing*, 28:3, 42–54.

Lasch, C. (1980) *The Culture of Narcissism: American Life in an Age of Diminishing Expectations*, London: Abacus.

Leidner, R. (1993) *Fast Food, Fast Talk: Service Work and the Routinization of Everyday Life*, London; University of California Press.

Lewis, D. and Bridger, D. (2000) *The Soul of the New Consumer: Authenticity – What We Buy and Why in the New Economy*, London: Nicholas Brearley.

McLean, C. and Knights, D. (1999) 'Taking Liberties with Personal Finance Education: Reconfiguring Citizenship and Welfare', paper presented at SCOS Conference 1999, Edinburgh.

Marcuse, H. (1964) *One Dimensional Man*, Boston, MA: Beacon Press.

Miller, P. and Rose, N. (1990) 'Governing Economic Life', *Economy and Society*, 19:1, 1–31.

Morgan, G. and Sturdy, A. (2000) *Beyond Organizational Change: Structure, Discourse and Power in UK Financial Services*, Basingstoke: Macmillan.

O'Malley, P. (1992) 'Risk, Power and Crime Prevention', *Economy and Society*, 21:3, 252–75.

Peters, T. and Waterman, R. (1982) *In Search of Excellence*, London: Harper & Row.

Regan, W. (1963) 'The Service Revolution', *Journal of Marketing*, 27:3, 247–53.

Rose, N. (1990) *Governing the Soul: The Shaping of the Private Self*, London: Routledge.

Rose, N. (1999) *Powers of Freedom: Reframing Political Thought*, Cambridge: Cambridge University Press.

Solomon, M. R. and Buchanan, B. (1991) 'A Role-Theoretic Approach To Product Symbolism: Mapping a Consumption Constellation', *Journal of Business Research*, 22:2, 95–109.

Warde, A. (1991) 'On the Relationship Between Production and Consumption', in Burrows, R. and Marsh, C. (eds), *Consumption and Class: Divisions and Change*, London: Macmillan.

8

Struggles for the Control of Affect – Resistance as Politics *and* Emotion

Andrew Sturdy and Stephen Fineman

Introduction

Emotion control, or 'face work', has long been an implicit feature of the way labour is shaped for productive ends. Particular emotions, such as pleasure, confidence, concern, anger and fear are faked, freed or frowned upon for strategic purposes or interactional gain (Fineman, 1993a; Goffman, 1959; Mills, 1951). To a degree, this process is unexceptional. It reflects the socio-cultural embededness of all emotions where individuals learn what emotions fit with what kinds of circumstances and the cultural rules which govern display (Harré, 1986; Harré and Gerrod, 1996; Hochschild, 1983). However, our concern in this chapter is the extent and form of normative control exerted over emotions and feelings in and through organisations. Much of this can be implicit, rules which are embedded in the nature of local power/status relationships at work. Recently, however, régimes of emotion control have become increasingly sophisticated, explicit and of institutionalised and international proportions especially in service encounters. Even if we do not fully accept the omnipotence of what Ritzer (1993) terms the 'McDonaldisation' of society (cf. Smart, 1999), we see a host of service industries incorporating detailed emotion scripts into their training programmes, often coupled with executively determined monitoring and surveillance systems. Emotion 'management' increasingly features in financial services (Fuller and Smith, 1991; Morgan and Sturdy, 2000; Wharton, 1993), hotels and leisure (Bryman, 1999; Van Maanen, 1991), supermarkets (Rafaeli, 1989) air travel (Hochschild, 1983; Wouters, 1989), fast food (Leidner, 1993), slower ('high class') food (Hall, 1993; Whyte, 1948) and health care (O'Brien, 1994; Wharton, 1993). Much of this activity is directed at women. Beyond services also, there have been organisational culture change programmes which aim to 'engineer' or 'transfigure' emotion (Gagliardi, 1986) towards 'appropriate' affective tones – such as being 'passionate' or 'enthralled' (Carlzon, 1987; Hopfl and Linstead, 1993; Kunda, 1992; Peters, 1989; Van Maanen and Kunda, 1989).

This objectification and commodification of emotion is problematic. It represents a significant scaling-up of institutional and executive privilege over the ownership of emotion. It attempts, often markedly, to limit individuals' social choices over what they should feel and emotionally express at their work and beyond, a potentially oppressive extension of the deployment of power and the locus of management control. In using people's emotions and feelings as a means to an end, it raises questions about the morality of such endeavours, as well as about the very notion of managing emotions (Grey, 1996; Hassard and Parker, 1994; Ray, 1986).

In this chapter we seek to explore some of the ideologies and techniques through which emotion engineering is formed, practised and experienced. Our interest is in highlighting the ways in which wider market relations and values interface with corporate competitive aims and authority arrangements, to produce régimes of emotion regulation. In these terms, we reveal how domination and consent is often 'written in' to organisations in non-obvious and emotional ways (e.g. Barley and Kunda, 1992). In doing so, we highlight how, despite increasing academic attention to emotion in organisations and to régimes of, and responses to, management control, the literature fails to address the *interdependence* of emotional and political action. In particular, we seek to show how emotion is important to the concerns of labour process analysis such as resistance and consent and how emotion in organisations is implicated in structures of power and inequality.

Emotions and the Labour Process

The writings on emotion in organisations are only partly helpful to a critical approach. While some (to which we shall return) explore the social construction of emotion, especially the mediating effects of control through gender, culture and/or multiple identities (e.g. Ashforth and Humphrey, 1993, 1995; Craib, 1995; Hochschild, 1979, 1983; Jackall, 1988; Kunda, 1992; Mumby and Putnam, 1992; Wharton, 1993; Wouters, 1989), most fail to locate hierarchy and control beyond organisational or group boundaries. Many are situated uncritically within a managerialist frame and/or aimed at technical and psychological questions – not explicitly moral/political ones (e.g., see Rafaeli, 1989; Rafaeli and Sutton, 1989; Sandelands and Buckner, 1989; Sutton and Rafaeli, 1988).

By way of contrast, labour process theorists have been especially vocal in critiquing wider loci and values of control in organisations, but have typically devoted very little attention to emotion as either a process or product of capitalist employment relations (e.g., Braverman, 1974; Burawoy, 1979; Edwards, 1979; Friedman, 1977; Littler, 1982). Labour process theory, broadly defined, views the organisation of labour through a wide-angle lens, informed by economic, moral, sociological and, to a much lesser extent, social-psychological insights. It recognises that controls over

work behaviour are located within forms of capitalism where the transformation of labour power and realisation of surplus value are a central
requirement.

But, for labour process theory (LPT), control is essentially problematic. In
particular, for the capitalist, control is always threatened in that there is
always some dependence on workers' co-operation and they 'retain their
power to resist being treated like a commodity' (Edwards, 1979:12; Friedman, 1977). We therefore find in LPT an important critical debate on worker
'resistance' and 'consent' to work controls, responses that may challenge
and/or unintentionally reproduce an existing organisational order (Burawoy, 1979; Edwards, 1990; Jermier *et al.*, 1994; Sturdy *et al.*, 1992; Thompson,
1983). Significantly though, consent and resistance are not represented as
'felt' or emotionalised concepts. 'Resistance' in particular, is what others –
labour process theorists, managers – see as interruptions to the flow of
work; it is often not what subjects themselves report (see Wray-Bliss and
Tyler and Taylor, this volume). The 'resister' is more likely to focus on his or
her feelings – of resentment, fear, anger or frustration (Fineman and
Gabriel, 1996; Terkel, 1975). These are feelings which themselves have been
partly shaped within the organisational power and status relations, expressed or suppressed according to the local and wider norms of display.

While labour process theorists have yet to engage fully with emotion,
some have edged towards it. Ethnographic accounts of paid employment
frequently reveal or describe emotional experiences (e.g., Collinson, 1992).
More explicitly, a stream of literature has focused on the neglect of
'subjectivity'. This is a legacy of Marxist essentialism, the homogenisation
of labour and its interests and an antipathy towards individualistic psy-
chologism (Knights, 1990; Thompson, 1983). By way of correction they have
sought to 'humanise' or, at least, give analytical space to, the employee – 'an
appreciation of how the constitution of subjectivity, as labour power, is both
a condition and consequence of the reproduction of monopoly capitalism'
(Willmott, 1990:371). The role of the socially constructed, often fragmented,
self is stressed, whereby self-control and self-identity are mediators of the
'tension' between capitalist forces and worker action. Some of these
analyses appear to introduce concepts of emotion, especially 'insecurity'
and 'anxiety', in relation to, for example, gender, sexuality, ethnicity, work
and leisure (Duncombe and Marsden, 1995; Jermier, 1995; Knights, 1990).
However, these 'emotions' are typically presented more as philosophical
constructs than experiential/feeling ones.

Post-modern approaches to organisations transcend or eschew capital–
labour relations. Some reveal how emotions at work and more broadly how
we see and feel about ourselves, are historically constituted through power–
knowledge régimes in all areas of life (Rose, 1989). These are represented by
discourses – such as those of 'rationality', 'enterprise' and 'masculinity'
(e.g., du Gay, 1996; Kerfoot and Knights, 1993). Grand formal narratives
such as Marxism and Globalisation are regarded as specific products of

these more pervasive processes rather than prime or core in themselves – so they merit less attention (Reed, 1997; cf. Knights, 1997). By focusing on the salience of the text or discourse, the worker and the distinction between managerial strategies and outcomes tend to be removed from the academic gaze (Thompson and Ackroyd, 1995; cf. du Gay, 1996). Where resistance is a focus, it is taken as an essential characteristic of discourses of control rather than of any intersubjective or emotional dynamics (Bendelow and Williams, 1998; Sturdy, 1998).

This takes an epistemological direction which is interesting, but not altogether helpful to our present quest. We would certainly not argue that social relations can be reduced to the conditions and consequences of capitalist and patriarchal structures, but we see the 'dull compulsion of economic relations' as a widespread experience, whatever the prevailing discourse. It is also important to highlight how the so called 'playfulness' and 'disposal of tradition' that apparently characterises post-modern society is itself becoming a commodity of capitalist control – such as 'love of the company', 'humour' and 'delayering' (Albrow, 1997; Willmott, 1992).

In sum, emotion control has yet fully to be exposed to significant critical examination, falling into mainly uncharted territory between emotion research and labour process theory. In what follows we aim to explore some of this terrain. We examine what the more critical emotion researchers have to say on the tacit and explicit features of control and we extend and develop these insights in labour process terms. Attention is also given to the ways in which emotion is 'capitalised' upon or commodified through marketing and consumption, an important extension to analyses of the labour process for critical organisational theory (Knights and Morgan, 1993). Types of resistance which are emotionally directed and/or consti-tuted – intrapsychic, distancing and open challenge – are examined. Finally we speculate on directions for theoretical and empirical development on emotions at work and beyond.

The Emotions of Control and Control of Emotions

There is a spectrum of contracts, rules, rewards and punishment systems which aim to regulate an employee's role behaviour and work performance. These systems are founded upon a concentration of power and ownership represented, as well as experienced, by management. Specific controlling techniques include job descriptions, promotions, demotions, raises, dis-missals, appraisals, technologies and forms of surveillance.

Many of these methods trade on workers' feelings – especially anxiety and fear. With employees' dependence on capitalist enterprises for both a living and social identity in consumer society, fear of material and existential deprivation run as close partners to the organisation's control systems (Featherstone, 1991; Fineman, 1987; Flam, 1993). Meanwhile, 'human resource management' speaks in positive, up-beat emotional tones, emphasising job satisfaction, the pleasures of individual and group achievement and the warmth of organisational belonging.

Social influence in organisations is also exerted through personal, persuasive, control. Managerial 'skills' at, for example, bullying, manipulating, demanding and evading can assist compliance, but once again principally through anxiety and fear (Jackall, 1988; Kets de Vries and Miller, 1991). More subtle influence strategies may operate through the play of different emotions, such as pride or love: flattering, commending and consulting all have this potential, where compliance or co-operation is more gently engineered (Atouf, 1995).

These 'emotions of control' may be contrasted with the 'control of emotions' (see Fineman and Sturdy, 1999). Emotions themselves have long been the target of management influence and feature particularly in early, 'sympathetic', human relations concerns with the 'sentimental worker' (Hollway, 1991; Stearns and Stearns, 1986). The 'tough love' of the late-twentieth century, however, has few frills in its emotion-management approaches (Legge, 1995). It disciplines emotion through techniques of selection, training, surveillance and appraisal (Hochschild, 1975; 1983; Leidner, 1993; Wouters, 1989).

Corporate emotion prescriptions for employees can be explicit, aimed at 'outward' display and/or 'inner' feeling. For example, employees of Marshall Figure Salons in the USA are instructed to use a personalised script to appear exuberant in flattering potential clients: 'Mary, I love your suit. I really admire how professional(ly) you dress . . . where do you buy your clothes?' (Lally-Benedetto, 1985:8). In a different setting, staff of the British Child Support Agency are taught to say 'I hear what you're saying' to suggest sympathy and concern in the face of angry and distressed clients (BBC, 1996). Similarly, Disneyland's deep indoctrination of its park employees' front-stage, back-stage and even off-stage emotional behaviours can trigger other emotions such as guilt in those who feel 'too tired to smile' (Van Maanen, 1991:74; see also Bryman, 1999).

Our research of customer service training in the UK and South East Asia illustrates some of the nuances of such controls. The following are drawn from direct observations of seminars (see also Sturdy, 2000a). The first example is from a meeting run by an independent training company, attended by a mixed group of public and private sector employees:

> Trainees are encouraged to imagine 'good things', positive mental images such as a 'thirty-second holiday' and 'self-talk' is advocated in order to produce and sustain a 'good mood'. If this fails, they are called upon to 'fake it 'til you make it' . . . Responsibility is placed on employees for their own 'discipline' – 'no-one makes you feel the way you do without

your permission'. This project, it is claimed, can be completed by 'lunching with positive people' and 'avoiding moaners who can be taught nothing and are a part of our negative [British] culture'.

The second illustration is from an in-house seminar within a telephone sales subsidiary of a large UK insurance company. The training-focus was on language and its emotional use:

> New staff are initially subjected to twelve hours of service training to invoke positive feelings from customers – 'making it easy for them to say "yes"' [training course title]. Here, certain common words or expressions such as 'sorry', 'no problem' and 'premium' are considered to have negative connotations – the wrong emotional tone. They are replaced by a range of positive, up-beat sounding, or 'sexy' words such as 'certainly', 'rest assured', 'immediate' and 'great' which are to be used in all areas of work – and even at home – to avoid getting 'out of the habit'. The aim is to leave customers with the impression that the salesperson was 'genuine' and 'natural' and, of course, to secure a sale.

Such programming efforts have the capacity to over-write affectivity on a grand scale (see also Cameron, 2000). For example, exhorting employees to regularly and/or 'sincerely' 'smile' or 'enthuse' at work can be counter to and/or play on norms – gender, ethnic, occupational – of wider social relations (Ashforth and Humphrey, 1995). In terms of national culture, we find the techniques of emotion control deployed often derive from American practice and companies, globalizing emotion performance. However they also reflect a particular economic form. Trainees for example, are left in no doubt about the competitive imperative of customer orientation, with job security and/or personal rewards explicitly conditional. In this manner, powerful corporations are able to produce and reproduce their own ideologies – such as those associated with 'loyalty', 'belonging' and 'enthusiasm' towards company and/or customer – wherever they happen to settle (Sturdy, 2001).

   The employee is a key target for such endeavour, but, as is evident in the insurance example above, so is the customer. Through catchy advertisements and persuasive marketing, corporations can also shape the kind of emotional experience customers 'ought' to both want and expect from their services or products. For example, we have Delta Airlines seductive 'Fly me, you'll like it' advertisements (Hochschild, 1983) and the US waste-treatment industry's enthusiastic attempts to persuade farmers to 'feel good' about buying and using sewage sludge (Stauber and Rampton, 1995). In stark contradiction to the ideology of the 'sovereign' consumer (Abercrombie, 1994; Knights *et al.*, 1994), corporations seek to mould popular perceptions of the pleasures of consumption (Abercrombie, 1994; Gramsci, 1971).

Capturing emotion

If the employee is able to 'give' the customer a momentary 'nice day', the more complete the corporate capture of emotion and the stronger the overall capitalist project. Either party may perform their parts 'deeply', on the 'surface' (Hochschild, 1983) or a mixture of the two. Indeed, we might expect different degrees of engagement with 'the act' according to felt pressure to perform, time constraints and features of mood and relative status and power (Edwards *et al.*, 1998). Should the sentiments be not 'really felt' by the parties, it need not compromise the control necessary for the transaction to be completed. For example, the customer who simply mirrors or mimics what the employee emotionally 'does' can experience instrumental rewards of more attention, a warmer encounter and faster service – potentially a tempting invitation to the corporation's culture and ways (Goffman, 1967; Rafaeli, 1989; Rafaeli and Sutton, 1989).

Cynical, sceptical and 'resistant' customers, as well as 'poorly' performing employees, ensure that this process will falter. But the broad tendency is to make 'as if natural' certain corporately controlled emotions – both in and out of commercial exchanges (Alvesson and Deetz, 1996; Giddens, 1979). They become reproduced in the fabric of both work and non-work structures, perhaps complicating existing social/structural tensions and inequalities, especially in relation to gender and sexuality (Filby, 1992; Parker, 1995; Tyler and Taylor this volume). This serves the capital-accumulation aims of a few while being taken for granted as 'normal' by the many (Giddens, 1979; Lukács, 1971).

The reconstruction of 'fear' as 'fun' is a case in point. A range of products and services aim intensely to stimulate actual or vicarious experiences of fear and terror, yet be 'safe' enough to be marketed as fun or 'entertainment': bunjee jumping; roller coasters; violent and highly sexualised movies; terror attractions. Fear becomes a desire 'itself subject to control, nurtured encouraged, stimulated so long as it affords pleasure' (Gabriel and Lang, 1995:106). So we may, paradoxically, go to a 'fun park' to experience and express terror, or violent acts of sado-masochism become a routine part of sexualised entertainment in clubs – like the London Torture Garden (Grant, 1996). And as we become sated, the terror may be progressively escalated (such as with ever more fearful 'rides') (Campbell, 1987). Such industries may powerfully influence social meanings of feeling and expressing fear, making little concession to the way they may act as communication in different cultures, nor how it may confuse emotional cues in actual high-threat situations.

Where an emotion is commercially appropriated, wrenched from its wider social and historical roots, there runs a danger of degrading or trivialising its signal function (Hochschild, 1979). So we might expect the long-term mass marketing of products through idealised or stereotypical images of, say, nostalgia, love, envy or anxiety eventually to be reproduced in the deeper structure of popular emotional beliefs (Sturdy and Knights, 1996). Our query here is less about the distortion of some essential or 'real' sense of emotion, but the glossily disguised authoritarianism – acceptable so long as it sells the product. This can be contrasted with more distributed and/or negotiated socio-political processes which affect the meanings of emotions such as intergenerational conflict over 'appropriate' emotional control and display. Similarly, emotions, to an extent, will reflect their particular historical time – such as the danger attributed to intense feeling, especially passion and anger, in the Victorian era (Gerth and Mills, 1953; Stearns, 1989).

'Struggles' for Emotion Control

The forms of emotion control we have described may more or less 'work' as management or marketing devices, but they should certainly not be seen as simple-to-apply to simple-minded 'victims'. In their different ways, the literature on emotion, the labour process and consumerism, reveal that emotional arenas are contested, resisted with unpredictable and sometimes self-defeating outcomes. The arenas are shaped by participants in the project, within and across divisions between managers and the managed (e.g., see Burawoy, 1979; Gabriel and Lang, 1995; Goldman, 1992; Jermier *et al.*, 1994; Knights and Collinson, 1985). Indeed, the extent to which resistance substantively challenges and/or reproduces patterns of domination is an important and recurring question for critical analysis.

At the risk of oversimplification, we have constructed three overlapping types of worker resistance (after Collinson, 1994) as political *and* emotional. Some forms are likely to be felt as *intrapsychic* – 'within the person' (cf. Williams and Bendelow, 1998). The employee experiences a personal struggle between pressures from, often powerful, others to display certain emotions and his/her feelings of being 'inauthentic'; not honestly displaying or knowing what is 'really felt'. Other forms of resistance may involve this dynamic, but are more proactive in socially re-negotiating emotional space in the job for the employee to reassert control and particular sense/s of self. A third form is explicitly confrontational and disruptive – directly *challenging* prescriptions, such as through employee strikes and consumer boycotts. We will examine these three forms in more detail in relation to both the control of emotions and the emotions of control.

Intrapsychic resistance

As we have suggested, the prescription of feeling rules are explicit in many face-to-face service jobs and implicit to a number of, if not all, occupations – such as the 'caring' nurse, the 'detached' researcher (Fineman, 2000). An individual may experience intrapsychic 'resistance' – felt discomfort, gloom, despair, pain, stress – when there is a contradiction or tension between private feelings about self and publicly required emotional display. When hidden or contained, such resistance is absorbed as emotional labour; the burden and numbness the employee bears in exchange for the instrumental rewards of the job (Hochschild, 1983; Vallas, 1993). This response is captured well in Van Maanen's oft cited observations of Disneyland employees:

> Much of the numbness is, of course, beyond the knowledge of supervisors and guests because most employees have little trouble appearing as if they are present even when they are not. It is, in a sense, a passive form of resistance that suggests there still is a sacred preserve of individuality left among employees in the park (1991:75; see also Gabriel, 1995).

But under relentless pressure to keep a 'false face', the mask may crack: the act falters, control is threatened, if not lost. This is consistent with reports of employee stress, disillusionment, identity confusion and burnout (Pines and Aronson, 1989). Resistance, in these terms, is an inwardly directed emotional activity that has 'negative' performatory consequences. It is often constructed by both managers and the managed as an employee's individual responsibility, especially a problem of failing to cope at work (Newton, 1995). But being a 'non-coper' has a wider context, reflecting the societal constitution of 'goodness' in emotion control (Elias, 1978; Stearns, 1993; Wouters 1991, 1989). The boundaries of what should and should not be displayed, and what is regarded as 'odd' or 'sick', are embedded in contemporary social definitions of affectivity and self, moulded by those who are powerful conduits for the control and labelling of emotion – such as medical practitioners, psychiatrists, teachers, media professionals, corporate executives, management consultants and academics (Hopfl, 1992; Illich, 1977, 1978; Rose, 1989).

The stress 'spill' from intrapsychic resistance typically is met with techniques which aim to re-manufacture consent and reproduce the extant organisational order. For example, 'buffering' temporarily camouflages the 'problem': the vulnerable employee is encouraged to take 'sick leave' or 'a holiday' (Ashforth and Humphrey, 1995; Fineman, 1985; 1995). Similarly, 'normalizing' reinstates the required emotion 'face' through further training, counselling and 'stress management'. Each reinforces a social definition of the employee as personally deficient, but in a manner that can be fixed. They foster an ideal of 'stress-fitness', a sentiment which resonates well with popular discourses on the 'evils' of stress (Newton, 1995; Thompson and McHugh, 1990:325) and lures the 'sick' or 'wounded' (Kunda, 1992) towards a new personal robustness. It provides a discourse on how best to control the emotions that interfere with those required for job performance.

Yet, in accepting stress management, the employee unwittingly helps shore-up régimes which themselves may be far 'sicker' than the employee. As Newton (1995:60) wryly observes:

> the subject in stress discourse begins to look rather like a Marxist caricature: an individual who is desperately concerned to remain stress-fit, a good coper who can, whatever the pressures, deliver the last drop of her labour.

Stress and other individualising programmes, such as those aimed at constituting a more 'enterprising' self (see du Gay, 1996), have developed into an industry that profits from intrapsychically resistant employees. It sells emotion-control knowledge, often drawn from other colonisers of affectivity such as academics. Even if commercial gain is not sought, with their various texts and interventions on stress and emotion-management, consultants and the like help reinforce and hegemonise a managerially aligned view of 'correct' emotionality. This is sometimes quite explicit in academic literature. For example, while Ashforth and Humphrey note that *others* may 'appropriate emotions as instruments of social objectives' (1995:109), they fail to reflect on their own role in this process, wishing to 'capture' emotion to serve 'organisational effectiveness' (1995:99, 102). In doing this, and in presenting research questions such as 'how can emotions be mobilised to increase receptiveness to organisational change' (1995:118), there is no recognition of competing definitions of effectiveness nor of management as anything other than a neutral practice or group.

Resistance through distance

Intrapsychic resistance both contains and personalises an individual's feelings of dislocation; distancing actively transforms it. Distancing as resistance (see Cohen and Taylor, 1976; Collinson, 1994; Goffman, 1959) creates a symbolic and/or physical separation from the organisational-cultural emotion imperatives that are experienced as distressing; a reformation of 'place' (Clark, 1990). Such distancing by the individual may not aim to challenge the dominant order: it tailors it to the person's preference or defensive interests, so camouflaging and partly ameliorating fears and anxieties.

Resistance of this type can take the form of the actor 'unofficially' re-scripting his or her role to create a degree of positive feeling, such as fun or joy. The dictates of the corporate script are actively rejected or subverted in favour of one which is more self-designed (Filby, 1992; Fineman, 1993b; Leidner, 1991; Wouters, 1989). As part author and director of the playlet, the actor is shielded from the stigma and psychological costs of full role-embracement – even though the wider stage is set by others, especially management.

Tolich's (1993) study of supermarket staff nicely illustrates this. They appeared to accept and even welcome management's ideology on the primacy of the customer and the surveillance of their own greetings, smiles and sincerity. However, the onerousness of the emotional labour could be reduced through departing from the required script, overlaying it with improvised routines of their own – often exercised with panache. They became skilled at the aesthetics of display (Fine, 1989; Nickson *et al.*, this volume). Customers were joked with, offered personal advice, even prayed for. This was constructed 'free space' by the clerks, where emotion management was experienced as autonomous and feelings were 'owned'; an 'escape into' an emotional arena which management had yet to displace or fully colonise – 'stressful satisfaction' (see also James, 1989; Sturdy, 1992; cf. Wray-Bliss, this volume).

There are key accomplices to this type of drama who define the wider framing of control. 'Fun' is essentially bounded by management's indulgency: the checkout tills must ring; customers must still buy. And customers need also be 'good' ones, willing to engage with the employee; to collude with the act (Hall, 1993; Leidner, 1993; Mulkay and Howe, 1994; Rafaeli, 1989). Customers' prior socialisation (e.g., from company advertisements which extol 'friendly', 'personal', service) and their experience of other service encounters, provide them with a ready set of (ever increasing) expectations on which to draw. Those employees who deviate too far, 'over' or 'under' performing (perhaps 'taking out' their frustrations on the customers), may be challenged directly by the customer, or otherwise 'caught' in 'off site' management techniques, such as customer 'satisfaction' surveys (Fuller and Smith, 1991).

More generally, customer compliance is crucial to sustaining the legitimacy of a corporate emotion order; the 'struggle' to control emotion is rarely just a bipartite, employee/employer, matter. The dissatisfied ('awkward', 'embarrassing', 'irate') customer can resist some of the strictures and standardisation of service encounters, blocking or disengaging from the employee's corporatised enthusiasm or learned techniques (e.g. Hochschild, 1983; Leidner, 1993; Van Maanen, 1991). More radically, some may express their discontent with the company's values by boycotting or 'misappropriating' its products (Gabriel and Lang, 1995:151; Smith, 1987; Willis, 1990). Consumer resistance to corporate emotion engineering has yet to be fully explored (Smart, 1999), but we would expect it to relate to what is deemed as socially acceptable or appropriate in commercial exchange. Such boundaries are always being tested and redefined. For example, in the mid-1990s the clothing manufacturer Benetton chose to use product-unconnected, high-realism, emotional shock images to promote its clothing. The prevalent consumer response appeared to be one of revulsion and rejection and talk of a boycott of Benetton products. Less dramatically, the more flexible sales script introduced to the trainees mentioned earlier was developed partly in response to negative customer reactions.

Employees are, of course, largely unable to 'boycott' employers as a collectivity, but resistance can be physically distanced; in work 'zones' which provide an amnesty from normal emotional labours. They are places where different feeling rules prevail (Fineman, 1993b; Gabriel, 1988; Goffman, 1956, 1959). Rest rooms, galleys, corridors and other 'off-stage' areas provide an opportunity for employees to drop their corporate mask, free from the scrutiny of supervisors and customers. 'Undesirable' emotions, such as fear, anger, hurt and frustration, can be vented or expressed. In such settings the otherwise consented-to social order can be attacked, deprecated or ridiculed in the presence of a 'willing', audience of colleagues (Boje, 1991; Gabriel, 1991; Sturdy, 2000a).

Cynicism is often an observed feature of this process. It is a way of maintaining a feeling of autonomous self, while also defensively preserving the 'necessary' motions of role prescriptions. The cynical employee maintains distance by looking somewhat jaundicely onto his or her role performance; it appears as a hollow game. A UK flight attendant explains:

> You try saying 'hello' to 300 people and sound as though you mean it towards the end. Most of us make a game of it. Someone – probably a manager – said 'This business is all about interpersonal transactions'. He was wrong. It's all about bullshit. If life is a cabaret, this is a bloody circus. (Hopfl, 1991:5–6)

The cynic's free space is highly conditional. It permits an assertion of one's own identity and control over work, but in ways which often reinforce management controls (Burawoy, 1979; Sturdy, 1992). Indeed, cynicism and related humour are often seen as generating a closed loop whereby employees are locked into their pessimism, unable to form a 'truly' critical stance on the emotional demands of their job or a sense of their own rights and power (du Gay and Salaman, 1992; Kunda, 1992; Leidner, 1993; Willmott, 1993). However this view is often overstated. Cynicism is much more than a psychological safety valve; it is a conduit for questioning and resistance which may produce alternative, *sceptical*, rationales and rhetorics. These can provide the basis for challenges to existing orders or, more simply, limit the scope of totalising control (Sturdy, 1998; Wray-Bliss, Tyler and Taylor and Sturdy, all in this volume).

Openly challenging the emotion order

The resistance approaches we have so far discussed may temporarily disturb the underlying configuration of managerial prerogative, ensure the continuity of the control 'problem' and inform oppositional ideologies and ethics. However, rarely do they radically re-define or democratise an emotion order. Intrapsychic resistance, in particular, can be a largely unconscious process which produces social defences and collective denial.

These tend to leave untouched the anxiety-provoking systems and struc-tures of work (Fineman, 1995; Menzies-Lythe, 1988). Furthermore, those who adopt what is 'appropriate' or customary for their hierarchical position in the organisation (e.g., as a trainee nurse or junior doctor) also inherit certain 'divisions' of emotional labour (James, 1993). To question these also challenges the fabric of an organisational/ professional order.

For these reasons, as well as the broader nature of the employment relationship, overt resistance is often muted. But there are some exceptions, especially when dissent is shared and when an employee feels morally compromised. Fuller and Smith (1991), for example, report a 'smile strike' by hotel desk clerks, 'angry' at being monitored through managerially 'planted' customers. Indeed, the planted 'mystery shopper' has achieved something of the status of a specialism within market research, a extension of the arm of surreptitious managerial control of emotion (Carty, 1996). Like Bentham's much cited panopticon, mystery shopping trades on subterfuge, creating a degree or apprehension or fear in many employees who know they might be its 'victim'. This may translate into mistrust, uncomfortable compliance or eventual defiance by the employee.

Open employee resistance in such circumstances may be triggered when a line of moral acceptability is crossed and when there is perceived safety (and greater power) with like-minded others. For instance, we have observed in our researches of customer service trainees that not all are prepared to acquiesce to, or embrace, the trainer's exhortations to 'always be friendly and caring' to customers. In the classroom at least, some are sceptical about the apparent corporate interest in consumer needs and publicly chastise the trainer for advocating a false niceness – when all that really seemed to matter was closing a sale or selling complementary products (Sturdy, 2000a).

Defiance of an emotion order can be more formally collectivised or institutionalised – such as through trade union action (see also Sturdy, this volume). The individualising of stress in the workplace is a case in point. US and British trade unions have sought to expose the 'incorrect' moral premise of corporations which, as noted earlier, blame their employees for not managing their stresses. The unions focus on 'managerial causes' of stress, alleging long work hours, team working, just-in-time methods of working and job insecurity (Fineman, 1995; TUC 1996). In turning the partisan tables in this manner, trade unions cast stress and its 'coping' rhetoric into a broader socio-political arena.

There are also resisters who 'go it alone'. Hochschild (1983:127) has graphically illustrated this with an overburdened, disillusioned, flight attendant who stops smiling at her customer; she cynically defies the customer's challenge to smile according to the rule book. Some individual employees express their resistance through feelings of deep outrage about what is being done to them in the workplace, such as with instances of sexual harassment (Collinson, 1994). Here, emotion rules and the emotions of control combine with facets of patriarchal power and bureaucratic and capitalist hierarchy. The following account, from Fineman and Gabriel (1996:168), illustrates this and the emotions of control more generally. The words are those of a young female management trainee employed in a shipping agency:

> At the beginning, my boss was helpful and polite . . . I greatly appreciated his kindness . . . As we spent more time working together, the status gap between us seemed to get smaller. He started to act in a less formal way . . . I thought it was only a indication of our improving friendship. Then things suddenly got worse . . . He started to talk to me in a different way. For example, he said I should wear tighter and shorter skirts. Also, he acted differently, such as putting his hand on my shoulder while he talked to me. He behaved in a way which made me feel very embarrassed . . . . [Then] he asked me explicitly to have a candle-lit dinner with him so that I would get a brilliant report. My anger exploded because I felt I was being insulted. By that time I could not restrain myself anymore. So, I replied, 'no way!' Then I walked out of the door and went straight to the toilet and just cried for nearly a hour.
>
> He paid my salary and now wanted something in return. He was enjoying his exclusive privilege and tried to control me . . . I should also be responsible for what happened since I did not protect myself. I should have been aware of what could happen. I encouraged his confidence . . . Now, I have learnt a big lesson. Do not trust anybody before enough information is obtained; and don't be misled by first-impressions, they can be very wrong.

The mix of resistance strategies and emotion work in this case are poignant. As the boss's implied emotion rules become more explicit, the trainee struggles (resistance as embarrassment) and eventually 'explodes' in open anger and exasperation. She then hides her feelings in a safe zone, privatising her distress, and with much injured pride begins to blame herself. Finally, the foundations are laid for distancing resistance and a new-found cynicism.

Sexual harassment is one extreme of exploitation of sexualisation in both the labour process and service encounters. Emotional 'performance' is purchased, either formally or in quiet 'deals' behind closed doors (Gardner, 1995; Gutek, 1985; Tyler and Taylor, this volume). The open expression of moral outrage by the harassed is partly informed by the wider social discourse on the meaning of harassment and male/female power differentials in and out of employment settings (Hearn *et al.*, 1989). For the individual employee however, an open challenge on grounds of harassment, whether from co-worker or customer, can still incur considerable emotional and material costs, especially in the absence of representation.

The apotheosis of individual, open, resistance can be found with the whistleblower. Here, the persistence and passion in refusing to be dominated or 'not heard' by the employer can be regarded as a moral/political act aimed at concrete change. Typically, it is a deep-felt sense of injustice or conscience that drives an individual employee publicly to expose an organisational 'wrong' (Glazer and Glazer, 1989; Miceli and Near, 1991; Westin, 1981). These feelings may be complemented by those of guilt or shame from not revealing what they (and others) regard as a harmful or repugnant organisational practice (e.g., unsafe products or processes, corruption, environmental damage and unfair employment practices). As they become more politicised in their mission (Collinson, 1994; Rothschild and Miethe, 1994), whistleblowers almost invariably run against the tacit emotion rules of the corporation. The employee as hired 'hand' is not free to voice open criticism of the organisational order; some anxieties and fears should not to be expressed, other than, perhaps, through well-insulated corporate channels.

To a considerable extent this is an unequal struggle as the more the passion, frustration and dismay of the whistleblower, the more management reasserts its control through its own defences, typically demonising and deprecating the 'disloyal' whistleblower. In the battle for the moral high ground and the manipulation of public sentiments, most corporations can muster a formidable legal and public-relations armoury. Against this, individual whistleblowers are very vulnerable, notwithstanding recent protective legislation in the UK. However, once they are prepared to sacrifice their place in the corporate order for their cause, the fear of non-compliance to management control no longer holds its usual sting (Rothschild and Meithe, 1994). The whistleblower's hand can also be considerably strengthened if others – trade unions, interest groups, the media – join the cause and help resist the corporation's (or industry's) 'disinformation' and vilification. This collectivisation may be regarded as being as much to do with the mobilisation of dissent and anger in the control of labour as with the manifest issues being contested.

Discussion and Conclusions

The homogenisation and commodification of emotion now appear to play an increasingly central role in the social reproduction of capitalism. We have suggested that in controlling both manifest and tacit emotion rules, corporations strive to engineer a degree of employee and consumer co-operation that can monopolise emotions and their signal functions – and thereby impoverish those affected. Control, however, is rarely complete. There is a mosaic of resistance, some of which is partly enriching for the individual, other less so. The most defensive resistance permits the work act to continue, but with the self/selves largely disengaged and critical vision impaired. Employee resistance is rarely able to tug hard at the roots of emotional labour, often held tightly in place by executive privilege and the fears inherent in the employment relationship. The worst oppressions of the commodification of emotion, therefore, may go largely, but not completely, unchallenged.

Labour process theory espouses an important virtue: that fairer and more liberating or equitable ways of working are desirable and more or less attainable, especially through transformative employee resistance. This moral stance is not part of managerially aligned organisational theories and is irrelevant to many post-modern theorists – who problematise or avoid the adoption of preferential positions. However, resistance is mainly a one-dimensional concept in labour process theory. Analytically it is not treated as emotionalised nor is it applied to emotions as 'products' to contest in the workplace. The act of resistance is more than an outcome of the contradictions of capitalism and control. The force and texture of a 'challenge' is from feelings – such as of hurt, affront, anger or fear. And how the challenge is enacted depends upon the emotion rules within particular organisational settings. The display of anxiety, embarrassment, outrage, anger, guilt, pride and other feelings are implicitly or explicitly shaped, prescribed or proscribed within the organisation–labour contract.

We need a better understanding of the moral and the structural order of emotions in organisations because both define the boundaries of what can be expressed and the way in which resistance is experienced. Open resistance is more likely to be suppressed by the individual where, for example, revealing one's fears and anxieties invites punishment or retribution – loss of job, reprimand, poor appraisal, ridicule. Yet it is precisely these emotions which underpin capitalist employment relations and their contradictions. Challenges to an oppressive order are more likely where there are structures which legitimise such fears and anxieties. Indeed, 'political consciousness' could be regarded as a blunt instrument of resistance without its mobilising passion and anger, and without a constituency that authorises the expression of those feelings. This is not to repeat the 1960s humanist calls, or the more recent proclamations of 'excellence' gurus, for freedom of emotional expression. Freedom, as we have noted, may be appropriated and always has its disciplinary form (Giddens, 1979; Hodgson, this volume; Rose, 1989). It is, however, to recognise conceptually and practically the enabling and constraining conditions of both power and resistance. Collective settings, such as trade unions and consumer groups may provide a structurally and morally based challenge to do just this. They offer one route to different, perhaps more liberating, emotion orders, particularly where they move beyond liberal pluralism and challenge the very structures of capitalism.

The kinds of resistance one is most likely to encounter are local, individual (or in loose coalitions) and temporary. In analysing these, there is a double imperative. First, that the phenomenon of resistance itself should be seen as socially-emotionally constituted; and second, that it will interact with the political context of emotion control that is imposed. Researching these issues, at the interface of emotion theory and labour process theory, extends and develops both bodies of knowledge: politicising the former, emotionalising the latter. This requires a wider development of their conceptual connections as well as imaginative descriptive studies of the nuances of resistance and consent (see Fineman, 2000; Sturdy 2000b). If our current picture is representative, then present forms of resistance are going to achieve, at most, modest change to the underlying structure of emotion engineering. We can help expose the reasons for the frailty of such resistance, as well promote alternatives which trade less on monolithic programmes of emotion management.

References

Abercrombie, N. (1994) 'Authority and Consumer Society', in Keat, R., Whitley, N. and Abercrombie, N. (eds), *The Authority of the Consumer*, London: Routledge.
Albrow, M. (1997) *Do Organizations Have Feelings?*, London: Routledge.
Alvesson, M. and Deetz, S. (1996) 'Critical Theory and Post-modernism Approaches to Organisational Studies', in Clegg, S. R., Hardy, C. and Nord, W. R. (eds), *Handbook of Organization Studies*, London: Sage.
Ashforth, B. E. and Humphrey, R. H. (1993) 'Emotional Labor in Service Roles: The Influence of Identity', *Academy of Management Review*, 18:1, 88–115.
Ashforth, B. E. and Humphrey, R. H. (1995) 'Emotion in the Workplace – A Reappraisal', *Human Relations*, 48:2, 97–125.
Atouf, O. (1995) 'The Management of Excellence: Deified Executives and Depersonalised Employees', in Pauchant, T. C. (ed.), *In Search of Meaning*, San Francisco: Jossey Bass.
Barley, S. R. and Kunda, G. (1992) 'Design and Devotion: Surges of Rational and Normative Ideologies of Control in Managerial Discourse', *Administrative Science Quarterly*, 37: 363–99.
BBC (1996) Televised programme 'The System', British Broadcasting Corporation, Channel 2, 26 September.
Bendelow, G. and Williams, S. J. (eds) (1998) *Emotions in Social Life*, London: Routledge.
Boje, D. (1991) 'The Storytelling Organisation: A Study of Story Performance in an Office-Supply Firm', *Administrative Science Quarterly*, 36: 106–26.
Braverman, H. (1974) *Labor and Monopoly Capital*, New York: Monthly Review Press.
Bryman, A. (1999) 'The Disneyization of Society', *Sociological Review*, 47:1, 25–47
Burawoy, M. (1979) *Manufacturing Consent*, Chicago: University of Chicago Press.
Cameron, D. (2000) *Good to Talk*, London: Sage.
Campbell, C. (1987) *The Romantic Ethic and the Spirit of Modern Consumerism*, London: Macmillan.
Carlzon, J. (1987) *Moments of Truth*, New York: Harper and Row.
Carty, P. (1996) *The Guardian*, 9 Oct, 3.

Clark, C. (1990) 'Emotions and Micropolitics in Everyday Life: Some Patterns and Paradoxes of "Place" ', in Kemper, T. D. (ed.), *Research Agendas in the Sociology of Emotions*, Albany, NY: State University of New York Press.

Cohen, S. and Taylor, L. (1976) *Escape Attempts: The Theory and Practice of Resistance to Everyday Life*, London: Allen Lane.

Collinson, D. (1992) *Managing the Shopfloor*, Berlin: De Gruyter.

Collinson, D. (1994) 'Strategies of Resistance: Power, Knowledge and Subjectivity in the Workplace', in Jermier, J., Knights, D. and Nord, W. R. (eds), *Resistance and Power in Organisations*, London: Routledge.

Craib, I. (1995) 'Some Comments on the Sociology of Emotions', *Sociology*, 29:1, 151–8.

du Gay, P. (1996) *Consumption and Identity at Work*, London: Sage.

du Gay, P. and Salaman, G. (1992) 'The Cult(ure) of the Customer', *Journal of Management Studies*, 29:5, 615–33.

Duncombe, J. and Marsden, D. (1995) ' "Workaholics" and "Whingeing Women" – Theorising Intimacy and Emotion Work – The Last Frontier of Gender Inequality?', *Sociological Review*, 43:2, 150–69.

Edwards, P. K. (1990) 'Understanding Conflict in the Labour Process: The Logic and Autonomy of Struggle', in Knights, D. and Willmott, H. (eds), *Labour Process Theory*, London: Macmillan.

Edwards, P., Collinson, M. and Rees, C. (1998) 'The Determinants of Employee Responses to TQM: Six Case Studies', *Organisation Studies*, 19:3, 449–75.

Edwards, R. (1979) *Contested Terrain*, New York: Basic Books.

Elias, N. (1978) *The Civilizing Process, Vol. 1. The History of Manners*, Trans. Jephcott, New York: Urizen Books.

Featherstone, M. (1991) *Consumer Culture and Post-Modernism*, London: Sage.

Filby, M. P. (1992) 'The Figures, The Personality and The Bums: Service Work and Sexuality', *Work Employment and Society*, 6:1, 23–42.

Fine, G. A. (1989) 'Aesthetic Constraints: The Culture of Production in Restaurant Kitchens', paper presented at the annual meeting of the American Sociological Association, San Francisco.

Fineman, S. (1985) *Social Work Stress and Intervention*, Aldershot: Gower.

Fineman, S. (ed.) (1987) *Unemployment: Personal and Social Consequences*, London: Tavistock.

Fineman, S. (ed.) (1993a) *Emotion in Organisations*, London: Sage.

Fineman, S. (1993b) 'Organizations as Emotional Arenas', in Fineman, S. (ed.), *Emotion in Organizations*, London: Sage.

Fineman, S. (1995) 'Stress, Emotion and Intervention', in Newton, T. (ed.), *Managing Stress: Emotion and Power at Work*, London: Sage.

Fineman, S. (ed.) (2000) *Emotion in Organizations*, 2nd edn, London: Sage.

Fineman, S. and Gabriel, Y. (1996) *Experiencing Organisations*, London: Sage.

Fineman, S. and Sturdy, A. J. (1999) 'The Emotions of Control – A Qualitative Exploration of Environmental Regulation', *Human Relations*, 52:5, 631–64.

Flam, H. (1993) 'Fear, Loyalty and Greedy Organisations', in Fineman, S. (ed.), *Emotion in Organisations*, London: Sage.

Friedman, A. (1977) *Industry and Labour*, London: Heinemann

Fuller, L. and Smith, V. (1991) ' "Consumers" Reports: Management by Customers in a Changing Economy', *Work Employment and Society*, 5:1, 1–16.

Gabriel, Y. (1988) *Working Lives in Catering*, London: Routledge.

Gabriel, Y. (1991) 'Turning Facts into Stories and Stories into Facts: A Hermeneutic Exploration of Organisational Folklore', *Human Relations*, 44:8, 857–75.

Gabriel, Y. (1995) 'The Unmanaged Organization – Stories, Fantasies and Subjectivity', *Organization Studies*, 16:3, 477–501.

Gabriel, Y. and Lang, T. (1995) *The Unmanageable Consumer – Contemporary Consumption and its Fragmentations*, London: Sage.

Gagliardi, P. (1986) 'The Creation of Change of Organisational Cultures: A Conceptual Framework', *Organisation Studies*, 7:2, 117–34.

Gardner, C. B. (1995) *Passing By: Gender and Public Harassment*, Berkeley: University of California Press.

Gerth, H. and Mills, C. W. (1953) *Character and Social Structure – The Psychology of Social Institutions*, San Diego: Harvest/HBJ.

Giddens, A. (1979) *Central Problems in Social Theory*, London: Macmillan.

Glazer, M. and Glazer, P. (1989) *The Whistleblowers: Exposing Corruption in Government and Industry*, New York: Basic Books.

Goffman, E. (1956) 'Embarrassment and Social Organisation', *American Journal of Sociology*, 62: 264–71.

Goffman, E. (1959) *The Presentation of Self in Everyday Life*, New Jersey: Anchor Books.

Goffman, E. (1967) *Interaction Ritual*, New Jersey: Anchor Books.

Goldman, R. (1992) *Reading Ads Socially*, London: Routledge.

Gramsci, A. (1971) *Selections from the Prison Notebooks*, London: Lawrence and Wishart.

Grant, L. (1996) 'Violent Anxiety', in Dunant, S. and Porter, R. (eds), *The Age of Anxiety*, London: Virago.

Grey, C. (1996) 'Towards a Critique of Managerialism: the Contribution of Simone Weil', *Journal of Management Studies*, 33:5, 592–611.

Gutek, B. A. (1985) *Sex and the Workplace: Impact of Sexual Behavior and Harassment on Men and Organisations*, San Francisco: Jossey-Bass.

Hall, E. J. (1993) 'Smiling, Deferring and Flirting: Doing Gender by Giving "Good Service"', *Work and Occupations*, 20:4, 452–71.

Harré, R. (1986) *The Social Construction of Emotions*, Blackwell: Oxford.

Harré, R. and Gerrod, P. (1996) 'Some Complexities in the Study of Emotions', in Harré, R. and Gerrod, P. (eds), *The Emotions*, London: Sage.

Hassard, J. and Parker, E. (eds) (1994) *Towards a New Theory of Organisations*, London: Routledge.

Hearn, J., Sheppard, D. L., Tancred-Sheriff, P. and Burrell, G. (eds) (1989) *The Sexuality of Organisation*, London: Sage.

Hochschild, A. (1975) 'The Sociology of Feeling and Emotion: Selected Possibilities', in Millman, M. and Kanter, R. (eds), *Another Voice*, New York: Anchor.

Hochschild, A. (1979) 'Emotion Work, Feeling Rules and Social Structure', *American Journal of Sociology*, 39 (Dec): 551–75.

Hochschild, A. (1983) *The Managed Heart: Commercialization of Human Feeling*, London: University of California Press.

Hollway, W. (1991) *Work Psychology and Organisational Behaviour*, London: Sage.

Hopfl, H. (1991) 'Nice Jumper Jim!: Dissonance and Emotional Labour in a Management Development Programme', paper presented at 5th European Congress – The Psychology of Work and Organisations, Rouen, 24–27 March.

Hopfl, H. (1992) 'The Making of the Corporate Acolyte', *Journal of Management Studies*, 29:1, 23–34.

Hopfl, H. and Linstead, S. (1993) 'Passion and Performance: Suffering and the Carrying of Organisational Roles', in Fineman, S. (ed.), *Emotion in Organisations*, London: Sage.

Illich, I. (1977) *Disabling Professions*, London: Marion Boyars.

Illich, I. (1978) *Deschooling Society*, London: Marion Boyars.

Jackall, R. (1988) *Moral Mazes*, New York: Oxford University Press.

James, N. (1989) 'Emotional Labour: Skill and Work in the Social Regulation of Feelings', *Sociological Review* 37:1, 15–42.

James, N. (1993) 'Divisions of Emotional Labour: Disclosure and Cancer', in Fineman, S. (ed.), *Emotion in Organisations*, London: Sage.

Jermier, J. (1995) 'Labour Process Theory', in Nicholson, N. (ed.), *Encyclopedic Dictionary of Organisational Behavior*, Oxford: Blackwell.

Jermier, J., Knights, D. and Nord, W. R. (1994) 'Resistance and Power in Organisations: Agency, Subjectivity and the Labour Process', in Jermier, J., Knights, D. and Nord, W. R. (eds), *Resistance and Power in Organisations*, London: Routledge.

Kerfoot, D. and Knights, D. (1993) 'Masculinity, Management and Manipulation', *Journal of Management Studies*, 30:4, 659–79.

Kets de Vries, M. F. R. and Miller, D. (1991) 'Leadership Styles and Organisational Cultures: The Shaping of Neurotic Organisations', in Kets de Vries, M. F. R. (ed.), *Organisations on the Couch*, San Francisco: Jossey Bass.

Knights, D. (1997) 'Organisation Theory in the Age of Deconstruction: Dualism, Gender and Post-modernism Revisited', *Organisation Studies*, 18:1, 1–19.

Knights, D. (1990) 'Subjectivity, Power and the Labour Process', in Knights, D. and Willmott, H. (eds), *Labour Process Theory*, London: Macmillan.

Knights, D. and Collinson, D. (1985) *Job Redesign: Critical Perspectives on the Labour Process*, Aldershot: Gower.

Knights, D. and Morgan, G. (1993) 'Organisation Theory and Consumption in a Post-Modern Era', *Organisation Studies*, 14:2, 211–34.

Knights, D., Sturdy, A. J. and Morgan, G. (1994) 'The Consumer Rules? The Rhetoric and Reality of Marketing', *European Journal of Marketing*, 28:3, 42–54.

Kunda, G. (1992) *Engineering Culture: Control and Commitment in a High-Tech Corporation*, Philadelphia: Temple University Press.

Lally-Benedetto, C. (1985) 'Women and the Tone of the Body: An Analysis of a Figure Salon', paper presented at the annual meeting of the Midwest Sociological Society, St. Louis, MO.

Legge, K. (1995) *Human Resource Management*, Basingstoke: Macmillan.

Leidner, R. (1991) 'Gender, Work and Identity in Interactive Service Jobs', *Gender and Society*, 5:2, 154–77.

Leidner, R. (1993) *Fast Food Fast Talk: Service Work and the Routinization of Everyday Life*, London: UCLA Press.

Littler, C. (1982) *The Development of the Labour Process in Capitalist Societies*, London: Heinemann.

Lukács, G. (1971) *History and Class Consciousness*, trans. Livingstone, R., Cambridge, MA: MIT Press.

Menzies-Lythe, I. (1988) *Containing Anxiety in Institutions – Selected Essays*, London: Free Association Books.

Miceli, M. P. and Near, J. P. (1991) 'Whistleblowing as an Organisational Process', *Research in the Sociology of Organisations*, 9: 139–200.

Mills, C. W. (1951) *White Collar: The American Middle Classes*, Oxford: Oxford University Press.

Morgan, G. and Sturdy, A. J. (2000) *Beyond Organisational Change*, Basingstoke: Macmillan.

Mulkay, M. and Howe, G. (1994) 'Laughter For Sale', *Sociological Review*, 42:3, 481–500.

Mumby, D. K. and Putnam, L. L. (1992) 'The Politics of Emotion: A Feminist Reading of Bounded Rationality', *Academy of Management Review*, 17:3, 465–86.

Newton, T. (ed.) (1995) *Managing Stress: Emotion and Power at Work*, London: Sage.

O'Brien, M. (1994) 'The Managed Heart Revisited: Health and Social Control', *Sociological Review*, 42:3, 393–413.

Parker, M. (1995) 'Working Together, Working Apart: Management Culture in a Manufacturing Firm', *Sociological Review*, 43:3, 518–47.
Peters, T. (1989) *Leadership and Emotion*, California: TPG Communications.
Pines, A. and Aronson, E. (1989) *Career Burnout*, New York: Free Press.
Rafaeli, A. (1989) 'When Cashiers Meet Customers: An Analysis of the Role of Supermarket Cashiers', *Academy of Management Journal*, 32:2, 245–73.
Rafaeli, A. and Sutton, R. I. (1987) 'Expression of Emotion as part of the Work Role', *Academy of Management Review*, 12(1): 23–37.
Rafaeli, A. and Sutton, R. I . (1989) 'The Expression of Emotion in Organisational Life', *Research in Organisational Behavior*, 11: 1–42.
Ray, C. A. (1986) 'Corporate Culture: The Last Frontier of Control?', *Journal of Management Studies*, 23:3, 287–97.
Reed, M. (1997) 'In Praise of Duality and Dualism: Rethinking Agency and Structure in Organisational Analysis', *Organisation Studies*, 18:1, 21–42.
Ritzer, G. (1993) *The McDonaldization of Society*, Thousand Oaks, CA: Pine Forge Press.
Rose, N. (1989) *Governing the Soul: The Shaping of the Private Self*, London: Routledge.
Rothschild, J. and Miethe, T. D. (1994) 'Whistleblowing as Resistance in Modern Work Organisations: The Politics of Revealing Organisational Deception and Abuse', in Jermier, J., Knights, D. and Nord, W. R. (eds), *Resistance and Power in Organisations*, London: Routledge.
Sandelands, L. E. and Buckner, G. C. (1989) 'Of Art and Work: Aesthetic Experience and the Psychology of Work Feelings', *Research in Organisational Behavior*, 11.
Smart, B. (ed.) (1999) *Resisting McDonaldization*, London: Sage.
Smith, N. C. (1987) 'Consumer Boycotts and Consumer Sovereignty', *European Journal of Marketing*, 21:5, 7–19.
Stauber, J. and Rampton, S. (1995) *Toxic Sludge is Good for You*, Monroe, ME: Common Courage Press.
Stearns, P. N. (1989) 'Suppressing Unpleasant Emotions: The Development of a Twentieth-century American', in Barnes, A. E. and Stearns, P. N. (eds), *Social History and Issues in Human Consciousness*, New York: New York University Press.
Stearns, P. N. (1993) 'Girls, Boys and Emotions: Re-definitions and Historical Change', *The Journal of American History*, 80:1, 36–74.
Stearns, P. Z. and Stearns, P. N. (1986) *Anger: The Struggle for Emotional Control in America's History*, Chicago: University of Chicago Press.
Sturdy, A. J. (1992) 'Clerical Consent', in A. J. Sturdy, D. Knights and H. Willmott (eds), *Skill and Consent*, London: Routledge.
Sturdy, A. J. (1998) 'Customer Care in a Consumer Society' *Organisation*, 5:1, 27–53.
Sturdy, A. J. (2000a) 'Training in Service – Importing and Imparting Customer Service Culture as an Interactive Process', *International Journal of HRM*, 11:6, 1082–1103
Sturdy, A. J. (2000b) 'Knowing the Unknowable? – Methodological and Theoretical Problems and Integration in Emotion Research and Organisational Studies', 16th EGOS Colloquium, Helsinki School of Economics, 2–4 July.
Sturdy, A. J. (2001) 'The Global Diffusion of Customer Service – Reasserting Generic Barriers and Contradiction', *Asia Pacific Business Review* (In Press).
Sturdy, A. J. and Knights, D. (1996) 'The Subjectivity of Segmentation and the Segmentation of Subjectivity', in Palmer, G. and Clegg, S. R. (eds), *Constituting Management: Markets, Meanings and Identities*, Berlin: De Gruyter.
Sturdy, A. J., Knights, D. and Willmott, H. (1992) (eds) *Skill and Consent*, London: Routledge.
Sutton, R. I. and Rafaeli, A. (1988) 'Untangling the Relationship Between Displayed Emotion and Organisational Sales', *Academy of Management Journal*, 31:3, 461–87.

Terkel, S. (1975) *Working*, Harmondsworth: Penguin.

Thompson, P. (1983) *The Nature of Work*, London: Macmillan.

Thompson, P. and Ackroyd, S. (1995) 'All Quiet on the Workplace Front? A Critique of Recent Trends in British Industrial Sociology', *Sociology*, 29:4, 615–33.

Thompson, P. and McHugh, D. (1990) *Work Organisations*, Basingstoke: Macmillan.

Tolich, M. B. (1993) 'Alienating and Liberating Emotions at Work', *Journal of Contemporary Ethnography*, 22:3, 361–81.

TUC (1996) *Trade Union Action at the Workface: Stress at Work*, London: Trades Union Congress.

Vallas, S. (1993) *Power in the Workplace: The Politics of Production at AT&T*, Albany, NY: State University of New York Press.

Van Maanen, J. (1991) 'The Smile Factory: Work at Disneyland', in Frost, P. J. *et al.* (eds) *Reframing Organisational Culture*, London: Sage.

Van Maanen, J. and Kunda, G. (1989) ' "Real Feelings": Emotional Expression and Organisational Culture', *Research in Organisational Behavior*, 11: 43–103.

Westin, A. (1981) *Whistleblowing: Loyalty and Dissent in the Corporation*, New York: McGraw-Hill.

Wharton, A. S. (1993) 'The Affective Consequences of Service Work: Managing Emotions on the Job', *Work and Occupations*, 20:2, 205–32.

Whyte, W. (1948) *Human Relations in the Restaurant Industry*, New York: McGraw-Hill.

Williams, S. J. and Bendelow, G. A. (1998) *The Lived Body – Sociological Themes, Embodied Issues*, London:Routledge

Willis, P. (1990) *Common Culture*, Milton Keynes: Open University Press

Willmott, H. (1990) 'Subjectivity and the Dialectics of Praxis: Opening up the Core of Labour Process Analysis', in Knights, D. and Willmott, H. (eds), *Labour Process Theory*, London: Macmillan.

Willmott, H. (1992) 'Post-modernism and Excellence: The De-differentiation of Economy and Culture', *Journal of Organisational Change Management*, 5:1, 58–68.

Willmott, H. (1993) 'Strength is Ignorance; Slavery is Freedom: Managing Culture in Modern Organisations', *Journal of Management Studies*, 30:4, 515–52.

Wouters, C. (1989) 'The Sociology of Emotions and Flight Attendants: Hochschild's "Managed Heart" ', *Theory, Culture and Society*, 6:1, 95–123.

Wouters, C. (1991) 'On Status Competition and Emotion Management', *Journal of Social History*, 24:4, 699–717.

9

The Customer is Always Right? Customer Satisfaction Surveys as Employee Control Mechanisms in Professional Service Work

Joan E. Manley

Introduction

The recent history of management innovations includes many programmes designed to improve the quality of goods or services and to increase levels of customer satisfaction. Plans such as total quality management (TQM) and others also claim to provide opportunities for organisations to improve levels of co-operation between managers and employees and to increase the commitment both groups offer to the organisation (Hackman and Wageman, 1995). As such they represent premise-setting opportunities, allowing (as here) a vehicle for administrators to try to re-focus the attention of professional staff on those problems that are of greatest concern to management. Customer satisfaction, as defined by management, can also serve to increase control over professional service work.

The current emphasis of TQM-like programmes in professional service organisations in the US is customer satisfaction. Surveys that measure levels of customer satisfaction have become widely used and are now a part of management strategies to influence professional practice in the clinical setting, the classroom and other locations of professional service work. TQM plans were popular in the 1980s and early 1990s and involved team-based normative strategies stressing customer satisfaction. Such plans were designed to improve quality and involve all employees. They have evolved and now emphasise the more measurement-oriented practices of performance improvement. In the case of hospitals, 'proof of performance improvement' includes measuring customer satisfaction, establishing new performance standards, and thereby gaining greater control over, and routinisation of, professional service work. At the same time, quality improvement through self-directed project teams has evolved into a practice whereby task forces adopt goals and use methods that are centrally determined. In this manner, 'success' is evaluated by others through institutionally defined performance improvement measures.

Professional organisations, such as hospitals, have typically offered employees a work atmosphere with rationalised formal structures and decentralised power and decision making. In turn, professionals provide expert knowledge, serving their own and the organisation's purposes and contributing to the legitimacy of both. Changes in the demand for this knowledge may mean that many actors (e.g. managers, administrators and professionals) seek greater control over its delivery. In manufacturing, TQM's techniques included strategies to encourage greater commitment to the organisation. Similarly, in professional environments, leaders attempt to bring their more loosely coupled systems under closer or tighter control by encouraging the transfer of commitment from work or occupation-directed concerns to more organisationally directed goals. In all environments, TQM offers the potential for increased legitimacy and power to organisational leaders as well as to the external agencies recommending such practices.

Increasingly, TQM programmes emphasise performance improvement as a function of customer satisfaction (rather than group or teamwork). In the case of US health care, hospitals often engage independent firms to administer customer (patient) satisfaction surveys after patients have been discharged. In fact, many hospitals have conducted such surveys for years and their results help to identify some of the problems and concerns of 'customers'. However, in the past, such instruments were the exclusive province of public relations departments. More recently, performance improvement 'councils' or other formal structures periodically review summaries of survey results to prioritise problem-solving efforts with administrators. In the process, administrators gain greater control over the way professional service work is organised, reorganised and measured. Customer satisfaction surveys yield results. But there is often a degree of subjectivity employed in deciding which problems merit attention, who is to be assigned the task of remedying them and how improvement will be recognised and evaluated. In other words and as is the case with TQM more generally (Manley, 2000), although problem solving efforts may be decentralised, the process depends on centralised evaluation of customer satisfaction concerns and centralised assessment of performance improvement.

This chapter begins with a brief summary of TQM and of the organisation of healthcare in the United States. Data for the study were gathered at a suburban hospital in the northeastern United States during 1993–94 and at an urban hospital in the southeastern United States during 1997. I attended council meetings, reviewed minutes of council proceedings and performance improvement reports and interviewed some council members. Neither case study was designed specifically to examine the use of customer satisfaction surveys. However, I will use information gathered at both research sites to describe the process of identifying problems, assigning responsibility for problem solving and measuring performance improvement. In both cases, hospital administrators introduced and implemented such management practices on the back of recommendations from a regulatory body.

These supported management efforts to measure professional work and to demonstrate improved performance, partly for accreditation purposes. I conclude with a brief discussion of the implications of employing customer satisfaction surveys to structure professional service work.

Total Quality Management and Control

With some exceptions, critical reviews of workplace transformations in the US, including the renewed interest in customer satisfaction, have focused on production-oriented enterprises (see Leicht, 1998) and Fortune 1000 organisations (Lawler *et al.*, 1992, 1995), neglecting the process of transforming professional service organisations. This chapter seeks to compensate for this neglect by describing the process of using customer satisfaction surveys to direct a portion of professional work and then speculate on the broader motives of administrators and regulators.

The theoretical constructs of TQM programmes are partly rooted in the concepts of statistical process control. Emanating from the philosophies of such quality 'gurus' as Deming, Juran and Crosby, programmes emphasise the systemic nature of organisations and the importance of leadership. Every member of an organisation is encouraged to identify problems as system errors and to work together towards achieving 'total quality' and continuous improvement (Anderson *et al.*, 1994; Kalleberg and Moody, 1996). However, TQM is also an ambiguous concept (Dean and Bowen, 1994), partly due to the great variation in the composition, breadth and techniques of various TQM programmes (Cole, 1995). The inconsistent use of TQM in professional organisations may reflect the still-unresolved conflict of whether indirect (professional) or direct (bureaucratic) controls better manage uncertainty in organisations (Barley and Tolbert, 1991).

Assessments of the effects of TQM on organisations and their workers can be (loosely) divided into two camps. The first argues that TQM solves many of an organisation's problems, expands the decision-making authority of workers and makes organisations more flexible, competitive and efficient (Brown and Reich, 1989; Lawler, 1996; Lawler *et al.*, 1995; Lincoln and Kalleberg, 1985, 1990; Safizadeh, 1991; Zwerdling, 1980). The second, which is more critical, terms this thrust toward lean production and improved quality as 'neo-Taylorist', noting that it requires greater standardisation and quanitification of work methods (Appelbaum and Batt,

1994; Klein, 1994; Vallas and Beck, 1996). Here it is argued that it is management who define quality, establish the premise upon which an organisation-wide focus on TQM is built, and often use such programmes as opportunities to recentralise or otherwise increase control and commitment as well as to decrease variability in the production process (Barker, 1993; Graham, 1993; Webb, 1996). In this way, TQM, functions as a justification for organisational change (Zbracki, 1998) which is at odds with some of the claimed objectives of optimising quality, learning and co-operation. The central role of management is often obscured amid the rhetoric of management consultants and popular 'success' stories (Appel-baum and Batt, 1994).

Some view TQM, and workplace transformation more generally, as part of a long-term, but incomplete evolution to new organisational forms (Cole, 1995; Heckscher and Donnellon, 1994). The work of Lawler *et al.* (1995) provides support for this view. They report that although some Fortune 1000 firms have dropped TQM programmes, their use has increased steadily overall since the 1980s. More recently, the emphasis on worker involvement and empowerment aspects of TQM has been overshadowed by concerns with quality and customer-satisfaction issues. The new emphasis on performance improvement or 'outcomes measure-ment' in health care organisations suggests a similar trend. Such efforts to gain greater control over professional work may now also be supported by institutional bodies such as government and other regulatory agencies. As we shall see, this is certainly the case with health care organisations in the USA.

The Organisation of Health Care in the United States

There are certain features that characterise the US hospital system (Stevens, 1989). The first is a diversity of hospital types ranging from private and for-profit enterprises, to public and profit hospitals affiliated with medical schools, to public, charitable not-for-profit concerns. In addition, hospitals range in size from very small (less than 50 beds) to very large (1,000 or more beds). Although pluralism is certainly a major characteristic of the American hospital system, most American hospitals focus on acute care and surgery. Social stratification of patients occurs according to their ability to pay as hospitals provide a range of services to patients. Ability to pay depends on access to private insurance, government subsidies or charity rather than personal wealth. As many as 40 million people in the US have no health insurance, without necessarily qualifying for government insurance.

Unlike traditional bureaucratic forms with pyramidal-shaped hierarchies of control, hospitals in the United States consist of alliances of professional and managerial authority (Goss, 1963; Hughes, 1996). Physicians claimed control over hospitals early in this century and their professional dominance extended beyond acute care and surgery to a subordination of other health care professionals such as nurses (Abbott, 1988; Manley, 1995). US hospitals are also in the midst of significant organisational change. Managed care organisations (MCOs), and health maintenance organisations (HMOs) are reorganising traditional professional/managerial relationships in hospitals. These include strategic alliances, partnerships and joint ventures between various types of health care organisations, professionals, and business interests.

Physicians add to the complexities of such organisations – they are often affiliated with, but are not direct employees of, hospitals. There has always been a sort of tension between the medical profession and hospital administrators in negotiating this dual system of control in hospitals. Hospitals need the 'product' physicians offer and physicians, in turn, need the services of the hospital. While physicians still act as independent contractors, with the rise of MCOs and HMOs, professional work is increasingly likely to come under direct control of the organisation (Dill, 1995; Mechanic, 1994). As direct employees of hospitals, nurses, administrators, technicians, cleaning people and others must deal with the bureaucratic authority of the organisation and with the professional authority of the physicians who continue to have the primary responsibility for deciding diagnoses and treatments. Thus, hospitals are complex organisations where those with the greatest expertise – professionals and semi-professionals – are increasingly likely to be organisationally subordinate to non-expert administrators (Abbott, 1991; Dill, 1995; Hafferty and Light, 1995; Leicht and Fennell, 1997; Mechanic, 1994; Tolbert and Stern, 1991).

In addition to this complex health care recipe, hospital administrators and professionals are under tremendous external pressure to cut costs, increase revenues and improve customer satisfaction (Leicht, 1998). Part of this pressure is experienced through regulatory bodies such as the Joint Commission for Accreditation of Healthcare Organisations (JCAHO), the most powerful in the sector. It issues guidelines for hospital accreditation and conducts surveys every three years to check and rate compliance. Failure to achieve a satisfactory rating could result in loss of accreditation, which would render many hospitals ineligible to receive much of their funding and reimbursement for services from state, federal and private insurers. In 1996, it introduced outcome and other performance measures into its accreditation process in order to stimulate continuous improvement (ie, TQM). Customer satisfaction surveys were not actually included in the JCAHO list. Despite this, many hospitals have incorporated the results of such surveys into the routine operations of their internal monitoring bodies. The JCAHO's initiative seems to have provided health care administrators with the opportunity to exert greater leverage or 'clout' when negotiating with professionals over new *management-sponsored* initiatives.

The Process of Measuring Customer Satisfaction

Southern General Hospital (a pseudonym) is a 300-bed acute care facility located in a city of approximately 300,000 people in the southern US. In 1992, Southern began gathering information from former patients shortly after discharge to determine whether their stay was satisfactory and to identify actions that might improve patients' overall evaluation of the hospital. Surveys included some general questions asked of all former patients and some more specific questions concerning the particular department in which the patient had been hospitalised. Since 1996, the survey process has been conducted by a consulting firm on behalf of the hospital. More recently the use of measurement techniques as part of a performance improvement initiative has been recommended by the JCA-HO. Southern institutionalised the JCAHO recommendation, forming the Performance Improvement Council. The council's 18 members include the chief operating officer, five physicians, four registered nurses (RN), representatives from a variety of other technical and clinical specialities and one representative from the hospital Board of Trustees. All other council members also hold positions of middle or upper-level management within the hospital.

Northern General (a pseudonym) is also an acute care hospital with capacity for 250 patients. It is located on the border of two densely populated counties in a northeastern US state. Northern's TQM Steering Council included 14 members. Council members (many of whom were department managers) were poised to select co-operative people to serve on TQM project teams. Team members were usually hand picked by project team leaders or were recommended by other steering council members. Although involvement of a cross-section of employees of differing ranks is part of the TQM philosophy, non-management employees were a distinct minority on problem-solving teams at both Northern and Southern General Hospitals.

In the beginning, the TQM steering council at Northern General received recommendations for problems to solve through a 'suggestion box' process by which any employee could bring a problem to the attention of the council. In practice, in the early stages, many problem-solving initiatives actually reflected the goals and concerns of council members or the chief operating officer (COO). These included problems of parking lot security, slow elevator service and night-time noise in patient areas. In one case, a 'solution' actually preceded a problem. A mini-bus was donated to the hospital to transport patients and visitors to and from the parking lot. A project team was formed and declared that the bus would solve the 'problem' of visitors' safety concerns.

In December 1993, the COO advised the steering council that TQM efforts would be more measurement-oriented and project teams would respond only to problems identified through customer satisfaction surveys. These would be conducted by an outside consulting service. In addition, Northern's steering council and project teams were to become part of the formal organisational structure under the direction of the existing Quality Assurance department.

Patient Satisfaction Surveys

Patient satisfaction survey documentation at Southern General Hospital conveys the impression of the current need to attract and retain a loyal client base in health care as in other competitive professional service arenas. The covering letter speaks of trust and the need for the hospital to 'continue to earn it – every day, with every patient – by offering only the highest attainable value in health care and personal service'. Southern General Hospital competes with four other acute care facilities, several of which have recently been acquired by a for-profit health care organisation. At the same time, one wonders just how much leeway patients have in selecting their providers given the restrictions of various private insurance plans and health maintenance organisations (HMOs). In such a climate, evidence of customer satisfaction and performance improvement are important not only to attract those patients who have a choice of health care providers, but also play an important role in negotiating with insurers.

The patient survey contains twelve sections and a total of 80 questions. In addition, each section provides an opportunity for open-ended comments. Patients are asked their opinion of the entire hospital experience beginning with the admission process, the condition of their room, quality of meals and ending with the discharge process. There are sections dealing with special services the patient may have received, personal issues and the overall impression/opinion of the hospital. The most interesting sections for the purpose of this paper concern the professional services rendered to the patient during their stay including those provided by nurses, physicians, tests and treatments.

Nurses and physicians

The survey section that deals with nurses asks patients their opinion on six indicators of nursing service rendered. On a five-point Likert scale ranging from 'very poor' to 'very good', patients are asked to indicate whether nurses were friendly and/or courteous, prompt in responding to call bells, displayed a good attitude toward patient requests, attended to patient's special needs and how well nurses kept patients informed. Finally, patients are asked to rate the skill of the nurses and are invited to provide additional comments on any particularly good or bad experience. Patients are given no indication of what would constitute skill on the part of nurses and therefore such ratings are purely subjective in nature. Nevertheless, they indicate the impression of high or low skill levels which, given that surveys are measuring customer satisfaction, is the critical indicator.

The section dealing with physician services asks patients how much time the physicians spent with them, whether or not the physician seemed concerned with the patient's questions or worries, how well the physician kept the patient informed and whether or not they were friendly or courteous. As in the section on nurses, questions regarding physicians end by asking the patient's estimation of the skill of the physician and for comments describing a good or bad experience.

Tests and treatments and special services

Patients are asked not how long they may have waited for treatment, but rather their opinions of the waiting time as well as whether personnel expressed concern for their comfort, whether or not professionals explained what would happen during the procedure and if the personnel dealing with the patient were courteous. Once more, patients are asked to rate the skill of professionals; however, in the case of blood testing and IV (intravenous) procedures, patients are given an indication of what would constitute skill. Specifically they are asked to indicate how quickly the professional drew blood or started an IV and whether or not the patient experienced pain. As most medical personnel will attest, while speed and absence of pain may indicate skill or technical expertise, they just as easily reflect 'an easy case' (ie, one where performing the required procedure was not complicated by poor physical condition or advanced age). The section on special services likewise asks patients to rate the overall performance of various specialised areas from cardiac rehabilitation to telephone operators and volunteers. In all cases, the criteria for what constitutes a 'very poor' or a 'very good' rating remain unspecified.

Assignment of Problem-solving Tasks

As was the case with the earlier research at Northern General, the Performance Improvement Council (PIC) meets monthly at Southern General Hospital. Members review results of customer satisfaction surveys together with those of internal quality control and other standard performance indicators. At the time of this research there were 30 project teams in operation to address, evaluate or monitor problems or areas of concern that were identified by customer satisfaction surveys or through existing hospital quality assurance procedures. The purpose of these teams ranged from very specific clinical concerns such as 'to ensure adequate and complete reporting of adverse drug reactions' to somewhat vague or general concerns such as 'to develop essential guest relations' expectations throughout the hospital' or 'to improve communications hospital-wide'. The results of patient satisfaction surveys were presented to the council together with results for each measure during each quarter of the previous year. If surveys reflect a significant difference on any indicator from one quarter year to the next, the council may decide to form a team to address the problem area. Teams are headed by members of the council or their designated representatives.

Despite such formal arrangements and as revealed in a previous case study on the implementation of TQM (Manley, 2000), it is often difficult to link directly the existence of a project team to a specific problem. During the meetings I attended at Southern General, not one team was established to deal with a problem identified either through customer satisfaction surveys or quality assurance practices. Instead, problem areas tend to be concerns shared by many hospital administrators (the exceptions being those problems identified through clinical quality control monitoring, such as high infection rates in a particular area, or a sudden increase in medication errors). Thus, project teams with somewhat general mandates (e.g., improve hospital communications) allow administrators wide latitude when establishing problem-solving teams. The earlier TQM efforts at Northern General reflected similarly loose connections between project team assignments and identification of actual problems (either through customer satisfaction surveys or the action request forms).

In both hospitals, specific complaints identified through the customer satisfaction surveys or received directly by the hospital are also referred to the department in question. Individual professionals identified in the customer satisfaction surveys (ie, those against whom a complaint is lodged or who are identified as having provided less than optimal service) receive additional training or counselling or are simply advised that a complaint has been registered against them by a former patient. Remedial actions are reported to the PIC.

Although questions regarding physicians are a part of the patient satisfaction surveys at Southern General, no discussion of complaints about physicians were reported during council meetings that I attended, nor were physicians mentioned in any of the previous minutes of the PIC (although the council had been established the previous year). In addition, of the five physicians on the PIC, only one regularly attended meetings. The council discussed ways to improve physician attendance such as changing the time of meetings. However, the tendency of physicians to ignore or to avoid these meetings was observed in my previous research at Northern General on the implementation of TQM. As one nurse wryly commented, 'a lot of the doctors have been here for a long time and have outlasted several administrations. They have seen plans come and go and figure if they wait long enough this one will go away, too'.

Perhaps a more accurate assessment would be that those professionals with more power and prestige also have more leeway in deciding which directives they will comply with, particularly in the case of administrative or management concerns rather than technical procedures. But for other professionals, with lesser ability to resist management imperatives, centrally directed improvement plans initiated under the rubric of customer satisfaction can result in disappointment and frustration. Two examples of this are of improving cafeteria service and reducing night-time noise in patient areas.

A long-standing complaint of patients and visitors (and employees) in hospitals is the quality of food. One of the earliest quality improvement efforts at Northern General Hospital was to improve the dining experience. The exact goals for the team charged with improving food service were vague. Over a one-year period, the team met regularly and made several suggestions for improving service. They added a salad bar, increased the variety of menu items, and initiated innovations such as days on which the menu offered types of ethnic food (including 'Italian day'). At the end of this period hospital administrators decided to 'outsource' or subcontract food service to a catering firm. The dietary manager was replaced (asked to resign) and a representative of the catering firm became a member of the project team overseeing improvement in food service. This action served to send a message to other managers that what happened to the dietary manager could happen to them as well. In fact, in a subsequent interview the COO admitted that one outcome of this action was an increase in the co-operation she received from other middle-level managers.

The case of the team charged with reducing night-time noise in patient areas provides another example. Patients often complained in surveys that they were unable to sleep or that their sleep was often interrupted because of noise. The assumption on the part of administrators, patients and others was that such noise emanated from the nursing staff who talked too loudly, especially during shift changes. A team was assigned the task of improving this problem and set about conducting a campaign to accomplish their goals. They made posters that depicted a nurse with lips pursed behind a raised index finger (a widely recognised symbol prompting people to whisper or talk softly). The team met with managers of each patient unit and urged them to counsel their night staff to be extra quiet. But the customer satisfaction in this area did not improve. Upon further study, it was determined that the most disruptive noises were not coming from the nursing staff, but were in fact noises made by other patients. Here, failure to improve does not necessarily imply that insufficient efforts were exerted. When the goals are vague, as was the case with the cafeteria improvement effort, or the problem one that is beyond the control of the professionals involved, a central committee has a great deal of latitude in evaluating success or failure and in structuring additional improvement efforts.

Discussion

Although many hospitals have employed customer satisfaction surveys for some time, incorporating the results of such instruments with outcomes measurement as required by JCAHO increases the likelihood that professionals will see such programmes as coercive strategies and as tools to increase the organisation's legitimacy. In the present case, this is accomplished by attempting to improve professional performance and customer satisfaction and, implicitly, to make more efficient use of professionals and their expert knowledge.

Citing the success of similar programmes in industry, critics call for professional organisations to be more *businesslike* and place emphasis on efficiency, performance improvement, customer satisfaction and continuous quality improvement (rather than post-hoc performance evaluation or simply meeting standards of care established by others). Introducing professionals to outcomes measurement and customer satisfaction as part of the bureaucratic structure reinforced the premise that quality was something that required improvement as defined by productivity and customer satisfaction. Project teams with vaguely specified or wide-reaching purposes, such as improving hospital-wide communication or developing essential guest relations throughout the hospital, provided administrators with wide latitude to structure and measure performance improvement. In this way performance improvement measures and problem-solving that responds to customer satisfaction surveys become institutionalised and combined with the existing quality assessment structure. Greater bureaucratic control over quality assessment as defined by management now exists alongside more technical (or clinical) quality assessment concerns.

Although conducted at different time periods, the experiences of both Northern General and Southern General Hospitals suggest that the specific premise established by outcomes measurement and customer satisfaction surveys is that oversight of such issues is the business of administrators. By adopting TQM and other performance improvement measures organisations can meet the requirements of regulators such as the JCAHO. Equally, hospital administrators gain legitimacy and power. In professional bureaucracies, such a shift towards greater bureaucratic control represents a decrease in the flexibility and autonomy of some professionals. More powerful professionals (physician employees and those in private practice) resisted such management directives by skipping meetings and through other passive strategies rather than with direct opposition. Less powerful ones (nurse managers, department heads such as pharmacists, radiologists, physical therapists and members of other technical specialties) incorporated outcomes measurement and responded to customer complaints within bureaucratic and professional authority structures.

When administrators introduce problem-solving strategies designed for industry to such professional environments, they are not simply planning for improved quality and customer satisfaction. In the process, professionals are encouraged to become more attuned to the organisation's problems and agenda and accept new programmes and initiatives. Designed to improve quality and reduce variability in manufacturing, quality improvement plans are also aimed at achieving increased centralised control and, as here, can serve to both facilitate and legitimate a shift in power from professionals to managers.

References

Abbott, A. (1988) *The System of Professions: An Essay on the Division of Expert Labor*, Chicago: University of Chicago Press.

Abbott, A. (1991) 'The Future of Professions: Occupation and Expertise in the Age of Organisation', *Research in the Sociology of Organisations*, 8:17–42.

Anderson, J.C., Rungtusanatham, M. and Schroeder, R.G. (1994) 'A Theory of Quality Management Underlying the Deming Management Method', *Academy of Management Review*, 19:3, 472–509.

Appelbaum, E. and Batt, R. (1994) *The New American workplace: Transforming work systems in the United States*, Ithaca: ILR Press.

Barker, J.R. (1993) 'Tightening the Iron Cage: Concertive Control in Self-managing Teams', *Administrative Science Quarterly*, 38: 408–37.

Barley, S.P. and Tolbert, P.S. (1991) 'Introduction: At the Intersection of Organisations and Occupations', *Research in the Sociology of Organisations*, 8: 1–13.

Brown, C. and Reich, M. (1989) 'When Does Union-management Cooperation Work? A Look at NUMMI and GM-Van Nuys', *California Management Review*, Summer, 26–44.

Cole, R.E. (1995) 'Introduction', in R.E. Cole (ed.), *The Death and Life of the American Quality Movement*, (3–10), New York: Oxford University Press.

Dean, J.W. and Bowen, D.E. (1994) 'Management Theory and Total Quality: Improving Research and Practice Through Theory Development', *Academy of Management Review*, 19:3, 472–509.

Deming, W.E. (1986) *Out of the Crisis*, Cambridge, MA: MIT University Press.

Dill, A. (1995) 'Case Management as a Cultural Practice', *Advances in Medical Sociology*, 6: 81–117.

Goss, M.E.W. (1963) 'Patterns of Bureaucracy Among Hospital Staff Physicians', in Freidson, E. (ed.), *The Hospital in Modern Society*, (170–94), New York: Free Press.

Graham, L. (1993) 'Inside a Japanese Transplant: A Critical Perspective', *Work and Occupations*, 20: 147–93.

Hackman, J.R. and Wageman, R. (1995) 'Total Quality Management: Empirical, Conceptual, and Practical Issues', *Administrative Science Quarterly*, 40: 309–42.

Hafferty, F.W. and Light, D.W. (1995) 'Professional Dynamics and the Changing Nature of Medical Work', *Journal of Health and Social Behaviour*, 36: 132–53.

Heckscher, C. and Donnellon, A. (1994) *The Post-bureaucratic Organisation: New Perspectives on Organisational Change*, Thousand Oaks, CA: Sage.

Hughes, J.J. (1996) 'Managed Care, University Hospitals, and the Doctor–Nurse Division of Labour', *Research in the Sociology of Health Care*, 13A: 63–92.

Kalleberg, A. L. and Moody, J. W. (1996) 'Human Resource Management and Organisational Performance', in Kalleberg, A. L., Knoke, D., Marsden, V. and Spaeth, J. L. (eds), *Organisations in America: Analyzing their Structures and Human Resource Practices*, 113–32, Thousand Oaks, CA: Sage.

Klein, J. (1994) 'The Paradox of Quality Management', in Heckersher, C. and Donnelon, A. (eds), *The Post Bureaucratic Organisation: New Perspectives in Organisational Change*, Thousand Oaks, CA: Sage.

Lawler, E. E., III (1996) *From the Ground Up: Six Principles for Building the New Logic Corporation*, San Francisco: Jossey-Bass.

Lawler, E. E., III, Mohrman, S. A. and Ledford, G. A. Jr (1992) *Employee Involvement and Total Quality Management: Practices and Results in Fortune 1000 Companies*, San Francisco: Jossey-Bass.

Lawler, E. E., III, Mohrman, S. A. and Ledford, G. A. Jr. (1995) *Creating High Performance Organisations: Practices and Results of Employee Involvement and Total Quality Management in Fortune 1000 Companies*, San Francisco: Jossey-Bass.

Leicht, K. T. (1998) 'Work (If You Can Get It) and Occupations (If There Are Any)? What Social Scientists Can Learn From Predictions of the End of Work and Radical Workplace Change', *Work and Occupations*, 25:1, 36–48.

Leicht, K. T. and Fennell, M. L. (1997) 'The Changing Context of Professional Work', *Annual Review of Sociology*, 23: 215–31.

Lincoln, J. R. and Kalleberg A. L. (1985) 'Work Organisation and Workforce Commitment: A Study of Plants and Employees in the US and Japan', *American Sociological Review*, 50: 738–60.

Lincoln, J. R. and Kalleberg A. L. (1990) 'Work Organisation, Culture, and Work Attitudes: Theoretical Issues', in Lincoln, J. R. and Kalleberg, A. L. (eds), *Culture, Control, and Commitment: A Study of Work Organisation and Work Attitudes in the United States and Japan*, 7–29, New York: Cambridge University Press.

Manley, J. E. (1995) *Border Wars: The Battle to Define and Direct Experts*, Doctoral dissertation, Rutgers University.

Manley, J. E. (2000) 'Negotiating Quality: TQM and the Complexities of Transforming Professional Organisations', *Sociological Forum*, 15:3.

Mechanic, D. (1994) 'Managed Care: Rhetoric and Realities', *Inquiry* 31: 124–8.

Safizadeh, M. H. (1991) 'The Case of Workgroups in Manufacturing Operations', *California Management Review*, Summer: 61–82.

Stevens, R. (1989) *In Sickness and in Wealth: American Hospitals in the Twentieth Century*, New York: Basic.

Tolbert, P. S. and Stern, R. (1991) 'Organisations of Professionals: Governance structures in Large Law Firms', *Research in Sociological Organisations*, 8: 97–117.

Vallas, S. P. and Beck, J. P. (1996) 'The Transformation of Work Revisited: The Limits of Flexibility in American Manufacturing', *Social Problems*, 43:3, 339–61.

Webb, J. (1996) 'Vocabularies of Motive and the "New' Management', *Work, Employment and Society*, 10:2, 251–71.

Zbracki, M. J. (1998) 'The Rhetoric and Reality of Total Quality Management', *Administrative Science Quarterly*, 43:3, 602.

Zwerdling, D. (1980) *Workplace Democracy: A Guide to Workplace Ownership, Participation, and Self-management Experiments in the United States and Europe*, New York: Harper and Row.

10
The Importance of Being Aesthetic: Work, Employment and Service Organisation

Dennis Nickson, Chris Warhurst, Anne Witz
and Anne-Marie Cullen

Introduction

The growing awareness of the sovereignty of the customer has a particular resonance in the service sector, most especially in those organisations involving face-to-face or voice-to-voice interaction. In recent years this has meant the emergence of numerous managerial programmes aiming to maximise 'service quality' and 'customer satisfaction', especially within the context of an increasingly competitive business environment. This chapter is concerned with an important, but so far under-appreciated and largely unexplored form of labour in interactive service work – what can be termed 'aesthetic labour'. Based on the exploratory research project outlined below, our inchoate conceptualisation of aesthetic labour and its relationship with wider debates about the nature of aesthetics and organisation is outlined more fully in Witz *et al.* (1998) and Warhurst *et al.* (2000a). Essentially though we see such labour as a supply of embodied capacities and attributes possessed by workers at the point of entry into employment. Employers then mobilise, develop and commodify these capacities and attributes through processes of recruitment, selection and training, transforming them into 'competencies' and 'skills' which are then aesthetically geared towards producing a 'style' of service encounter deliberately intended to appeal to the senses of customers, most obviously in a visual or aural way. Although analytically more complex, 'looking good' or 'sounding right' are the most overt manifestations of aesthetic labour. In essence, then, with aesthetic labour employers are seeking employees who can portray the company's image through their work, and at the same time appeal to the senses of the customer for those firms' commercial benefit.

This nascent concept builds on, but significantly extends, the seminal work of Arlie Hochschild (1983) whose research on flight attendants led her to coin the term emotional labour. The concept of emotional labour refers to the management or display of appropriate emotions while working, which require service employees to 'induce or suppress feeling in order to sustain the outward countenance that produces the proper state of mind in others' (ibid.:7) again with commercial benefit the aim. Yet, while Hochschild's work referred to 'the management of feeling in order to create a publicly observable facial or bodily display' (ibid.), the corporeal dimensions of emotional labour remained undeveloped. We would argue that the performance of employees can require not just emotion management but the management of appearance. The negation of the corporealness of service employees seemed to us to be increasingly unacceptable given our identification of an increased awareness of this issue on the part of employers (for a fuller explanation of our point of departure from the work of Hochschild, see Witz *et al.*, 1998).

Interestingly, and also with regard to flight attendants, Hancock and Tyler (2000) have analysed the corporeal aspect of employment and work. This work is a useful step forward though is limited for two reasons. First, the aesthetic dimensions of this employment and work is said by these authors to be unrecognised and unacknowledged by management and therefore its labour is implicit (rather than explicit as we have discovered). Indeed, it is 'invisible' to all; management, customers and employees (ibid.:120). Contradictorily but tellingly, it is peer pressure and self-surveillance, rather than management, which then act to enforce any organisational aesthetic code. Second, Hancock and Tyler employ a particular conceptualisation of aesthetic that is beauty and gender specific. As a consequence, their analytical focus is really the 'integral relationship between the aesthetic, the corporeal and the gendered nature of work and employment' (ibid.:113), with the latter skewed towards meaning '*feminine subservience*' (ibid.:109).

To fully understand the nature of aesthetic labour, this chapter will outline and critique existing debates about the nature of services and the service labour process. It will then consider the implications of these aesthetics for the way that employees are recruited, selected and trained for, and work within, the 'style' labour market in Glasgow. Finally, the chapter suggests how the labour of aesthetics is not only produced but also consumed, and by both employees and customers.

The Nature of Services and the Service Labour Process

Much of the services' marketing and management literature points to a range of broadly similar and 'special' characteristics (see, for example, Bowen and Schneider, 1988; Lashley and Taylor, 1998; Schneider, 1994). These characteristics, first noted by Regan (1963), are usually described as intangibility, inseparability and heterogeneity.

Generally services are intangible or at least much less tangible than physical goods or products. This lack of possession means that services generally cannot be owned in the same way that manufactured goods can, they can only be experienced, created or participated in, with the result that customers may find it difficult to evaluate the services rendered (Edgett and Parkinson, 1993). Essentially, 'pure' services are more concerned with a performance rather than an object and unsurprisingly this has engendered the use of theatrical metaphors to characterise service work, an example being Disney's well-known use of 'back-stage' and 'on-stage'. Campbell and Verbeke (1994:96) suggest that a lack of a tangible product makes it difficult for service organisations to differentiate themselves 'since customers do not always understand what information is being conveyed by different competitors'. In response to such problems they suggest that service companies may seek to 'tangiblise' (Bowen and Schneider, 1988:50) the intangible via such things as standardising the exterior and interior of buildings to create an image which customers will immediately recognise, a strategy pursued with some success by McDonald's.

This process can be considered as a reflection of what Segal-Horn (1993) calls the 'hard', more tangible, elements of service that may be more responsive to standardisation. This is a useful distinction that allows us to examine the strategies adopted by service organisations in relation to the 'hard' or 'hardware' and the 'soft' or 'software'. The hardware approach highlights the significance of corporately designed representations of an organisation and its products – for example through marketing material, corporate logos, product design and packaging, and corporate buildings (Schmitt and Simonson, 1997). Within the context of the service sector, hardware can be broadly conceptualised as the physical product (for example, the interior and exterior of a hotel, its rooms, meals, beverages and leisure services). The software consists of the more amorphous notions of service quality, service delivery and the emotional interaction between the producer and consumer. Thus, it could be suggested, that both the hardware and the software comprise the overall product and in the normative view held by much of the services management literature must successfully coalesce to ensure organisational success. Nonetheless, it is widely recognised that within the notion of intangibility, service organisations which offer a product that is, in the words of Lashley and Taylor (1998), 'intangible dominant', increasingly seek to differentiate themselves on the basis of the software aspects such as seeking high quality and 'authentic' service interactions for the increasingly discerning customer.

The key feature of inseparability is the high level of face-to-face or voice-to-voice interaction between buyer (that is, the customer) and seller (that is, the employee) resultant from the simultaneous production and consumption within the service process. This process has been variously described in hyperbolic terms as the so-called 'Moment of Truth' (Carlzon, 1987) as enacted by what Tom Peters has called 'service stars' (Armistead, 1994) or more prosaically as the 'service encounter' (Czepiel *et al.*, 1985). Carlzon's description neatly fits in with the theatrical metaphor. Indeed, this drama-turgical view of service suggests that the organisation, via its front-line staff, has to 'get it right first time' in order to ensure a flawless performance which will result in the customer returning to any given service business. More measured and less prescriptive accounts of the service encounter are concerned to recognise a number of elements that pose a range of issues for organisations, particularly on the issue of quality assurance where 'the consumer finds it difficult to isolate service quality from the quality of the service provider' (Enderwick, 1992:139). Organisations, then, may face significant problems in attempting to manage and control interaction between their front line employees and customers. These problems are given a particular focus when we recognise the notion of heterogeneity.

Heterogeneity refers to possible variations in service quality due to the labour intensity of most service production, such that 'the quality and essence of a service can vary from producer to producer, from customer to customer, and from day to day' (Zeithaml *et al.*, 1985, cited in Edgett and Parkinson, 1993:26). As a result of this possible variance in employee–customer interactions, service organisations may face difficulties in ensuring uniform quality of service between outlets, especially in branded services. Enderwick (1992) suggests that one of the ways in which organisations have sought to resolve this problem is to reduce the human element in service production by the use of mechanisms such as Automatic Teller Machines in banking for example. An alternative to this approach is to 'industrialise' services, by breaking down service operations into minute and discrete simple tasks to enable semi- and unskilled front-line staff to follow a routinised, simple, standardised and often scripted approach to each service encounter, typified by fast food outlets such as McDonald's. This approach has engendered a wide literature which can broadly be seen as polarising between those who see this paradigm as one to be admired and copied (for example Levitt, 1972; Zemke and Schaaf, 1989) and those who excoriate its dehumanising effects (for example, Leidner, 1993; Ritzer, 1996). Enderwick (1992) suggests that increasingly, in addressing this problem of heterogeneity, a key strategy adopted by many service organisa-tions is extensive employee training and development, which recognises and acts upon the idea of front-line staff being crucial to organisational success and, as a result, support for human resource management (HRM), internal marketing, total quality management and empowerment (see, for example, Baum, 1995; Collins and Payne, 1994; Lashley, 1997).

Prescriptive accounts that have supported the adoption of these practices have usually done so on the basis of recognising that the source of competitive advantage for many service firms is likely to stem from a perceived difference in the quality of the service offered to the customer. Thus, differentiation comes from organisations not only meeting, but 'exceeding' customer expectations. Much of the research that has emerged has pointed to a polarisation between, on the one hand, differentiation in terms of service quality (premised on high levels of multi-skilling, staff development and training) and on the other hand, rational standardisation of product and service delivery (with its concomitant deskilling, low pay, low status and alienating work). These strategies could be crudely characterised as McDonaldisation or an empowerment-based strategy to managing employees (cf. Korczynski, this volume). Depending on their market positioning, organisations will respond by pursuing particular human resource management strategies (Lashley and Taylor, 1998).

Increasingly though, more searching research is beginning to emerge that seeks to go beyond prescriptive accounts of the relationship between product market strategies and their concomitant HRM approaches. This more critical analysis of the service labour process is particularly concerned to address the question of the extent to which, even within the context of ostensibly 'empowered' organisations, employees enjoy 'real' autonomy from managerial surveillance, prescriptions and control (see for example, Jones *et al.*, 1997; Sturdy, 1998; and Taylor and Tyler, 2000). A feature of this work is the passing recognition, or more usually the complete elision, of discussions of aesthetic labour. For example, Macdonald and Sirianni (1996:4–5) note how the increasing scope of interactive service work 'has given rise to particularly invasive forms of workplace control and has led managers to attempt to oversee areas of workers' personal and psychic lives that have heretofore been considered off limits'. They further recognise that workers' personal characteristics are increasingly linked to their 'suitability' for particular organisational responses to the quality service imperative. Specifically, they recognise that an 'empowerment' approach, based on the careful recruitment, selection, training and motivation of employees who are likely to make decisions in the service encounter, means 'managers must first select the right kinds of people for the job, often using gender, class, age and other status markers to serve as a proxy for required personality types' (ibid.:7). Nevertheless, Macdonald and Sirianni then concentrate on organisations' attempts to induce attitudinal changes, rather than explore the use of such proxies by organisations.

We recognise here that other work has pointed to the importance of appearance in organisations in the past. Hopfl (2000) offers a fascinating insight into the importance of aural and visual characteristics of individuals in the Society of Jesus – the Jesuits. As she notes, 'Self-presentation – the cultivation of appearance, even a certain theatricality – as a key constituent of organisational success is not a recent invention' (ibid.:191). Thus, as long ago as the sixteenth century, 'the Society was extremely selective in whom it recruited and retained as members . . . it looked in candidates to the Society a pleasing manner of speech and verbal facility, and also good appearance in the absence of any notable ugliness, disfigurement or deformity' (ibid.:203–4). In a more contemporary vein Mills (1951:175), discussing 'salesgirls', utilises a typology developed by Gayle, which includes 'The Charmer', who 'attracts the customer with a modulated voice, artful attire and stance', and in the words of one such salesgirl, 'It's really marvellous what you can do in this world with a streamlined torso and a brilliant smile'. Continuing on a retail theme, in her work on retailing and local economic development Lowe (1991) briefly notes the importance of appearance and image in the recruitment and selection processes of retailers, and particularly high fashion retailers. This leads her to suggest the development by retailers of 'customised service provision' which is provided by suitably 'customised workers' (ibid.:42). More generally, the work of Benét (1972) and McNally (1979) on respectively, secretaries and female office workers, points to the importance of appearance in the workplace.

Thus, there has been and continues to be allusions to the commercial benefit from aesthetics as part of the 'software' of the workplace but analysis of it remains limited. This neglect stems partly from a noting, but little else, of managerial use of aesthetic proxies (Macdonald and Sirianni, 1996; Warhurst *et al.*, 2000a) and partly because any analysis that does occur, quickly progresses into one about women and sexuality within the workplace. Often this shift is legitimate, though sometimes not, as the labour of aesthetics is a broader appeal to customers' senses. The main reason, though, is the lack of *explicit* recognition of employees' appearance and self-presentation as a source of commercial utility for service organisations and that this is intentionally and, we discovered, sometimes systemically, mobilised, developed and commodified by these organisations.

Tyler and Taylor (1998; see also Taylor and Tyler, 2000) are more detailed about the commercial nature of aesthetics in their review of emotional labour in the airline industry and develop this through the conceptualising of the 'exchange of aesthetics' as a 'gift exchange'. This conceptualisation of aesthetics in work is narrower than ours because they analyse it only insofar as it represents a commodification of the female body and it is defined in terms of the commodification of sexual difference. We suggest, on the other hand, that aesthetic labour *valorises* embodiment, so need not be treated as a distinctive mode of exchange beyond contract, and that while there are indeed important gendered dimensions to aesthetic labour, it is by no means only female embodiment that is being commodified as aesthetic labour.

Nonetheless, Tyler and Taylor's work is notable because it draws attention to the commercial utility of the use of aesthetic labour by organisations (see also Hancock and Tyler, 2000). We would argue that, in recognising the notion of both hardware and software described earlier, a number of organisations are increasingly viewing their employees as not only offering competitive advantage in relation to the process of service and the service encounter but, equally, as becoming an integral part of the hardware (that is, literally embodying the image of the company). In this way, for some companies in the 'style' labour market, such as design-led hotels, style bars and cafés and designer fashion retailers, staff are intended to be the embodiment of the company, at which point the human software is transformed into the corporate hardware and becomes in this process an important part of what the customer consumes. Thus, while appearance and the presentation of the self has always been important within organisations it is the more recent attempts to systematically mobilise, develop and commodify these phenomena as an organisational resource that means analysis of contemporary service organisations has to take cognisance of aesthetic labour.

Consequently, the labour of aesthetics now forms a vital part of the aesthetics of service organisation as it is experienced by customers, whether dining in a restaurant, staying in a hotel, drinking in a café bar or browsing in a shop. There is now a growing literature that explores organisational practices *as* aesthetic practices (Gagliardi, 1990, 1996; Strati, 1990, 1996, 1999). Here, we draw on Gagliardi's concept of organisational aesthetics as comprising a 'material culture' and develop this notion to include its animate as well as inanimate components. The labour of aesthetics forms the animate component of the aesthetics of organisation. As we suggested earlier, there is now a conflation of hardware and software, or at least a blurring of a distinction between the two, as organisations seek to mobilise, develop and commodify employees' physical capital (Bourdieu, 1984) into a style of aesthetic labour. The aesthetic labourer becomes 'human hardware'. The labour of aesthetics not only valorises embodied work, but also functions to materialise the aesthetics of service organisation. Gagliardi (1996) refers to the material culture of an organisation as its corporate landscape. Aesthetic codes are written into corporate landscapes in two ways: *in situ* or in the physical place and *in visu* or into the eye:

> The first way consists of writing the aesthetic code onto the physicality of the place, populating it with artifacts; the second consists in educating the eye, in furnishing it with schemata of perception and taste, models of vision, 'lenses' through which to look at reality (ibid.:572).

We will return to this point later. Suffice to note here that in this materialisation, the producers of aesthetic labour must also be sensitive to aesthetic consumption so that a blurring is apparent of aesthetic production and consumption. Interestingly, our research also indicated that customers too both consume and produce the material culture of the service organisation in those organisations in which the labour of aesthetics is most systematically utilised.

Research Locale and Methodology

In any examination of service sector work and employment, Glasgow is an apposite research location. The city is currently reinventing itself, as manufacturing declines and services now account for 84 per cent of employment in the city. Policy-makers would like the new jobs to be the much-vaunted 'knowledge work' or iMacJobs, involving 'thinking' skills. However, most of the jobs being created are in routine interactive services or McJobs, involving 'person to person' skills (for more details, see Thompson *et al.*, 2000; Warhurst and Thompson, 1999).

The research was conducted in Glasgow as the city's employment in services were expanding rapidly, particularly in the retail and hospitality industries. Glasgow ranks second only to London's West End in the Experian Retail Vitality Index with the second largest retail floor space in the UK, excluding new city centre retail developments. The city has the highest concentration of hotel accommodation in Scotland – and the best annual average occupancy rates (Glasgow Development Agency, 1999a). £580m was invested in retail and £555m in hotel and leisure development in the city over 1997–98 (Glasgow Development Agency, 1998a). Tourism increased by 81 per cent during 1991–98 with 1.5m visitors to the city in that last year (*Glasgow Technologist*, 2000). As this boom continues, there were 35 applications to open new bars in Glasgow city centre and 20 applications for new hotels in 1999 alone.

Within this expansion, we have identified an emerging style labour market that encompasses designer-type retail and hospitality outlets, and which is attracting much media and practitioner attention (see, for example, Agate, 1999; Davis, 2000; Frewin, 1999; Henderson, 1999). These perceptions are encapsulated by the labelling of Glasgow as 'the style capital of Scotland, if not all of Britain' (*Sunday Mail*, 1999:25). It is this style labour market from which we developed our conceptualisation of 'aesthetic labour'.

Our research into aesthetic labour is based upon a small pilot project conducted over 1997–98. In addition to the analysis of company documentation and other such secondary sources, a qualitative research methodology was adopted comprising a series of interviews with management and representatives of local tourist boards as well as four focus groups of male and female managers and employees involved in routine face-to-face or voice-to-voice customer interaction work. This primary research encompassed the retail, hospitality and banking industries. There were three main areas of interest, namely: recruitment and selection; training, working and management practices; and the service encounter. These practices were analysed within a triangular configuration of employer–employee relations, employee–employee relations, employee–customer relations (note that 'employer' and 'management' are used interchangeably here for convenience only). More detail of the research methodology and methods can be found in Warhurst *et al.* (2000a). While our resulting conceptualisation is tentative, the results of the research have clear implications for academic understanding of contemporary work and employment in restructuring formerly manufacturing-based economies in the UK and have already been incorporated into policy debates and practitioner initiatives addressing labour markets, social inclusion, training and skills development (see Nickson *et al.*, 2000; Warhurst *et al.*, 2000b).

Research Findings

Aesthetic labour is the mobilisation, development and commodification of the embodied capacities and attributes of employees to produce a favourable interaction with the customer. There is some evidence from our research that the aesthetic skills and competencies being sought by employers from the 'style' labour market – involving, for example, boutique hotels and designer retailers – are now occurring though less systematically in other high street retailers, banks and hospitality outlets (and analysis of this development requires further research). Employer demand for aesthetic skills and competencies is becoming more prevalent because of its perceived commercial utility. These employees are increasingly regarded by employers as part of the service product. It is no surprise therefore that a recent survey of company dress codes in the *IRS Employment Trends* (2000) highlights the importance companies now place on their employees' appearance when dealing with customers. Relatedly, it is important to note that the form of aesthetic being offered may vary from one type of service organisation to another. Aural and visual aesthetics are both important for organisations involved in face-to-face or voice-to-voice customer interaction respectively, for example retail and call centre operations. Similarly, there are different visual aesthetics desired and being produced through their employees by different service companies.

Moreover we would suggest that aesthetic skills do not replace but complement social and technical skills. In the style labour market, management need, and employees use, a matrix of skills: technical, social and aesthetic. Previous research has emphasised the first, current research has brought greater attention to the second, but the third – aesthetic – has been largely overlooked to date. In this respect, we would argue that the term 'person to person' skills noted earlier should be conceived as encompassing not just the social but also the aesthetic. Affecting a desired service encounter requires the use of both types of skills in the style labour market.

Our findings indicate that employers in retail and hospitality are not, in the first instance, seeking potential employees with technical skills. Technical skills tend to be developed once employees are in the organisation, and then usually derived from 'on the job' training. This findings affirm those of the Work Wise report (Farquhar, 1996) that technical skills rank low with Glasgow employers as criteria for recruitment and selection, in fact twenty-third out of twenty-four – just above being a member of a youth organisation!

Faces (and voices) that fit – recruiting and selecting aesthetic labour

At the point of entry it was person to person skills that employers' desired, and it was in the area of recruitment and selection that aesthetic labour had the most obvious resonance, as this process allows for the filtering out of 'inappropriate' people. Each firm had a 'model' employee that management sought to recruit. Sometimes this ideal was informal and implicit; 'it's very much, you know, they walk in through the door and you have a look at them and if they don't walk in presentable then you know, that's it really. You won't give them the chance again' asserted one bar manager, continuing, 'I know that sounds terrible but that's just the way it seems to go in the industry'. In other cases it was formal and explicit. In the recruitment literature of the hotel within the study, it was a person description not a job description that featured, asking prospective employees to assess themselves by the thirteen words that were claimed to characterise that company's image; 'stylish' and 'tasty' for example.

A review of job advertisements in the Glasgow newspapers revealed that employers were using a variety of strategies to signal the type of people they would wish to employ. A number of key phrases occurred regularly in job adverts for the leisure and retail sectors. Examples of these phrases include 'well spoken and of smart appearance' and 'very well presented'. A significant number of adverts asked applicants to enclose a photograph with their application. This practice is strongly countenanced against by the UK Employment Service due to possible discriminatory practices. Indeed, the personnel manager of a hotel within the study acknowledged that the hotel would have utilised such a practice, but had reservations as to its legality.

A number of the participants in the focus group also suggested that there had been a distinct shift in what organisations were now seeking in the potential employee. In particular, they noted the need for applicants to have the ability to present a certain type of persona which encompassed many of the 'dispositions' suggested by Bourdieu (1984); language and dress codes; manner; style, shape and size of the body. Consequently, organisations were looking for the 'right' sort of appearance and 'disposition', and before any technical skills requirement. For example, the personnel manager of a self-proclaimed 'stylish, contemporary' boutique hotel – Hotel Elba,[1] in discussing the recruitment of staff for a new café within the hotel, commented that: 'we didn't actually look for people with experience . . .

because we felt that wasn't particularly important. We wanted people that had a personality more than the skills because we felt we could train people to do the job'.

Allied to this was the way that a certain type of image was portrayed in their recruitment material. The advert (which interestingly for a waiting job was placed in the *Sunday Times*) for these positions contained a picture of a physically attractive young woman (in reality a model) who was felt to embody the desired iconography of the company and its 'ideal' worker. The individuals being sought by the company 'had to be pretty attractive looking people . . . with a nice smile, nice teeth, neat hair and in decent proportion,' explained the personnel manager. Male employees were subject to the same criteria, with a 'neat appearance . . . clean shaven . . . [making] an effort to look neat and tidy and presentable'. For both men and women, the hotel was ideally looking for graduates between 19 and 25 years old. 'There is probably a Hotel Elba look', said the manager, 'not an overly done up person but very, quite plain but neat and stylish . . . young, very friendly . . . people that look the part . . . fit in with the whole concept of the hotel'. The selection of the right individuals was necessarily explicit, the personnel manager stated: 'it's his [the owner's] image and he's very stuck on the whole image thing and it [an employee's appearance] had to be the right image.'

During the interviews, candidates were asked specifically about their attitudes and behaviour with regard to personal appearance: 'You know, it was things like 'Do you care about the way you look or do you only dress up for special occasions?'. . . That was to get an idea of whether people were stylish or did they take care over their appearance'. For other companies in the hospitality industries, employees also had to be 'well groomed, smart, clean and tidy . . . well spoken . . . trendier people . . .', as one bar manager explained. This manager also explained that during recruitment drives, staff poaching was commonplace by restaurants and bars: 'You walk in and if you got a good looking member of staff behind the bar that's [sic] good then you'll try and get them to come and work for you.'

Corporealness was not the only desired aesthetic in recruitment. The voice and accent of employees were also important. In the hotel, the personnel manager was adamant: 'We didn't want someone who spoke in a very guttural manner.' In the banks, again, one respondent claimed that having a 'clear accent' was an absolute essential. Another said 'if you are speaking to people from down south they say "Oh, that's a lovely accent." They always comment, it's the first thing they say to you, "Oh, I love phoning Glasgow. It's a lovely accent." One participant recalled that as part of the interview process for a job in telephone banking, the bank would call them at home to check 'your normal answering phone voice'. Furthermore as one respondent noted, 'You have to be the friendly face at the end of the phone . . . people can hear a smile in your voice'. This also supports evidence from our focus groups where, again, accents were seen to form an integral part of communication processes – an 'aural smile'. Indeed, it is a point often referred to in relation to locating call centres in Scotland. Purportedly, a Scottish accent resonates favourably with customers, implying prudence, friendliness and reliability (Glasgow Development Agency, 1998b; Johnstone, 1997).

Training the aesthetics of labour

Aesthetic labour is not only concerned with *getting into* a job but *doing* the job as well. Beyond recruitment and selection, a common theme that emerged was the extent to which organisations, through training, sought to mould people into the desired personas. This moulding was most obvious in the boutique hotel. After the telephone interview, application with CV and then face-to-face interview to be selected as waiting staff, there was a ten-day induction in which extensive grooming and deportment training was given to the staff by external consultants. Such sessions encompassed hair cuts/styling, 'acceptable' make-up, individual make-overs, how men should shave and the standards expected in relation to appearance. The sessions were intended to relay 'this is what we want you to actually look like . . . you have to understand what "successful" looks like . . . what "confident" looks like'.

As noted before, for employees, this knowledge of aesthetics and the development of their skills and competency in delivering aesthetic labour was intended to complement any social and technical skills. Resonating with those desired by employers identified in Hesketh (1998), the usual people (communication, verbal, personal and teamworking) skills were all important in the companies studied here. Once employed, technical skills and product knowledge were imparted on-the-job to employees; how to present food, take orders, use till equipment and so on, and, in most cases, provided at a very basic level and often through new employees shadowing existing employees – a marked contrasted from the effort and resources put into aesthetic training.

Managerial attention to appearance was also prevalent in several retail outlets. One focus group participant talked about her up-market fashion retail company's prescription of 'model' employees: 'The Leviathan Girl', 'The Leviathan Boy'. This initiative involved the company circumscribing the appearance of their employees such that, for example, 'If I was to have my hair done or anything . . . if you're going to cut your hair in any way, well drastically or highlights, you've got to discuss it with the manager first'. In a supermarket, one employee was sent home to shave her legs. This regulation of appearance and adherence to company standards was, in another company, overseen by the 'grooming standards committee', or in the words of one of the employees, the 'uniform police'. The function of the 'uniform police' was to monitor things such as the employees' skirts, shoes, stockings and jewellery to ensure they all conformed to the company ideal. Role playing was a recurring feature of employees' training. These methods sought to impress upon employees the importance of their own aesthetic capacities and attributes from the customers' perspective and also then develop and mobilise these capacities and attributes as knowledges, skills and competencies so as to be able to differentiate and so better serve customers. The companies instructed their employees in how to approach customers by 'reading' those customers' signifiers, for example body language. An employee of another up-market fashion retail company, Donnatello, related how 'the supervisors do a wee act kind of thing and pretend they are a customer and say "This is a bad example" and "This is a good example" and the good example is when you smile at them as soon as they walk in'. Another retail manager said her staffs' own body language 'can tell you a lot . . . they may not realise the body language that they're giving over is the wrong thing . . . her eye contacts wrong . . . shrugging her shoulders . . . [flicking] the hair'. Working for Leviathan, another respondent claimed, 'is a bit like acting. I mean it's like being in drama school' being taught how to stand and how even to look at customers.

Labour as a manifestation and representation of company image

Companies that deliberately employed aesthetic labour did so believing that it provided competitive advantage. As one manager stated: 'whether it's the bar, the restaurant, the café or whatever . . . if you want to bring people into your pub, if you've got nice looking staff then it brings in people.' This strategy in turn had implications as to who is allowed to present the public face of the organisation. In the financial services focus group, one of the participants noted that, 'In the branch I work in there's nine of us and there's two of them that you wouldn't dream of putting out on the front desk . . . [due to] . . . their appearance, just the way they look'. Similarly the same person recounted how a new employee had been sent by personnel to work in her branch:

> On paper her application was fine [and] she'd been interviewed by our personnel people . . . [but] . . . this woman walked in . . . How she looked and how she spoke . . . it was even the way she wore her uniform, the way her hair and her make up was . . . my manager took an instant dislike to her and the woman lasted seven weeks . . . I mean she was brilliant at [bank telling] but because of the way she looked and the way she spoke he took an instant dislike to her and it all went against her.

Similarly, within a well known restaurant chain, a respondent recalled how a colleague was dismissed for being 'too common', although the ostensible reason was poor performance. In questioning the decision, the respondent (an assistant manager at that time) was told that, 'She wasn't what they considered right for the company, what the customers were expecting'.

When not serving or replenishing stock, employees in one retail outlet were required to stand at 40 degrees near to the entrance of the store, smiling invitingly at prospective customers. Posture here was also prescribed as part of appearance: 'You're not allowed to stand with your arms crossed, cause that's closed,' said a respondent. In another retail store, employees were required to stand in front of a mirror and go though a prescribed appearance checklist before entering the shopfloor. As noted before, many of the retail employees talked of the 'performance' involved in their work, not only managing their emotions, as Hochschild (1983) and others have noted, but also their appearance. 'I think that we've all got the qualification how to present ourselves. I mean that how we're getting training, part of your training is actually how to perform,' said one such employee, continuing; 'we've all got to present the company now. We're not workers as such we're ambassadors now.' Perhaps even more than this. Some companies, such as Hotel Elba, want their staff to be the embodiment of the company.

All management and staff acknowledged the direct – via wandering about – and indirect – via video surveillance – monitoring by management of aesthetic labour and the disciplining of staff that did not conform to company expectations. The bar manager stated bluntly: 'I have on occasions sent people to the toilet to wash their hair or brush their teeth and things like that . . . It's just the image.' Interestingly, the employee who described the operation of the 'uniform police' in her company found it largely unproblematic: 'But I think it's necessary for someone who is in uniform, you know the fact that they have to have their hair tied back or whatever. What's the point in giving somebody a corporate image and then having big bits of hair everywhere'. The 'uniform police are constantly out and about' monitoring employees' image and it was 'a good thing', she insisted. Moreover several participants, representing a range of service industries, suggested that peer pressure would also ensure conformity to company standards on appearance and deportment as individuals who did not comply were felt to be letting their colleagues down. This socialisation was reflected in the view of a participant when she explained how she had confronted management on this issue; 'I said that I feel as though I'm being watched and they said "Well it's making sure the Leviathan standards are being kept up. If someone fails, the whole shop is affected by it." And it's true,' she reflected.

Arguably, employees' acceptance of their company's aesthetic demands might reflect a blurring of the line distinguishing producers and consumers of aesthetics. This blurring begins in the post-entry training intended to develop the new recruits' aesthetic awareness in terms of their existing capacities and attributes, that required by the company and that required of employees. Thus the training developed employees' awareness of their own and the company's image as well as the techniques to conflate the two. At

Elba Hotels, the extensive grooming and deportment training included sessions in which the newly recruited employees were required to walk around Glasgow city centre taking photographs of people and objects which they regarded as being manifestations and representative of the thirteen key words that 'summed up the type of people we wanted working at [the hotel]' said the personnel manager. Words such as such as 'stylish', 'passionate', 'energetic' and 'successful'. A debriefing session was then held with the company personnel manager and the training consultants. 'When we came back we then mixed up all of the photos . . . the groups swapped photos . . . and the other group . . . had to pick out the one that was 'successful' and whether they actually got it right, so that you could key, you know, that look.'

Employees in the retail outlets had also become sensitive through their training and work to the aesthetic labour of employees in other service organisations, noting how other employees used their body language for example. Indeed, there was some evidence that both management and staff had become more reflective about their work and employment, and as a consequence, their actions and attitudes in their non-working lives had changed, as they became more patient and empathetic with staff who served them, and more confident in life generally to approach people. They also became very sensitive to aesthetics generally. This sensitivity extended beyond the workplace to their domestic space as well. Of her involvement in the recruitment, selection and training of her staff, the Hotel Elba personnel manager said 'I was quite aware of it, erm, and I thought if I'm going to be part of this I have to. People are going to look at me and think this is the person who has worked for the company since it began . . . you know if you don't look right then how can you expect these other people to follow in your footsteps.' She admitted that she had 'got caught up in the whole concept of [Elba]', even to the extent of becoming aware of the aesthetics of her domestic food consumption.

The Blurring of the Production and Consumption of Aesthetics

Hotel Elba's new recruits are aesthetically produced to blend in harmoniously with the 'corporate landscape' (Gagliardi, 1996) through training of their appearance and its presentation as manifestation and representation of the company image. Emphasis is placed upon how to look the part and 'get the style right'. Thus, embodied workers are styled, transformed and 'made up' (see du Gay, 1996) during the induction and training period in order to function as the animate components of the corporate aesthetic of Elba Hotels. As aesthetic labourers, they are literally the embodied materialisation of the Elba aesthetic or style.

In addition, managers and employees had become not only sensitive to aesthetics as producers but also as consumers, and the production and consumption of aesthetics became blurred for both. Two retail employees discussed their appreciation of the production of aesthetic labour from the point of view of its consumption. 'You've got to be presentable', one said. 'Like a customer wouldn't trust someone if you're standing there looking awful', the other continued. 'You're sort of PR for the shop', the first opined, continuing, 'Before you start . . . you actually think: "Right, I'll do a once over. Do I look the part?"' Through their training and work, their aesthetic capacities had been mobilised and developed and they realised how much they now critiqued the aesthetics – hardware and software – of other service organisations when they were customers. Their employing organisations wanted their employees to be both producers and consumers of aesthetics, for the latter would help the former. For her interview for the job, for example, one retail employee had to demonstrate her aesthetic knowledge and noted the novelty of such selection techniques in her experience of retail employment:

> I had to go upstairs and make up an outfit for like a day like if a woman wanted to get a suit for work but was going out to a party at night, just change two items . . . I think they were looking to see if I had any sense of what matches, of what can go . . . Stuff like that I thought was quite daunting. I'd never done stuff like that before in retail.

In order for embodied workers to function as aesthetic labourers they must consume the style which is aestheticised in the production of the Elba experience – the *in situ* and *in visu* experience of customers. In order for aesthetic labourers to perform the labour of aesthetics they must first *consume* Elba style in order to engage in its *production*. They must, in other words, learn to present and inhabit their selves in particular ways in order to learn to inhabit their jobs in specifically Elba ways. Appearance, gesture, mannerism and so on – all features of embodied dispositions (Bourdieu, 1984) – are 'made over' or 'made up' in specifically Elba ways. We would suggest that in this respect Elba demonstrates a systematic utilisation of aesthetics on the part of employees and customers in relation to the company image, but the general approach was increasingly being taken by other service organisations judging by the experiences of other respondents.

Because the ideal customer, as with the ideal employee, does not exist without some organisational intervention, some educating of the customer is also required, not least because the market niche within which such organisations operate is still emergent. In relation to the customer's *in situ* (Gagliardi, 1996) experience of a service organisation, the pleasure and satisfaction of the customer depends crucially upon managing to see things 'through the eyes' as they are designed to be seen and experienced. In other words, part of the process of 'consumption' involves taking things *in visu*, through the eyes. The pleasure and satisfaction of the customer is secured by aestheticising a specific *pattern of sensibility*. The 'Elba experience' depends upon a *particular* pattern of sensible responses to the aesthetics of Elba as a *distinctive* way of 'organising service'.

Discussion and Conclusion

What we have demonstrated in this chapter is the existence and significance of aesthetic labour in service organisation. Our pilot research has allowed us to develop and articulate a conceptualisation of this form of labour. Researching the emergent style labour market of Glasgow indicated that aesthetic labour is increasingly being systematically utilised in interactive service work and employment. Examining recruitment and selection, training, working and management practices, and the service encounter, we found that some employers now seek labour that in its appearance and self-presentation appeals to the senses of customers. Moreover, aesthetic skills and competencies required to deliver aesthetic labour are a key feature of such work, more so, at the point of entry, than technical skills. On this basis they should at least be incorporated into notions of the 'people to people' skills noted earlier. In these retail and hospitality jobs, employers require employees who can produce the desired service encounter not simply by managing their feelings, but also by managing their corporealness. In the search for commercial benefit, the utilisation of aesthetics provides for organisational differentiation and/or embodies the specifically desired company image. Within this process we have noted a conflation of the hardware and software aspects of organisational aesthetics.

Though the concept of aesthetic labour has most resonance in the style labour market, we also found that aesthetic labour is becoming more prevalent in more prosaic segments of the service sector, for example in banking. Here, the different aesthetics required by employers becomes most apparent. In banking, emphasis on aural aesthetics is not surprising given that much of this work, especially in Glasgow, is becoming call centre based. To date, the importance of the vocal aesthetic has been under-appreciated and explored within literature examining call centre work (cf. Taylor, 1998) and should be a future focus of such research, we would suggest, as it is a clear feature of employees' experience of employment and how they 'do' their work.

If appreciating and analysing aesthetic labour provides a more nuanced understanding of both the service labour process and current developments in the economic restructuring of cities, then there are not just academic but also policy-making issues arising from our research. Two in particular seem salient; first, the potentially discriminatory practices that might accompany the use of aesthetic labour and, second, the training required for potential and actual employees.

Within the context of Glasgow, as service sector employment rises, so too do the number of non-residents working in the city. The proportion of Glasgow-based jobs held by Glasgow residents has declined to around 50 per cent of the total as the city economically restructures and is projected to decline to 45 per cent by 2007 (Glasgow City Council, 1997; Glasgow Development Agency, 1999b). There is some indication that jobs in the style labour market are being filled by students and suburban commuters. Inner city youth appears excluded. Either employers are excluding these individuals because of a lack of skills or they exclude themselves believing themselves to be not suitably skilled for the jobs available because they are not 'posh' enough (Training and Employment Research Unit, 1999). The danger is that stylish Glasgow forgets about unemployed Glasgow. Past state-driven provision of IT and more IT training for the unemployed, expecting them to then plug into iMacJobs of the knowledge economy, would seem to be less fruitful than expected. By contrast, a Glasgow-based charity, the Wise Group, is attempting to address the exclusion, seemingly evident in the style labour market, by developing a training programme to help unemployed people (for further details, see Nickson *et al.*, 2000). It will be based on understanding the opportunities available and helping participants to develop a presentation style that matches the new expectations of employers.

Having demonstrated the existence and significance of aesthetic labour and the important contributions that it can make to both academic and policy-making debates, it is necessary to assess the extent of aesthetic labour, both within particular city locales and across economically restructuring regions and countries. Our research identified a style labour market in Glasgow, but there were suggestions that features of aesthetic labour are occurring less systematically in other service organisations. Both emergent style labour markets and similar developments, for example in recruitment and selection and training, in other service organisations need to be examined. We are not suggesting that 'some day all service organisations will be this way'. Instead, we believe that the aesthetic will, for the foreseeable future, contribute to the matrix of skills demanded by employers and so significantly affect the experience and nature of work and employment in contemporary service organisation. As a consequence it needs to be further explored and understood.

Notes

1   Pseudonyms are used throughout for the companies drawn from the empirical research.

References

Agate, N. (1999) 'Glasgow's Aisles Better', *Sunday Herald*, 28 November, 24–6.

Armistead, C. (1994) *The Future of Services Management*, London: Kogan Page.

Baum, T. (1995) *Managing Human Resources in the European Tourism and Hospitality Industry – A Strategic Approach*, London: Chapman Hall.

Benét, M. (1972) *Secretary – Enquiry into the Female Ghetto*, London: Sidgwick and Jackson.

Bourdieu, P. (1984) *Distinction: A Social Critique of the Judgement of Taste*, London: Routledge.

Bowen, D. and Schneider, B. (1988) 'Service Marketing and Management: Implications for Organisational Behaviour', *Research in Organisational Behaviour*, 10, 43–80.

Campbell, A. and Verbeke, A. (1994) 'The Globalisation of Service Multinationals', *Long Range Planning*, 27:2, 95–102.

Carlzon, J. (1987) *Moments of Truth*, Cambridge, MA.: Ballinger Publishing.

Collins, J. and Payne, A. (1994) 'Internal Marketing: A New Perspective for HRM', *European Management Journal*, 9:3, 261–70.

Czepiel, J., Solomon, M. and Suprenant, T. (1985) *The Service Encounter: Managing Employee/Customer Interaction in Service Businesses*, Lexington, MA: D. C. Heath.

Davis, A. (2000) 'Bonnie on Clyde', *Caterer & Hotelkeeper*, 9 March, 35.

du Gay, P. (1996) *Consumption and Identity at Work*, London: Sage.

Edgett, S. and Parkinson, S. (1993) 'Marketing for Service Industries: A Review', *Service Industries Journal*, 13:3, 19–39.

Enderwick, P. (1992) 'The Scale and Scope of Service Multinationals', in Buckley, P. and Casson, M. (eds), *Multinational Enterprises in the World Economy – Essays in Honour of John Dunning*, Aldershot: Edward Elgar.

Farquhar, C. (1996) *Altered Perspectives*, Glasgow: Work Wise.

Frewin, A. (1999) 'Hospitality Staff Find Their Faces Don't Fit', *Caterer & Hotelkeeper*, 18 November, 4.

Gagliardi, P. (ed.) (1990) *Symbols and Artifacts*, Berlin: de Gruyter.

Gagliardi, P. (1996) 'Exploring the Aesthetic Side of Organisational Life', in Clegg, S. R., Hardy, C. and Nord, W. (eds), *Handbook of Organisational Studies*, London: Sage.

Glasgow City Council (1997) *Regenerating the Economy: Economic Development Strategy and Programmes*, Glasgow: Glasgow City Council.

Glasgow Development Agency (1998a) *Glasgow's Renewed Prosperity*, Glasgow: Glasgow Development Agency.

Glasgow Development Agency (1998b) *Glasgow Calling*, Glasgow: Glasgow Development Agency.

Glasgow Development Agency (1999a) *Upbeat Glasgow*, Glasgow: Glasgow Development Agency.

Glasgow Development Agency (1999b) *Glasgow Economic Monitor*, Spring, Glasgow: Glasgow Development Agency.

Glasgow Technologist (2000) 'Glasgow Tourism', 21.

Hancock, P. and Tyler, M. (2000) 'The Look of Love – Gender and the Organization of Aesthetics', in Hassard, J., Holliday, R. and Willmott, H. (eds), *Body and Organization*, London: Sage.

Henderson, C. (1999) 'Help wanted: only the hip and trendy need apply', *Sunday Herald*, 7 November, 24.

Hesketh, A. (1998) 'Reward in This Life', *Guardian*, Higher supplement, 24 February, 11.

Hochschild, A. (1983) *The Managed Heart*, Berkeley: University of California Press.

Hopfl, H. (2000) ' "*Suaviter in modo, fortiter in re*": Appearance, Reality and the Early Jesuits', in Linstead, S. and Hopfl, H. (eds), *The Aesthetics of Organisation*, London: Sage.

IRS Employment Trends (2000) 'Dressed to impress', 695, 4-16.

Johnstone, A. (1997) 'An Engaging New Line in Sales Talk', *Herald*, 14 August, 13.

Jones, C., Nickson, D. and Taylor, G. (1997) 'Whatever it Takes? Managing "Empowered" Employees and the Service Encounter in an International Hotel Chain', *Work, Employment and Society*, 11:3, 541-55.

Lashley, C. (1997) *Empowering Service Excellence – Beyond the Quick Fix*, London: Cassell.

Lashley, C. and Taylor, S. (1998) 'Hospitality Retail Operations Types and Styles in the Management of Human Resources', *Journal of Retailing and Consumer Services*, 5:3, 153–65.

Leidner, R. (1993) *Fast Food, Fast Talk, Service Work and the Routinization of Everyday Life*, Berkeley: University of California Press.

Levitt, T. (1972) 'Production-line Approach to Service', *Harvard Business Review*, 50:5, 41–52.

Lowe, M. (1991) 'Trading Places: Retailing and Local Economic Development at Merry Hill, West Midlands', *East Midland Geographer*, 14, 49–60.

Macdonald, C. and Sirianni, C. (1996) 'The Service Society and the Changing Experience of Work', in Macdonald, C. and Sirianni, C. (eds), *Working in the Service Society*, Philadelphia: Temple University Press.

McNally, F. (1979) *Women for Hire: A Study of the Female Office Worker*, Basingstoke: Macmillan.

Mills, C. Wright (1951) *White Collar – The American Middle Class*, New York: Oxford University Press.

Nickson, D., Warhurst, C. and Watt, A. (2000) 'Learning to Present Yourself: 'Aesthetic Labour' and the Glasgow Example', *Hospitality Review*, 2:2, 38–42.

Regan, W. (1963) 'The Service Revolution', *Journal of Marketing*, 2:3, 247–53.

Ritzer, G. (1996) *The McDonaldization of Society: An Investigation into the Changing Character of Contemporary Social Life – Revised Edition*, London: Pine Forge Press.

Schmitt, B. and Simonson, A. (1997) *Marketing Aesthetics*, New York: Free Press.

Schneider, B. (1994) 'Human Resource Management: A Service Perspective', *International Journal of Service Industry Management*, 5:1, 64–76.

Segal-Horn, S. (1993) 'The Internationalization of Service Firms', *Advances in Strategic Management*, 9, 31–55.

Strati, A. (1990) 'Aesthetics and Organisational Skill', in Turner, B. (ed.), *Organisational Symbolism*, Berlin: de Gruyter.

Strati, A. (1996) 'Organisations Viewed Through the Lens of Aesthetics', *Organisation*, 3:2, 209–18.

Strati, A. (1999) *Organisation and Aesthetics*, London: Sage.

Sturdy, A. (1998) 'Customer Care in a Consumer Society: Smiling and Sometimes Meaning It', *Organisation*, 5:1, 27–53.

Sunday Mail (1999) 'When Helena Pops Out She Heads for Scotland', 24 October, 25.

Taylor, S. (1998) 'Emotional labour and the new workplace', in Thompson, P. and Warhurst, C. (eds), *Workplaces of the Future*, Basingstoke: Macmillan.

Taylor, S. and Tyler, M. (2000) 'Emotional Labour and Sexual Difference in the Airline Industry', *Work, Employment and Society*, 14:1, 77–95.

Thompson, P., Warhurst, C. and Callaghan, G. (2000) 'Human Capital or Capitalising on Humanity? Knowledge, Skills and Competencies in Interactive Service Work', in Prichard, C., Hull, R., Chumer, M. and Willmott, H. (eds), *Managing Knowledge: Critical Investigations of Work and Learning*, Basingstoke: Macmillan.

Training and Employment Research Unit (1999) *Jobs Growth: From Perception to Reality*, University of Glasgow.

Tyler M. and Taylor, S. (1998) 'The Exchange of Aesthetics: Women's Work and "The Gift"', *Gender, Work and Organisation*, 5:3, 165–71.

Warhurst, C. and Thompson, P. (1999) 'Why the McJob and not the iMacJob Threatens to Dominate our Economy', *Sunday Herald*, 21 November, 18.

Warhurst, C., Nickson, D., Witz, A. and Cullen, A. M. (2000a) 'Aesthetic Labour in Interactive Service Work: Some Case Study Evidence from the "New" Glasgow', *Service Industries Journal*, 20:3, 1–18.

Warhurst, C., Nickson, D., Witz, A. and Watt, A. (2000b) 'Employment, Skills and Training in "Aesthetic Labour"', *Journal of Lifelong Learning Initiatives*, 17, 22–3.

Witz, A., Warhurst, C., Nickson, D. and Cullen, A. M. (1998) 'Human Hardware: Aesthetic Labour in the New Workplace', paper to the Work, Employment and Society Conference, University of Cambridge.

Zeithaml, V., Parasuraman, A. and Berry, L. (1985) 'Problems and Strategies in Services Marketing', *Journal of Marketing*, 49 (Spring) 33–46.

Zemke, R. and Schaaf, D. (1989) *The Service Edge: 101 Companies that Profit from Customer Care*, New York: American Library.

11
Relationship Marketing, E-commerce and the Emancipation of the Consumer

James Fitchett and Pierre McDonagh

This short chapter considers three related areas. It starts with a comment on the emerging practice known as relationship marketing; goes on to consider this in the context of the e-commerce phenomenon; and extends this discussion to include the consumer, whose interests may be threatened by both of these initiatives. Here we argue that relationship marketing should be considered as a hegemonic practice in relation to consumers. We then develop this idea in relation to citizenship more generally and the notion of a 'computer mediated cyborg citizen'. This product of human and computer synergy, typified by e-commerce, can seem as emancipated from organisational power, but, in 'virtuality' at least, is more often characterised by high levels of social control.

The Evolution of Relationship Marketing

The 'classics' of marketing began to emerge during the middle of the last century from American scholars with clear economic interests (e.g. Kotler, 1972; Smith, 1956; see also Ennis and Cox, 1988). They tended to emphasise the importance of competitive business strategies based on factors other than price. 'Exchange' based views of the market emerged later, where the consumer transaction and the satisfaction of customer needs and wants were offered as an alternative to the product and sales driven approach (see Morgan and Sturdy, 2000).

But markets change. Even when profitable, they may mature and saturate. It seems likely that the 'exchange' paradigm itself is doomed to share the fate of sales and pricing driven philosophies. Even now, the notion of relationship marketing, which initially developed from the exchange-based view, has started to supplant its progenitor. Relationship marketing's principal attraction is the possibility of 'mutually beneficial' exchanges. It boasts sophisticated consumers; avoids the limited returns available from a single transaction; considers the cost of retaining versus the

191

cost of recruiting consumers; enthusiastically embraces new technological opportunities allowing for the rapid transmission, storage and analysis of market data; and, in return, is rewarded by commercially beneficial 'trust' and 'loyalty'. Given these advantages, it is hardly surprising that relationship marketing (RM) and 'Customer Relationship Management (CRM),[1] have entered the rhetoric of marketing decision making, marketing theory and management generally (see Sturdy, this volume).

Reading these two paradigm shifts together, it is interesting to note how the emergence and subsequent establishment of, first, transaction and then, relationship marketing have relied heavily on emancipatory rhetoric. Both paradigms aim to offer the consumer more and both use notions such as consumer sovereignty to legitimise the (r)evolutionary changes proposed. The exchange-based paradigm stated that organisations must market, not what they can produce and sell, but what consumers want and need. RM, conversely, states that organisations must look beyond the individual exchange and recognise their duty and purpose as supporting mutually beneficial relationships with customers. This has very significant implications for the way work is organised and experienced. If the trend is indeed towards greater homogeneity between competing products and services, then the *only* method of long-term competitive differentiation is the mode and standard of service delivery (see also Korczynski, this volume). Customer service is, according to RM, the only means of sustaining competitiveness and ensuring market survival. It may be, as a consequence, that marketing generally is moving towards greater appreciation of consumer power, as well as greater respect for, and understanding of, consumers (see also Hodgson, this volume). Higher levels of service quality are said to emerge as a necessary condition and consequence of this market.

E-commerce and the Fulfilment of the Dreams of RM

The debates within marketing over the potential application of RM principles were initially limited due to a general failure to identify any practical and applicable means of implementing RM. Seeing consumers in terms of long-term relationships or focusing on service quality are all very well in theory, but they are hard to put into practice given the existing ways in which business success is seen and evaluated. In other words, while it may seem perfectly reasonable to sacrifice short-term market achievements in the present for long-term growth and market presence in the future, orthodox methods of organisational performance evaluation (e.g., market share, growth and sales volume) remain. These require (at least a quasi) compliance to tried, tested and accepted marketing procedures. However, the emergence of new technologies in the form of internet-based electronic commerce (e-commerce) have had a significant impact on accelerating the transition from exchange to relationship marketing philosophies. In addition to the commonly discussed marketing implications of the World Wide Web, such as larger markets, 'mass customization' (Whiteley 2000), collapsed distribution channels and so on; e-commerce has provided a *practical* medium through which to further the potential benefits of RM.

Various claims have been made about the relational basis of the organisation – customer connection. For example, it is suggested that:

> E-commerce means a major shift in the balance of power, much more efficient mechanisms for searching among potential suppliers means much more information into the hands of greatly empowered consumers (Microsoft 2000 in the *Economist*, 2000).

Potentially, as well as giving customers access to a market, the world of online commerce can provide the information marketers need to do so more effectively, both in terms of customer feedback and from recording their behaviour as they 'surf' and search. However, given the potential that such information has, it is not clear whether there is an obligation on the part of the organisation to explain to the general public just what their 'cookies'[2] are, why they exist, and what impact they have on market research and organisational decision-making?

These technologically based developments and the associated changes claimed for the customer–organisation relationship are occurring in what has come to be known as 'cyberspace'. But 'cyberspace' itself is rather an elusive concept:

> A consensual hallucination experienced by billions of legitimate operators, in every nation, by children being taught in mathematical concepts . . . . Unthinkable complexity. Lines of light ranged in the nonspace of the mind, clusters and constellations of data (Featherstone and Burrows, 1995:6 from Gibson, 1994).

More straightforwardly, it can be seen as 'a new . . . parallel universe created and sustained by the world's computers and communication lines' (Venkatesh, 1998:664). What is important here is that, through cyberspace, the customer-organisation relationship is transforming. This expansion is part of the business community's move to computer mediated communication and may be a product of what Besser (1995) sees as technology increasingly replacing public spaces and human interaction. This is part of a broader process of social change characterised by globalisation; a shift towards an economy based on knowledge and information; and the increasing prominence of technology and Information and Communication Technologies (ICTs) in everyday life (see OECD, 2000).

E-commerce is defined as trade which takes place over the Internet, usually through a buyer visiting a seller's website and making a transaction there (*The Economist*, 2000:6). It is expected that the effects will be strong in terms of more competitive pricing, but it is less often acknowledged that such price gains may have other costs. Whether the predictions of the more optimistic commentators of ICT will be realised and e-commerce really will 'right the wrongs' of the past, by making organisation–customer power relations more equal, has yet to be seen. Nor is it clear that e-commerce itself is the apotheosis of all that is best and most desirable in RM.

As we have seen, RM is considered distinctive in marketing, in the sense that it focuses on a continuum of transactions and a series of repeat purchases rather than a series of discrete and perceptually singular exchanges. Instead of pinning organisational success to the principle of customer satisfaction, RM emphasises the notion of customer retention (Rosenberg and Czepiel, 1984). In place of discursive practices such as *need satisfaction* to represent consumer motivation, RM introduces new terms such as *promise fulfilment* and constructing *good relations* with customers. Similarly, while traditional marketing discourse has presented consumer-complaining behaviour as a negative outcome of exchange (the very term *'complaining'* brings with it a host of negative associations), RM depicts it as a potentially positive interaction which, if managed correctly, can lead to greater customer loyalty and retention which, in turn, reduces overall marketing costs (DeSouza, 1992).

These characteristics of RM are seen as especially suited to e-commerce. It not only continues to provide consumers with opportunities to establish direct contact with front-line personnel in an organisation (and vice versa), but opens up the back office as well. Consumer histories, preferences and buying habits can be recorded and may provide the information needed to manage a continuum of exchanges. Moreover, the interactive character of this process should allow organisations to develop more effective consumer retention strategies through monitoring, rewarding and reminding consumers about their products and services. This same interactive feature allows consumers to voice concerns, complaints and suggestions in a direct manner and, more importantly, enables the organisation to respond directly and specifically to individual consumer inputs (Turban *et al.*, 1999).

Whereas prior conventions in marketing tended to represent the consumer as a passive and receptive unit that was acted upon (i.e., someone marketers sought to satisfy, who could be influenced attitudinally and behaviourally by communications), RM views the consumer as a highly active agent. This seemingly liberal (and liberating) principle seeks to acknowledge consumers' own productive endeavours and personal motivations for engaging in relationships with organisations and, at the same time, brings the idea of negotiation and partnership to the forefront of the marketing discourse (Goodwin, 1988).

The application of e-commerce technologies and the incorporation of RM ideas can be seen as providing organisations with both a justification for, and the means to establish, effective and legitimate expressions of the market and market relations. And these advantages come in addition to long-term growth through customer retention and the stability provided by customer loyalty. To customers, it grants organisational acknowledgement of consumer intention and motivation by identifying the constructive and productive aspects of consumption. Further, it is claimed that, the marriage of RM and e-commerce offers a greater voice and input into organisational strategic decision-making for employees, suppliers and stockholders (Reingen and Kernan, 1986; Schlesinger and Heskett, 1991). In this account then, RM, CRM and the Internet are depicted as progressive and positive for marketing theory, overcoming the problems inherent in micro-focused, managerialist-orientated, exchange-based models.

Reading RM as a Hegemonic Practice

Yet such claims are more rhetorical than real. Marketing principles may proclaim the consumer is now really the 'king' and argue the organisation will only prosper if the consumer's *long-term* desires and dreams are considered central to its activities, but in practice, organisation strategy and marketing activity are *inevitably* determined by managers, as agents of the organisation, not representatives of the customer.

Whatever emancipatory discourse is ascribed to RM and e-commerce, and whatever the supposed benefits for the consumer, these notions, neither challenge, nor explicitly confront the prevailing ideology. RM lays out an agenda of consumer commitment on the part of the organisation which explicitly seeks to redress existing inequalities in this 'relationship'. The rhetoric surrounding e-commerce and its emancipatory potential is probably the clearest example of this. However, the ideology of RM, mediated through 'cyberspace' via technologies such as the Internet, serves only to socialise and naturalise power differentials (Fitchett and McDonagh, 2000). The rhetoric of the *social-relationship* to position organisation-consumer interactions is hegemonic (Baudrillard, 1998). By assessing the implications of the RM discourse on the redefinition on the citizen as 'collaborator/partner' (see Zineldin, 1998) rather than self-motivated need satisfier, we contend that RM has failed to achieve greater representation of the individual.

It should be noted that it is organisations and organisational interests that have chosen to move towards the idea of a 'relationship'. It is the agents of organisations rather than consumers, which choose to describe interactions in the market as a partnership. With the exception of O'Malley (1999), there has been little effort to establish whether consumers actually want *relationships* with the organisations they have come to rely on for products and services. Indeed, e-commerce actually offers them the opportunity to be less loyal – they can exercise far greater promiscuity, deceit and subterfuge when using the Internet as a channel of exchange than was the case before.

Even where 'relationships' exist, there is little evidence of 'equality' either between organisation and customer or between customer and customer. While the firm may choose to define their customers as 'partners', select those groups of people with whom it is prepared to establish relationships, and prohibit relationships considered undesirable or unprofitable; the consumer is much less able to make such demands. As a result, it is difficult to believe in the mutuality of this relationship. Wherever the public rhetoric may lead us, it is important to remember that the RM discourse tends to be justified to the extent that it enhances organisational objectives. Indeed, it has been sold to decision makers on the basis that it will increase profits and market share, facilitate stability through establishing long term 'switching costs' (DeSouza, 1992) for customers, make marketing expenditure more efficient and so on (see Sturdy, this volume). The following quote from Buchanan and Gilles (1990:525) provides a good example:

> By chasing new customers at the expense of retaining existing ones, companies are, quite literally, missing a golden opportunity. Our clients have found that if they increase the rate at which customers are retained by as little as 5 per cent, profitability can move in some cases, by over 100 per cent. In other words: Customer Retention adds profit to the bottom line.

It seems that the terms and conditions of any relationship between organisation and consumer are not determined or negotiated mutually, but rather imposed by the organisation (see Gabriel and Lang, 1995, Chapter 7). And this, despite the apparently greater opportunities offered by e-commerce for consumers to express their views and opinions.

Nor is this imbalance of power ameliorated as the 'relationship' progresses. Rather, once the consumer has agreed to the conditions imposed by the organisation, he or she has little ability to renegotiate them. Inevitably all relationships, whether they are between consumers and organisations, colleagues, or spouses, have the potential to become conflictual. Either party may become dissatisfied and seek to adjust, resolve or dissolve understandings. However, unlike most social pairings, consumer–organisation relationships attribute judicial responsibilities unequally. The organisation typically has both the legislative authority and economic power to resolve disagreements in its own favour. While the individual consumer must personally accept the consequences of such adjudications, the organisation does not (McMurty, 1998).

On the Cyborg Citizen

It seems, from the examination of the underlying character of organisation–consumer relationships above, that the promise of greater consumer power through media such as e-commerce is, at best, severely limited and, at worst, actively misleading. RM began as a comparatively neutral concept in Business-to-Business exchanges, where mutual benefits could be secured through long-term commitments in product delivery and service provision. But it is far less appropriate in situations where resources and power bases are unequal and where interests vary considerably. Internet technologies may offer new opportunities and choices to consumers, but they do not provide a revolutionary means of addressing the political economy of consumption. By incorporating technology at a distance into the consumption act, the consumer has merely become a 'cyborg citizen' whose virtual control is limited through a typed or clicked role-play, a marriage of human and machine, a closely monitored computer mediated transaction.

RM logic denies the role of citizenry and regulation and, in the process, reinforces existing imbalances of power which favour the corporation over the customer in any relational episode (cf. Hodgson, this volume). E-commerce is a market rather than a radical new paradigm. The rhetoric of developing relationships can be applied in many contexts, some of which seem to be rather more credible and authentic than others. The relational terms of e-commerce transactions have some unique and contradictory features which do not necessarily favour or enhance consumer representation and expression. Some cyborg citizens argue they can perform many personally emancipatory acts through e-commerce: sexual promiscuity, gender or role swapping may be expressed through the web's biggest exchange item, the consumption of pornography. But such relations in their current form do not, and cannot equalise the power imbalance between consumers and organisations since it is organisations themselves that have greatest access to technologies and organisations that have the most influence over the way those technologies are developed. It seems, here, that the relations between organisation and consumer are based on rather more asymmetrics of power and are significantly more complex and contradictory than the RM literature often assumes.

Notes

1 On-line case studies are offered to browsers on *microsoft.com* of companies using CRM to improve service quality (e.g., Murphys, The Royal Bank of Scotland, NTL and Barclays Bank)

2 'Cookies' are electronic 'tags' that can be programmed to attach to an individual's computer when they access certain websites. They may contain

information about preferences or personal details that can be used (among other functions) to target marketing campaigns. Since individuals can programme their computers to reject 'cookies' this process is deemed to be consensual.

References

Baudrillard, J. (1998) *Consumer Society: Myths and Structures*, London: Sage.

Besser, H. (1995) 'From Internet to Information Superhighway' in Brook, J. and Boal, I. A. (eds), *Resisting the Virtual Life: The Culture and Politics of Information*, 59–69, San Francisco: City Lights.

Buchanan, R. and Gilles, C. S. (1990) 'Value Managed Relationships: The Key to Customer Retention and Profitability', *European Management Journal*, 8:4, 523–6.

DeSouza, G. (1992) 'Designing a Customer Retention Plan', *The Journal of Business Strategy*, 13:2, 24–8.

The Economist (2000) 'Shopping Around the Web: A Survey of E-commerce', 26 Feb–3 Mar, 354.

Ennis, B. M. and Cox, K. K. (1988) *Marketing Classics: A Selection of Influential Articles*, 6th edn, London: Allyn and Bacon.

Featherstone, M. and Burrows, R. (eds) (1995) *Cyberspace, Cyberbodies, Cyberpunk: Cultures of Technological Embodiment*, London: Sage.

Fitchett, J. A. and McDonagh, P. (2000) 'A Citizens Critique of Relationship Marketing in Risk Society', *Journal of Strategic Marketing*, 8, 209–22.

Gabriel, Y. and Lang, T. (1995) *The Unmanageable Consumer: Contemporary Consumption and its Fragmentations*, London, Sage.

Gibson, W. (1994) *Neuromancer*, London: Harper Collins

Goodwin, C. (1988) ' "I Can Do It Myself": Training the Service Consumer to Contribute to Service Productivity', *Journal of Services Marketing*, 2:4, 71–8.

Kotler, P. (1972) 'A Generic Concept of Marketing', *Journal of Marketing*, 36 (April), 46–54.

McMurty, J. (1998) *Unequal Freedoms: The Global Market as an Ethical System*, Connecticut: Kumarian Press.

Morgan, G. and Sturdy, A. J. (2000) *Beyond Organisational Change – Discourse, Structure and Power in UK Financial Services*, London: Macmillan.

OECD (2000) *Economic and Social Implications of E-commerce*, Paris: OECD [available online at www.oecd.org].

O'Malley, L. (1999) 'Consumer–Organisational Relationships as "Interpersonal Relationship": A Study of Consumer Views', in McLoughlin, D. and Horan, C. (eds), *Interactions, Relationships and Networks: Towards the New Millennium*. Working Paper presented at the 15th Annual IMP conference, Dublin: UCD.

Reingen, P. H. and Kernan, J. G. (1986) 'Analysis of Referral Networks in Marketing Methods and Illustration', *Journal of Marketing Research*, (November), 370–8.

Rosenberg, L. J. and Czepiel, J. A. (1984) 'A Marketing Approach to Customer Retention', *Journal of Consumer Marketing*, 1, 45–51.

Schlesinger, L. A. and Heskett, J. L. (1991) 'Enfranchisement of Service Workers', *California Management Review*, (Summer), 83–100.

Smith, W. R. (1956) 'Product Differentiation and Market Segmentation as Alternative Strategies', *Journal of Marketing*, July, 3–8. Reprinted in Ennis, B. M. and Cox, K. K. (eds) (1988) *Marketing Classics*, 6th edn, London: Allyn and Bacon.

Turban, E., Lee, J., King, D. and Chung, H. M. (1999) *Electronic Commerce: A Managerial Perspective*, London: Prentice Hall.

Venkatesh, A. (1998) 'Cybermarketscapes and Consumer Freedoms and Identities', *European Journal of Marketing*, 32: 7/8, 664–76.

Whiteley, D. (2000) *E-commerce: Strategy, Technology and Applications*, London: McGraw-Hill.

Zineldin, M. A. (1998) 'Towards an Ecological Collaborative Relationship Management – A 'Co-operative' Perspective', *European Journal of Marketing*, 32: 11–12, 1138–64.

12
Epilogue: Servicing as Cultural Economy

Paul du Gay

For a long time, as a number of the contributors to this volume acknowledge, the growth of service work – in all its plurality – did not receive the attention its burgeoning social and economic importance demanded or required. There were of course, a number of reasons for the relative neglect of servicing, including its (gendered) representation as somehow less than 'productive'(Allen and du Gay, 1994). Over time, however, neglect gave way to selective reappropriation, as industrial sociologists (as they used to be called), among many others, began to latch on to the possibilities of representing service work as a derivative of manufacturing labour. Here the focus of attention was on the task-based elements of certain forms of routine service-work (McJobs) and the conceptual vocabulary was one of 'rationalisation', 'instrumentalisation', 'commodification', 'economisation' and so on and so forth.

In other words, 'servicing' grew in analytic importance only insofar as it was able to be represented as another form of industrial – basically manufacturing derived – labour (du Gay, 1996; Macdonald and Sirianni, 1996). No doubt it would be foolish to suggest that such continuities did not and do not exist. Quite obviously many forms of work classified as 'service' – catering, say – contain significant elements of manufacturing labour. Equally, while manufacturing may well involve the production of tangible objects, those products needed to be researched, designed, financed and marketed. Forms of 'service' work are therefore a constitutive feature of doing 'manufacturing'.[1] Indeed, we can and should go further and say that both 'hard' – plant and equipment, for instance – and 'soft' – forms of cultural know-how and inventiveness relating to the organisation of production, say – technologies are present in both service and manufacturing production to varying degrees depending on context. The point here is not simply that differences between activity in manufacturing and in services are frequently exaggerated but rather that activity in both fields of production is not readily amenable to the sorts of economic (and more recently 'cultural') reductionism it has frequently been subject to.

This isn't the same thing as saying that economic relations – whether performed in 'manufacturing' or 'services' – are always already embedded within specific sets of social relations. It is a rather different claim: that

200

economic and cultural categories are inextricably merged within the structures of market relations and microeconomic action. Let us take an example from services, that of advertising. Advertising is frequently represented within mainstream economic discourses as a departure from perfect competition. It is seen as a form of non-price competition by which firms attempt to exert influence over demand for their products through a range of psychological and cultural interventions. It therefore signifies a shift away from formal economic rationality (Slater, 2000). Relatedly, within critical social theory and cultural studies, advertising often appears simply as a cultural intervention in the domain of the economic and is rarely seen as a mundane commercial enterprise. Although advertising is frequently represented here as an activity whose goal is to sell things to people it is not analysed first and foremost as a commercial practice. Rather its function as a producer of 'sign values' and its role in the so-called 'dematerialisation' of economic relations are highlighted (Wernick, 1991). The problem here is that neither economic nor cultural reduction gets to the heart of advertising as a particular form of commercial practice. Advertisers do actively conceptualise goods and markets in terms of use and sign values. The work they perform requires them to deploy forms of cultural expertise. But only for the purposes of increasing sales and beating competition (Slater, 2000:8). Markets and market relations are not the economic given within which more cultural 'advertising' choices are made. Rather, advertising practitioners define markets and market relations within a broader set of cultural calculations. At the same time, ostensibly cultural relations do not provide the settled back-drop to rational economic action. On the contrary, they are reconceptualised and reconfigured within an instrumentally rational attempt to increase sales and secure competitive advantage (du Gay and McFall, 1999; McFall, 2000; Slater, 2000).

The point here is that advertising is a form of commercial practice that inextricably combines economic and cultural rationalities. Simply put, advertising practice could not be conducted under neo-classical assumptions in which economics is purified of 'cultural' white noise. As Slater (2000:8) argues, advertising practitioners do not work with assumptions of homogeneous markets or products with essentialised meanings for the simple reason that they cannot identify any markets without understanding the cultures of consumption that generate relations between goods nor can they understand these goods independently of the competitive relations through which they are marketed. As he suggests, 'the entire business of advertising is defined as precisely in terms of making mincemeat of all the categories that economics hold dear: rational economic action within culturally stable frameworks. Their aim is to destabilize markets by redefining use values and vice versa' (2000:8).

The same is true of any number of other forms of economically relevant activity. A crucial feature of many of the forms of interactive service work discussed in this book, for example, is the more or less direct relationship they involve between one or more service provider and one or more service consumer. The inseparability of the production and consumption of such services makes it difficult for both the manager of the service organisation and the service consumer to isolate service quality from the quality of the service provider. In other words, the process of 'disentangling' necessary to the realisation of a market transaction is obviously a problem in a context where the interpersonal links, the attachment, are inscribed in the service relation itself (Callon, 1998:34). The present volume attests to the wide range of calculative techniques and technologies that have emerged to address this 'problem', each of which is aimed at increasing the ability of producers to frame the service relation and each of which relies upon, albeit in different ways and to different degrees, the subtle imbrication of cultural and economic – so called 'soft' and 'hard' – knowledges.

Take, for instance, the case of certain forms of retail service work. As the quality of interactive service delivery has been represented as a crucial determinant of a firm's competitive success or failure, employees involved in such work have found themselves being recruited and trained on the basis of their propensity to exhibit particular capacities and dispositions aimed at winning over the hearts and minds of customers. Through sustained exposure to an often weird and wonderful range of interpersonal and communication management techniques – such as Transaction Analysis – these service workers have found themselves being trained in how to fashion their conduct – bodily comportment, aural and visual characteristics and so forth – in order to produce certain meanings for customers and thus a sale for the company. In addition, however, as those training them make clear, they are also being equipped with a set of skills that will stand them in good stead not only inside the workplace but also in the context of other forms of social interaction (du Gay, 1996; Nickson *et al.*, this volume).

Focusing on such forms of service work indicates how difficult it is to disentangle 'economic' categories from 'cultural' categories in economically relevant practices. This observation holds for work in the marketing, financial and commercial service industries as much as it does for the more direct servicing work found in parts of the retail, hotel and tourist related trades. The links between economic categories and cultural categories in the marketing and advertising industries, where the core task concerns managing, or attempting to manage, the relationship between products and consumers, may be quite readily apparent. These links are of equal, if less obvious, significance in other industries. In finance, for example, particularly merchant banking, the elements of communication, display and presentation are not simply restricted to the culture of the 'deal'. Financial networks can be viewed as socio-cultural networks in which 'relationship management' holds the key to economic success (Abolafia, 1998; Morgan and Sturdy, 2000; Thrift, 1994). In so far as international financial centres are effectively characterised by streams of information, each of which is open to interpretation and each with its own contacts, one of the significant skills within international finance is the ability to make and hold contacts, to construct relationships of trust, and to be part of the interpretation of what is really happening. As Thrift (1994) points out, far from a reduction in the need for face-to-face contact in the international financial centres, even allowing for the profusion of 'hard' electronic technologies, there is now greater emphasis on the presentation of self, face work, negotiating skills and so forth in large part because of the increasing requirement to be able to read people as well as the increasingly transactional nature of business relationships between firms and clients. Similarly, the work of Abolafia (1998) shows us traders obsessed with networking, 'multiplying entanglements', as Callon (1998:40) puts it, the better to calculate economic advantage.

Even if we take an example of service work that contrasts markedly with the customer–oriented services or those of international finance, that of contract security work, the qualities of display, communication and presentation emerge as crucial elements of guarding work (Allen and Pryke, 1994). Security work is reactive, whether on day or night shift. During the day, guards monitor arrivals and departures, often through a variety of 'hard' technologies, with a brief to control entries and exits. Social contact, however, is not often a significant aspect of security work. The latter is primarily performance, involving a standardised body and a range of ritualised and codified gestures. Security guards produce a controlled space simply through their uniformed presence (being male and six foot does, of course, add authority to the performance!). There are few spoken lines to the performance, as it is the body itself which generates the controlled space rather than verbal interaction. In this instance, the skills involved are those of presentation management and relationship management referred to earlier in relation to quite different forms of service work.[2]

In each instance, servicing can be seen as simultaneously an economic and cultural phenomenon. At the level of micro analysis, as opposed to macro-critique, there is little to be gained from analysing servicing practice in terms of an opposition between economic value and cultural value.[3] As we have seen, the most technical calculations of economic value in services are internally connected to cultural values and vice versa. Advertisers, for example, constitute their economic categories and activities through discursive representations of consumption practices. These representations make up that which they purport to reflect. They should not therefore be approached primarily in terms of their empirical veracity but in terms of how they constitute practical conduct. How an advertiser or a retailer thinks and acts only makes sense in relationship to their practical intent, and the institutional framework of competition through which those intents are constituted. As Slater (2000:8) suggests, the point is, though, that we need to conceive of this in terms of the internal relation between economic and cultural value within the very logic of market relations.

Notes

1　Contemporary programmes of organisational reform in both services and manufacturing are frequently formatted and framed in relation to some particular ideal of 'Customer' authority that enjoins all manner of firms and the individuals employed by them to foster and develop ostensibly similar forms of marketised conduct.
2　Here I am drawing on co-authored work with John Allen. See Allen and du Gay (1994).
3　What goes for micro-economic analysis also applies to macro-economic analysis. Thinking for a moment about that object we refer to as 'the economy', it seems obvious that when seeking to manage such an entity one of the first things we need to do is build a clear picture of what an economy looks like. We need to ask ourselves what are its main components, and how do these work, how are they related? In other words, before one can even seek to manage something called an 'economy', it is necessary to conceptualize or represent a set of processes and relations as an 'economy' which are amenable to management. We therefore need a discourse of the economy and this discourse, like any other, will depend upon a particular mode of representation: the elaboration of a language and a set of technical devices and hence constructing an object in a certain way so that object can then be deliberated about and acted upon.

References

Abolafia, M. (1998) 'Markets as Cultures: An Ethnographic Approach', in Callon, M. (ed.), *The Laws of the Markets*, Oxford: Blackwell.

Allen, J. and du Gay, P. (1994) 'Industry and the Rest: On the Economic Identity of Services', *Work, Employment and Society*, 8:2, 255–71.

Allen, J. and Pryke, M. (1994) 'The Production of Service Space', *Environment and Planning D, Society and Space*, 12:4, 453–76.

Callon, M. (1998) 'Introduction: The Embeddedness of Economic Markets in Economics', in Callon, M. (ed.), *The Laws of the Markets*, Oxford: Blackwell.

du Gay, P. (1996) *Consumption and Identity at Work*, London: Sage.

du Gay, P. and McFall, E. (1999) 'Reappraising the Culture–Economy Dualism: Critique/Meaning/History', paper presented to the Consuming Markets, Consuming Meanings Conference, University of Plymouth, September.

Macdonald, C. and Sirianni, C. (1996) 'The Service Society and the Changing Experience of Work', in Macdonald, C. and Sirianni, C. (eds), *Working in the Service Society*, Philadelphia; Temple University Press.

McFall, E. (2000) 'A Mediating Institution? Using an Historical Study of Advertising Practice to Rethink Culture and Economy', *Cultural Values*, 4:3, 314–38.

Morgan, G. and Sturdy, A. J. (2000) *Beyond Organisational Change – Discourse, Structure and Power in UK Financial Services*, London: Macmillan.

Slater, D. (2000) 'Capturing Markets from the Economists', paper presented to the Cultural Economy Workshop, Open University, January.

Thrift, N. (1994) 'On the Social and Cultural Determinants of International Financial Centres: The Case of the City of London', in Corbridge, S. , Martin, R. and Thrift, N. (eds), *Money, Space and Power*, Oxford: Blackwell.

Wernick, A. (1991) *Promotional Culture: Advertising, Ideology and Symbolic Expression*, London: Sage.

Author Index

Abbott, A.   161
Abercrombie, N.   18, 20, 23, 25, 140
Abolafia, M.   202, 203
Ackroyd, S.   138
Adkins, L.   65
Adorno, T. W.   120
Agate, N.   177
Albrow, M.   138
Allen, J.   4, 200, 203
Alvesson, M.   26, 29, 141
Anderson, J. C.   159
Anthony, P.   67
Appelbaum, E.   159, 160
Armistead, C.   172
Aronson, E.   143
Ashforth, B. E.   6, 7, 18, 20, 22, 30, 60, 136, 140, 143, 144
Assiter, A.   62
Atouf, O.   139

Bain, P.   7, 67
Baldry, C.   3, 7
Barker, J. R.   160
Barley, S. P.   159
Barley, S. R.   136
Barrett, M.   54
Barry, A.   123
Barry, B.   65
Batt, R.   83, 84, 159, 160
Baudrillard, J.   102, 120, 195
Baum, T.   173
Bauman, Z.   3, 10, 39, 51–3, 55, 57, 66, 82, 109, 120
BBC   139
Beck, J. P.   160
Beck, U.   109, 129
Bell, D.   2, 82
Bendelow, G.   138, 142
Benét, M.   175
Benhabib, S.   63, 64–5, 71, 73, 74
Benson, S.   79
Berger, P.   54
Besser, H.   193
Bettencourt, L.   60
Bierstecker, T. J.   3
Bitner, J.   80

Boje, D.   146
Bourdieu, P.   120, 176, 179, 185
Bowen, D.   6, 18, 20, 22, 30, 80, 159, 171, 172
Boyd, C.   67
Boyne, G.   8
Braverman, H.   2, 103, 136
Bridger, D.   122
Brown, C.   159
Brownlie, D.   9
Bryman, A.   2, 4, 135, 139
Buchanan, B.   121
Buchanan, R.   196
Buckner, G. C.   136
Burawoy, M.   8, 136, 137, 142, 146
Burchell, G.   118, 123, 125, 129
Burrell, G.   34
Burrows, R.   193
Burton, D.   8

Callon, M.   202
Cameron, D.   140
Campbell, A.   172
Campbell, C.   141
Carlzon, J.   80, 135, 172–3
Carty, P.   147
Clark, C.   144
Cobble, D. S.   9
Cohen, S.   144
Cole, R. E.   159, 160
Colling, T.   67
Collins, H.   51, 57
Collins, J.   173
Collins, P. H.   65
Collinson, D.   10, 39, 48–51, 56, 137, 142, 144, 148, 149
Connell, R. W.   74
Cox, K. K.   191
Craib, I.   136
Czepiel, J. A.   172, 194

Danet, B.   18
Datamonitor   83
Davis, A.   177
De Certeau, M.   122

Subject Index